Variational Methods in Optimum Control Theory

This is Volume 45 in MATHEMATICS IN SCIENCE AND ENGINEERING
A series of monographs and textbooks
Edited by RICHARD BELLMAN, University of Southern California

A complete list of the books in this series appears at the end of this volume.

VARIATIONAL METHODS IN OPTIMUM CONTROL THEORY

Iu. P. PETROV

LENINGRAD, USSR

Translated by M. D. FRIEDMAN with the assistance of H. J. ten Zeldam

ACADEMIC PRESS NEW YORK AND LONDON 1968

Originally published in the Russian language under the title "Variatsionnye Metody Teorii Optimal'nogo Upravleniia" by "Energiia" Press, Moscow–Leningrad, 1965.

ACADEMIC PRESS INC.
111 Fifth Avenue, New York, New York 10003

United Kingdom Edition published by
ACADEMIC PRESS INC. (LONDON) LTD.
Berkeley Square House, London W.1

LIBRARY OF CONGRESS CATALOG CARD NUMBER: 68–18678

PRINTED IN THE UNITED STATES OF AMERICA

From the Preface to the Russian Edition

The purpose of this book is to elucidate the variational methods underlying optimum control theory, especially for the electrical engineer, and to acquaint the reader with the application of these methods to the solution of specific technical problems. The book assumes that the reader has the proper mathematical background such as the customary mathematical curriculum of the majority of engineering schools.

The author does not attempt to achieve complete mathematical rigor. A number of theorems are presented without proof. In these cases a reference is supplied in which the proof may be found.

The simplest sections of the calculus of variations, such as the necessary conditions for the extremum of an open domain, are treated in the first two chapters.

On the basis of these divisions, in Chapter III, solutions are generated for a number of applied cases of optimum control.

More complicated questions of the calculus of variations, the sufficient conditions for the extremum, methods of solving problems taking account of the constraints imposed on the desired functions, inevitable in practice, degenerate and nonstandard functionals are treated in Chapters IV and V.

In Chapter VI, the reader is acquainted with a wider range of practical problems than in Chapter III, the areas of electric motors, energy methods, and electrical transportation methods, the solution of which requires the methods of optimum control theory explained in Chapters IV and V.

The main part of the material in Chapters III and VI is the result of original research by the author. Besides assisting the reader in analyzing the methods available for the solution of optimum control problems, the examples presented are of special interest.

The book includes a brief historical survey concerned with the development of variational methods in mathematics and their application to the solution of engineering problems.

IA. G. NEUIMIN

Contents

This page intentionally left blank

Variational Methods in Optimum Control Theory

This page intentionally left blank

I Fundamental Concepts of the Calculus of Variations

1. Functionals

The object in the calculus of variations is to find functions achieving the extremal (maximum or minimum) value of some quantities which depend on these functions; they are called functionals.

A functional may be considered the generalization of the well-known concept of a function, i.e., a function of a special kind in which another function plays the part of the independent variable.

The following definite integral

$$J = \int_0^1 y \, dx \tag{1}$$

is the simplest example of a functional.

The value of the functional J can be represented by a constant which will correspond to each integrable function $y(x)$. Thus, if $y = x$, then $J = \frac{1}{2}$; if $y = x^2$, then $J = \frac{1}{3}$; if $y = e^x$, then $J = 1 - e = 1.718$, etc.

The length of a curve is a functional. Let us consider curves in the x, y plane connecting the points $x = 0; y = 0$ and $x = 1; y = 1$. Let the equations of these curves be given in the form $y = y(x)$. Then an infinitesimal linear element of the length of the curve ds will equal

$$ds = (dx^2 + dy^2)^{1/2} = (1 + y'^2)^{1/2} \, dx, \tag{2}$$

and the total length of the curve will be the integral

$$S = \int_0^1 (1 + y'^2)^{1/2} \, dx. \tag{3}$$

Here the functional depends not only on the value of the function $y(x)$ itself, but also on its derivative y'.

The expression

$$J = \int_a^b F(x; y; y')\, dx, \tag{4}$$

which is the definite integral of some function F dependent on an independent variable x, the desired function $y(x)$, and its derivative y', is another example of a functional of still more general form.

Henceforth, we shall consider only functionals of the form (4) almost exclusively, although in general, functionals exist which cannot be reduced to such form.

Let us present several examples of functionals encountered in engineering.

(1) The path traversed by an automobile in the time T is a functional of the velocity of the automobile. In this case

$$S = \int_0^T v\, dt,$$

where S is the traversed path, and v is the velocity.

(2) The cost of laying out a railroad track between two points is a functional of the distance to be covered. The efforts of designers are directed towards finding the cheapest way which would make the functional a minimum. For the flat earth case the solution is obvious; it is a straight line. In the presence of hills and ravines, finding the best solution is not so simple.

(3) The time of motion, the fuel consumption, and other parameters in aircraft or ship dynamics are functionals of the elevator and rudder control laws. Problems of the optimum control of the rudders, i.e., such control as would assure the highest velocity and greatest economy, are again problems of the calculus of variations.

(4) The drag force of water opposing ship motion depends on the shape of the ship's hull and is, in turn, a functional of a function of two variables, the surface of the ship's hull. For many years that surface of a ship was sought which would make the functional a minimum, i.e., would assure minimum drag in the water.

Let us note that the calculus of variations might be considered as an extension of the differential calculus for n variables. For instance, the function $y(x)$ in the functional (4) could be approximated by broken lines with end points $y_0 = y(x_0)$; $y_1 = y(x_0 + \Delta x)$; $\cdots$; $y_n = y(x_0 + n\,\Delta x)$ and the functional (4) itself, by the sum

$$J = \sum_{i=1}^{n} F\left(x_i;\, y_i;\, \frac{y_i - y_{i-1}}{x}\right) \Delta x. \tag{5}$$

Hence, the variational problem may be considered about equal to the conventional problem of finding the extremum of the functional $J(y_1, y_2, \ldots, y_n)$ of n variables. The approximation will naturally be very coarse for a small number of ordinates, but as n increases we will obtain a more and more exact approximation to the solution of the variational problem.

The functional may therefore be considered as a function of an infinite set of variables (the values of the function $y(x)$ at individual points), and the calculus of variations as the generalization of differential calculus which would permit finding the maximum and minimum in "infinite-dimensional" space.

It must be noted that the approximate solutions of problems for the maximum and minimum of functions of a small number of variables may be found without applying mathematics, but by utilizing the intuition of two and three-dimensional spaces developed by man. At the same time, an intuitive concept of n-space does not exist in practice, hence, even an approximate solution of variational problems on the basis of intuition is quite difficult. Examples exist where engineers erred for many years in the selection of the function achieving the extremum.

2. Admissible Lines. Function Classes

In the calculus of variations, functions are used which give the functional an extremum value as compared to its value in some other functions. Naturally, it is necessary to determine among which functions we shall seek the extremum, i.e., to determine the classes accessible for a comparison, the admissible functions (admissible lines).

It would be most natural to seek the extremum in the class of continuous functions. In this class are functions with no discontinuities, i.e., they smoothly change from one value to another. A continuous function is shown in Fig. 1, and an example of a function with discontinuities in

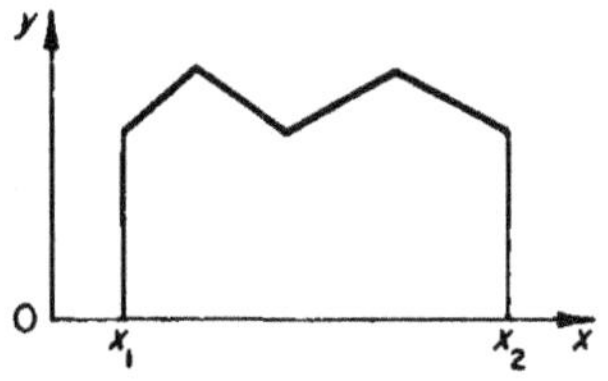

FIG. 1

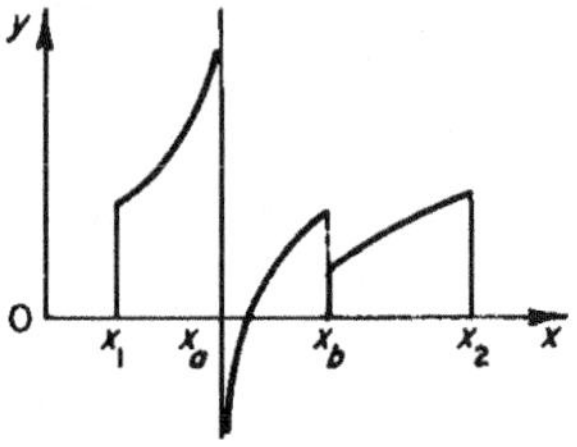

FIG. 2

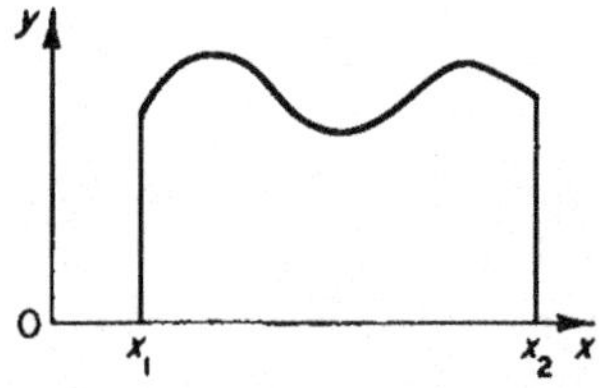

FIG. 3

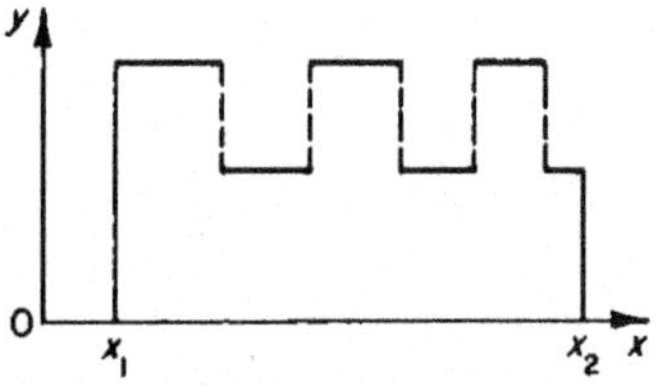

FIG. 4

Fig. 2 (infinite discontinuities when the values of the function tend to infinity as the point of discontinuity is approached, as well as finite, jump discontinuities).

It is expedient to seek the extremum in a rather narrower class of functions, i.e., in the class of continuous functions which have continuous first derivatives. Such functions are called smooth functions. An example of a smooth function is shown in Fig. 3. Smooth functions cannot have breaks because the continuity of the first derivative is violated at such break points. However, functions with breaks are often encountered in technical applications, and are called piecewise-smooth functions (see Fig. 1). Piecewise-continuous functions, with discontinuities (jumps) at individual points (Fig. 4), are also encountered.

Further, as a rule we shall seek the extremum in a class of piecewise-smooth functions. But sometimes (when it is necessary) we shall do it in a wider class of piecewise-continous functions. The majority of technical problems have solutions just in these classes of functions.

3. Nearness of Functions

In seeking the extremum we must compare values of a function for two "nearby" functions. Let us hence refine the concept of "nearness." Let two functions be given by the equations

$$y = y(x); \qquad y_1 = y_1(x).$$

Let the maximum of the absolute value of the difference $|y_1(x) - y(x)|$ designate the distance between these functions.

The functional

$$J = \int_a^b F(x; y; y')\, dx$$

depends not only on the function itself, but also on its derivative $y'(x)$. Hence, the values of the functional for functions between which the distance is small (less than any previously assigned number ε) may differ radically. Let us present an example. Take the functional

$$J = \int_0^{\pi} y'^2\, dx, \tag{6}$$

and consider the function

$$y = (1/n) \sin nx \tag{7}$$

whose distance from the horizontal axis (i.e., from the function $y = 0$) is $1/n$ and tends to zero as n increases without limit. Meanwhile, the value of the functional (6) for the function (7) is independent of n and equals $\pi/2$, but the value of the functional is zero for $y = 0$.

Hence, for "nearby" functions the values of the functional may differ substantially. In order to avoid this, it is necessary to refine the definition of "nearness" of functions.

Let the greatest of the maximums of the differences:

$$\begin{gathered} |y_1(x) - y(x)|; \\ |y_1'(x) - y'(x)|; \\ \cdots\cdots\cdots \\ |y_1^{(n)}(x) - y^{(n)}(x)|; \end{gathered} \tag{8}$$

be designated the nth-order distance for two functions.

Therefore, the smallness of the zeroth-order distance means that the functions are quite near each other. The smallness of the first-order distance means that both the functions and their first derivatives are quite near to each other.

In the example with the functions $y_1 = (1/n)\sin nx$ and $y = 0$, which we considered, the zeroth-order distance actually tends to zero as $n \to \infty$, but the first-order distance

$$\max |y_1' - y'| = \max |\cos nx - 0| = 1 \tag{9}$$

does not tend to zero. Hence, the values of the functionals were also different. Values of the functional (6) will be near each other on curves within first-order nearness of each other.

4. Classification of Extremums

Let a high mountain be located between two points. We must connect these two points by the shortest possible road. Naturally, the road should not pass over the mountain peak, but should go around it to the right or left. The shortest of all roads going around the mountain to the right is first found, and then the shortest of all roads going around the mountain to the left is found. Let the road to the left be shorter than the road to the right. Then the shortest of the roads going around the mountain to the left will yield an absolute extremum. The shortest of roads going around the mountain to the right will not yield an absolute extremum, but a relative extremum, i.e., it will be shorter compared to roads near it.

Hence, if a given curve gives a functional an extremum as compared with all curves of a given class, the extremum is absolute. If the extremum is achieved only in comparison with nearby curves, it is a relative extremum.

Strong and weak relative extremums are distinguished. A strong maximum of a functional is considered to be achieved on a curve if the value of the functional on the given curve is greater than on all other curves to which the zeroth-order distance is small. Also, a weak extremum is considered to be reached on a curve if the value of the functional on the given curve is greater than on curves to which the first-order distance is small. Let us elaborate the distinction between weak and strong extremums by a graphic example.

A sailboat, equipped with oars, moves over a lake from point *A* to point *B* against the wind. The velocity of the boat under sail is much greater than the velocity under oars, but it is impossible to go directly into the wind under sail. Hence, a weak minimum in the sailing time is achieved on the straight line connecting *A* and *B*. Actually, the transition of the line into a curve to which the first-order distance from the line will be small (Fig. 5a), will only increase the travel time because the sail will not be effective and the pathlength will increase. However, the sailing time may be shortened if we move in short tacks under sail (Fig. 5b). For a very large number of tacks, the ship's course will be within zero order nearness to the line *AB*. A strong minimum is not achieved on the line *AB*.

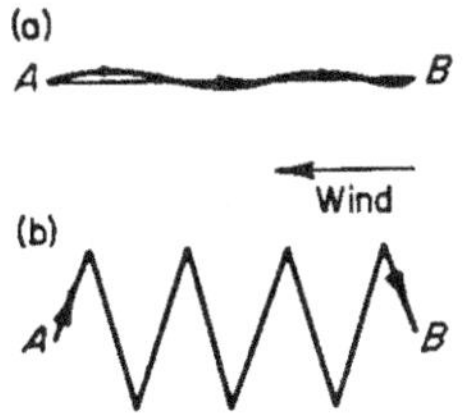

FIG. 5

Let us note that every absolute extremum is simultaneously a relative extremum, any strong extremum is simultaneously a weak extremum, but not conversely.

Indeed, in order to determine whether an absolute extremum has been reached on a given curve, it must be compared with all curves of a given class. In order to determine a relative extremum, it must be compared only with curves near it. A strong extremum is verified by a comparison with curves in zero-order nearness, while a weak extremum is proved from a comparison with a narrower class of curves in first-order nearness to the given curve. Hence, if some condition is necessary for a weak relative extremum to be achieved on a curve, this condition will be even more necessary for a strong extremum and much more necessary for an absolute extremum.

5. Euler Equation

We now consider the fundamental question of the calculus of variations, the derivation of necessary conditions for an extremum. To simplify the considerations further, we shall speak about seeking the minimum of the functional. The necessary conditions, as can be easily seen, remain the same. We shall investigate what conditions a function $y(x)$ should satisfy in order that an increment in the functional be positive upon its transition to any function $y_1(x)$. Exactly these conditions will later permit us to find the desired functions which will yield the extremum of the functional.

To simplify the investigation so as to be able to neglect higher order infinitesimals, we shall compare the desired function $y(x)$ with functions near to it rather than with just any functions, and for this we shall need a further refinement of the "nearness" concept of the previous sections.

Thus, let us assume that a weak relative minimum of the functional

$$J = \int_a^b F(x; y; y')\, dx$$

is achieved on some smooth curve passing through the points a and b, where we assume the function $F(x; y; y')$ to be continous and to have continuous partial derivatives to second order inclusive.

Let us determine the conditions that the function $y(x)$ must satisfy so that a minimum might be achieved.

Instead of the function $y(x)$, we shall therefore consider another function $y + \alpha\eta$, where α is a number and $\eta(x)$ is an arbitrary smooth function, subject only to the conditions $\eta(a) = \eta(b) = 0$.

The difference in the functionals (or the increment in the functional J)

$$\Delta J = \int_a^b F(x; y + \alpha\eta; y' + \alpha\eta')\, dx - \int_a^b F(x; y; y')\, dx \tag{10}$$

will be a function of α.

Let us expand it in a Taylor series in powers of α:

$$\Delta J = \alpha \frac{dJ}{d\alpha} + \frac{\alpha^2}{1 \cdot 2} \frac{d^2 J}{d\alpha^2} + \cdots . \tag{11}$$

The expression $\alpha\, dJ/d\alpha$, where the derivative $dJ/d\alpha$ is taken at $\alpha = 0$, is denoted by δJ and is called the first variation of the functional J. Therefore, the first variation is the main smooth, linear portion of the increment in the functional (it depends linearly on α).

Analogously, $\delta^2 J$ denotes the expression $(\alpha^2/2)(d^2J/d\alpha^2)$, and is called the second variation.

As α tends to zero, the terms containing the square and higher powers of α decrease more rapidly than the linear term, and the sign of the increment agrees, for small α, with the sign of the linear term, i.e., for small α

$$\Delta J \approx \delta J .$$

At the same time, since the minimum of the functional is achieved on the curve $y(x)$ by assumption, the difference ΔJ may not be negative, i.e., the inequality

$$\Delta J \approx \delta J = \alpha\, dJ/d\alpha \geqslant 0 \tag{12}$$

must be satisfied.

In order for the inequality (12) to be satisfied for any α, either positive or negative, it is necessary that

$$dJ/d\alpha = 0 , \tag{13}$$

and thereby, $\delta J = 0$ (if $dJ/d\alpha > 0$, we will then have $\Delta J \approx \alpha\, dJ/d\alpha > 0$ for positive and sufficiently small α, and $\Delta J < 0$ for negative and sufficiently small α).

Hence, the necessary condition for the extremum is that the first variation of the functional be zero. But

$$\begin{aligned}\frac{dJ}{d\alpha} &= \int_a^b \frac{d}{d\alpha} F(x; y + \alpha\eta; y' + \alpha\eta')\, dx \\ &= \int_a^b \left[\frac{\partial F}{\partial y}\frac{d(y+\alpha\eta)}{d\alpha} + \frac{\partial F}{\partial y'}\frac{d(y'+\alpha\eta')}{d\alpha}\right] dx \\ &= \int_a^b \left(\frac{\partial F}{\partial y}\eta + \frac{\partial F}{\partial y'}\eta'\right) dx . \end{aligned} \tag{14}$$

Let us integrate the second member in (14) by parts:

$$\int_a^b \frac{\partial F}{\partial y'}\eta'\, dx = F_{y'}\eta \Big|_a^b - \int_a^b \eta \frac{d}{dx} F_{y'}\, dx .$$

(From now on we shall use the abbreviated notation for the partial derivative; we shall write $F_{y'}$ for $\partial F/\partial y'$, etc.) It was assumed earlier that the function $\eta(x)$ vanishes at the points a and b. Therefore

$$\int_a^b F_{y'}\eta'\,dx = -\int_a^b \eta \frac{d}{dx} F_{y'}\,\mathrm{dx}$$

and

$$\delta J = \int_a^b \left(F_y - \frac{d}{dx} F_{y'}\right) \alpha\eta\,\mathrm{dx}. \tag{15}$$

We now apply the Lagrange lemma.

This lemma states: If a continuous function $M(x)$ possesses the property that

$$\int_a^b M(x)\,\eta(x)\,dx = 0 \tag{16}$$

for any smooth function $\eta(x)$, then there certainly exists a $M(x) = 0$ for all x $(a \leqslant x \leqslant b)$.

Indeed, let us assume the opposite: let $M(c) > 0$ in at least one point c $(a \leqslant c \leqslant b)$, and let us select the function which is greater than zero in the neighborhood of the point c and equal to zero in the rest of the interval (Fig. 6) as the function $\eta(x)$. Then the product $M(x)\,\eta(x)$ will

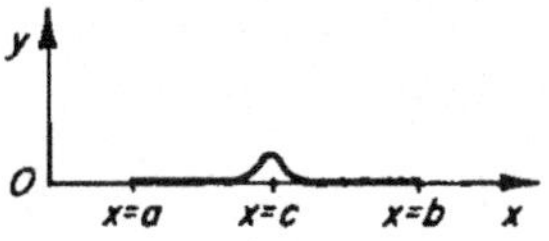

FIG. 6

be positive in the neighborhood of the point c and zero in the rest of the interval, and the integral (16) will not be zero. The obtained contradiction proves the lemma.

On the basis of the Lagrange lemma, the following deduction may be made from (15): If $y(x)$ achieves an extremum of the functional

$$\int_a^b F(x; y; y')\,dx,$$

then it is necessary that

$$F_y - \frac{d}{dx} F_{y'} = 0. \tag{17}$$

Equation (17) is called the Euler equation. This was found by Euler in 1744 [1] and it plays the central role in the calculus of variations. Its importance is that the function at which the extremum may be reached may actually be determined by its utilization.

An example will better illustrate this.

To determine the shortest line $y(x)$ connecting two points $(0; 0)$ and $(1; 1)$ on a plane it is possible to express the length of the connecting curve by means of the integral

$$S = \int_0^1 (1 + y'^2)^{1/2}\, dx,$$

i.e., in this case $F = (1 + y'^2)^{1/2}$; $F_y = 0$; $F_{y'} = y'/(1 + y'^2)^{1/2}$, and the Euler equation becomes

$$y'' = 0, \tag{18}$$

i.e., $y = Cx + C_1$, where C and C_1 are integration constants.

Hence, the Euler equation has permitted us to determine that the shortest path connecting two points in a plane may only be a straight line. The two arbitrary constants in (18) are found from the condition that the line passes through the two given points. In this case $C_1 = 0$; $C = 1$ and $y = x$.

Because of the fundamental role which the Euler equation plays in all the calculus of variations, we present another derivation of the same equation.

We replace the function $y(x)$ on which the extremum of the functional (4) is achieved, as has been assumed, by a broken line with vertices $y_0, y_1, \ldots, y_{n+1}$ (Fig. 7). Hence (see Section 1), the functional transforms

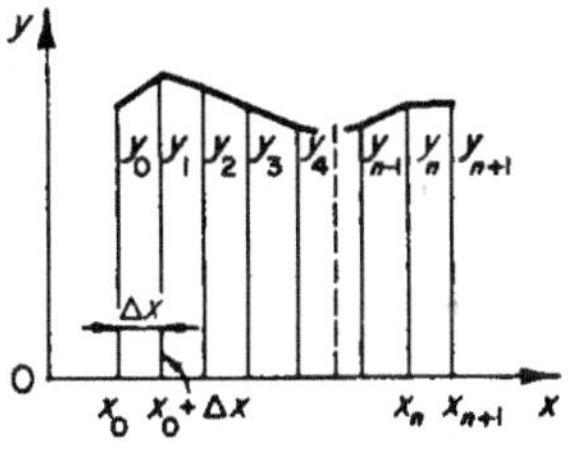

FIG. 7

into a function of n variables

$$J_n = \sum_{i=0}^{n} F(x_i; y_i; y_i')\,\Delta x,$$

where $y_i' = (y_{i+1} - y_i)/\Delta x$ (Fig. 7), and $J_n \to J$ as $n \to \infty$.

If the extremum is achieved on the broken line, then all the partial derivatives $\partial J_n/\partial y_i$ should be zero, as is known from differential calculus.

Only the terms $F(x_{i-1}; y_{i-1}; y_{i-1}')\,\Delta x$ and $F(x_i; y_i; y_i')\,\Delta x$ in the sum J_n depend on y_i, where the ith member contains y_i both directly and in terms of the third argument y_i', and the $(i-1)$th term only in terms of the third argument:

$$y_{i-1}' = (y_i - y_{i-1})/\Delta x.$$

Therefore

$$\frac{\partial J_n}{\partial y_i} = F_y(x_i; y_i; y_i')\,\Delta x - F_{y'}(x_i; y_i; y_i') + F_{y'}(x_{i-1}; y_{i-1}; y_{i-1}'). \qquad (19)$$

Now (19) may be transformed into

$$\frac{\partial J_n}{\partial y_i} = \left[F_y(x_i; y_i; y_i') - \frac{\Delta F_{y'}(x_i; y_i; y_i')}{\Delta x}\right]\Delta x,$$

where

$$\Delta F_{y'} = F_{y'}(x_i; y_i; y_i') - F_{y'}(x_{i-1}; y_{i-1}; y_{i-1}').$$

Now passing to the limit as $n \to \infty$; $x \to 0$, we obtain that the Euler equation $F_y - d/dx\, F_{y'} = 0$ must be satisfied in order for the smooth curve $y(x)$ to yield the extremum of the functional (4).

Precisely thus, by a passage to the limit, did Euler derive the equation in 1744. The validity of the passage to the limit is needed in the foundation, hence, the derivation considered earlier, utilizing the concept of the variation and the Lagrange lemma, is more rigorous.

However, the derivation of the Euler equation in terms of the Lagrange lemma also contains an inaccuracy which Dubois-Raymond pointed out in the 19th century: This derivation is complete if we assume, in advance, that both the first derivative $y'(x)$ and the second derivative $y''(x)$ of the function $y(x)$ on which the extremum is achieved, are continuous.

Another derivation of the Euler equation exists (it may be found in the work of Lavrent'ev and Liusternik [2]) which utilizes the Dubois-

Raymond lemma instead of the Lagrange lemma. This derivation does not require a preliminary assumption on the continuity of $y''(x)$. On the other hand, by utilizing this lemma it may be proved that the curve yielding the extremum of a nondegenerate functional has a continuous second derivative except at certain points.

6. Discussion of the Euler Equation

Consider the total differential of the second member of the equation

$$F_y - \frac{d}{dx} F_{y'} = 0 .$$

Here it is necessary to take into account that $F_{y'}$ is a function of three arguments: x, y, and y', and that y and y' are, in turn, functions of x. Therefore

$$\frac{d}{dx} F_{y'} = \frac{\partial F_{y'}}{\partial x} \frac{dx}{dx} + \frac{\partial F_{y'}}{\partial y} \frac{dy}{dx} + \frac{\partial F_{y'}}{\partial y'} \frac{dy'}{\partial x}$$

and the Euler equation may be written as

$$F_y - F_{y'x} - F_{y'y} y' - F_{y'y'} y'' = 0 . \tag{20}$$

This means that in the general case the Euler equation is a nonlinear second-order differential equation.

Solutions of the Euler equation are called extremums.

In general, it is not easy to find the solution of a second-order nonlinear differential equation. We now consider some particular cases where the integration is simplified.

Case 1. Let the value of F be independent of y. In this case the Euler equation reduces to the expression

$$\frac{d}{dx} F_{y'} = 0$$

from which

$$F_{y'} = \text{const} . \tag{21}$$

It is possible to determine y' as a function of x from (21), therefore, the desired function $y(x)$ may be expressed as an integral.

Case 2. Let the value of F be explicitly independent of x, $F = F(y; y')$. In this case (20) becomes

$$F_y - F_{y'y}y' - F_{y'y'}y'' = 0.$$

Multiplying all terms of the equation by y', we obtain an expression which, as is easily verified, may be written as

$$\frac{d}{dx}(F - y'F_{y'}) = 0$$

from which it follows that the desired function should satisfy the equation

$$F - y'F_{y'} = C. \tag{22}$$

It is customary to designate (22) as the first integral of the Euler equation.

Equation (22) does not contain x explicitly, and may always be integrated.

Let us note that all the terms of the equation may be multiplied by y' only if y' is not zero. Otherwise, by multiplying by y' we could lose the solution $y' = 0$, $y = A$, where A is a root of the equation $F_y(A; 0) = 0$.

Case 3. Let the value of F depend only on y'; thus the Euler equation is

$$\frac{d}{dx}F_{y'} = 0$$

and, therefore, $F_{y'}(y') = \text{const}$, from which $y' = \text{const} = k$, i.e., $y = kx + b$.

Hence, if the functional depends only on the derivative of the desired function, the extremum will always be straight lines.

Case 4. Let $F_{y'y'} = 0$ identically. This can only be if $F = F(x; y)$ or $F = M(x; y) + N(x; y)\,y'$, i.e., when the functional is either independent of the derivative of the desired function, or depends on it linearly. Such functionals are called degenerate; they possess special properties and will be considered separately.

Let us make a number of remarks apropos the Euler equation.

(1) First, let us note that the Euler equation should be satisfied by as small a segment of the function $y(x)$ as desired. Each piece of an extremal is also an extremal. The converse is false; a curve composed of pieces of

extremals may not, as a whole, yield the extremum. Section 26 devoted to the Jacobi condition contains more details on this.

(2) Formula (20) may be written as

$$y'' = \frac{F_y - F_{y'x} - F_{y'y}y'}{F_{y'y'}}. \tag{23}$$

But $F_{y'y'}$ does not equal zero identically for all functions (except the degenerate), and it may vanish only at discrete points. With the exception of these points, the value of the second derivative may be evaluated by means of (23). Therefore, the extremal of a nondegenerate functional is always a smooth line with a continuous second derivative.

There may be breaks in the curve yielding the extremum only at discrete points.

These cases will be examined individually later. Except for the singular points, the extremal will always be a smooth curve.

(3) Compliance with the Euler equation is only the necessary condition for an extremum. Extremals may sometimes yield neither a maximum nor a minimum, just as points where the derivative vanishes in differential calculus may also not be extremums, but inflection points, say. However, if the Euler equation is not generally satisfied for any function (there is a contradiction), this then indicates that an extremum does not exist for this functional.

Thus the Euler equation for the functional

$$J = \int_a^b y\,dx \tag{24}$$

(the area under the curve y) has the form $1 = 0$, and no function can satisfy it. This is natural since the maximum value of the integral (24) is infinity, and the least is minus infinity, i.e., there are no extremums. In more complicated cases when the lack of an extremum is not detected at once, an investigation of the Euler equation permits clarification.

(4) Let us turn to (15). In this formula $\alpha\eta(x)$ is the variation of the function ordinarily denoted by δy (Fig. 8) and (15) is written as

$$\delta J = \int_a^b \left(F_y - \frac{d}{dx} F_{y'}\right) \delta y\,dx.$$

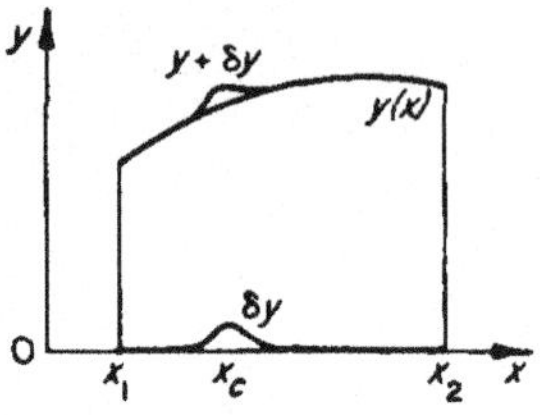

FIG. 8

Written thus, it recalls the well-known formula for the differential

$$dy = y'\,dx,$$

and, just as the latter, may be used for an approximate estimation of the change in the functional. Indeed, to the accuracy of higher-order infinitesimals, the increment in the functional agrees with its first variation, and the variation of the functional equals the integral of the variation of the function δy multiplied by the expression $F_y - d/dx\,F_{y'}$, which is sometimes called the functional derivative.

The functional derivative vanishes on the extremal, exactly as its ordinary derivative vanishes at maximum or minimum points of a function. Hence, for small deviations from the extremal, the changes in a functional will be higher-order infinitesimals. This fact is of great practical value.

7. The Legendre Condition

In order for $y(x)$ to yield the extremum of the functional $J = \int_a^b F(x; y; y')\,dx$, it is necessary that still another condition, the Legendre condition, be satisfied in addition to the Euler equation. Moreover, this condition will permit us to distinguish between a maximum and minimum.

In fact, as the expansion (10) shows, if the first variation vanishes, the sign of the increment of the functional ΔJ will agree with the sign of the second variation

$$\delta^2 J = (\alpha^2/2)\,(d^2 J/d\alpha^2), \tag{25}$$

since higher-order terms will decrease more rapidly than the quadratic term for sufficiently small α.

Therefore, in order for the function $y(x)$ to yield the minimum of a functional, compliance with the inequality $\delta^2 J \geqslant 0$ is necessary, and for a maximum, with the opposite inequality, i.e.,

$$\delta^2 J \leqslant 0.$$

But

$$\frac{d^2 J}{d\alpha^2} = \int_a^b \frac{d^2}{d\alpha^2} F(x; y + \alpha\eta; y' + \alpha\eta')\, dx$$

$$= \int_a^b (F_{yy}\eta^2 + 2F_{yy'}\eta\eta' + F_{y'y'}\eta'^2)\, dx. \tag{26}$$

The second member of the variation may be transformed by integrating by parts. Since $\eta(a) = \eta(b) = 0$, then

$$2\int_a^b F_{yy'}\eta\eta'\, dx = \int_a^b F_{yy'}\, d\eta^2 = F_{yy'}\eta^2 \Big|_a^b - \int_a^b \frac{d}{dx} F_{yy'}\eta^2\, dx$$

$$= -\int_a^b \frac{d}{dx} F_{yy'}\eta^2\, dx.$$

Therefore

$$\frac{d^2 J}{d\alpha^2} = 2\int_a^b (P\eta^2 + R\eta'^2)\, dx, \tag{27}$$

where

$$P = \frac{1}{2}\left(F_{yy} - \frac{d}{dx} F_{yy'}\right); \qquad R = \frac{1}{2} F_{y'y'}.$$

But since $\eta(x)$ is an arbitrary function, in order for the inequality $d^2J/d\alpha^2 = 0$ to be satisfied, it is necessary that $F_{y'y'} \geqslant 0$. Actually, it is easy to select a function $\eta(x)$ such that η^2 would be small and η'^2 large. To do this it is sufficient to select a rapidly varying function with a small absolute value. The sign of the second variation for such a function will agree with the sign of $F_{y'y'}$, and we arrive at the following necessary condition (the Legendre condition): In order for the curve $y(x)$ to yield the minimum of the functional $J = \int_a^b F(x; y; y')\, dx$, compliance with the inequality

$$F_{y'y'} \geqslant 0 \tag{28}$$

is necessary; and for a maximum, compliance with

$$F_{y'y'} \leqslant 0 \tag{29}$$

is necessary.

Hence, the investigation of the sign of $F_{y'y'}$ plays a most important role in the study of the functional: If $F_{y'y'}$ is negative, a maximum of the functional may be achieved on the extremals, and if it is positive, a minimum is achieved. Finally, if $F_{y'y'}$ is zero identically, we have a degenerate functional with singular properties.

Example 1. Let us investigate the functional $J = \int_1^2 (y' + x^2 y'^2)\, dx$ under the boundary conditions $y(1) = 1$; $y(2) = 2$.

Let us evaluate the derivatives

$$F_{y'} = 1 + 2x^2 y'; \qquad F_{y'y'} = 2x^2.$$

Since $F_{y'y'} > 0$ in the range $1 \leqslant x \leqslant 2$ we consider, the functional is nondegenerate and a minimum of the functional may be reached on the extremals. From the Euler equation

$$\frac{d}{dx}(1 + 2x^2 y') = 0,$$

we find that the extremals are hyperbolas

$$y = (C_1/x) + C_2.$$

From the boundary conditions we obtain the two equations

$$\begin{aligned} 1 &= C_1 + C_2 \\ 2 &= \tfrac{1}{2}C_1 + C_2 \end{aligned}$$

from which we find $C_1 = -2$; $C_2 = 3$, and the equation of the extremal is

$$y = 3 - (2/x).$$

Example 2. Let us investigate the functional $J = \int_0^\pi (y'^2 + 2y \sin x)\, dx$ under the boundary conditions $y(0) = 0$; $y(\pi) = 0$.

Since $F_{y'y'} = 2 > 0$, a minimum of the functional may be reached on the extremals.

The Euler equation

$$2y'' - 2 \sin x = 0$$

has the general solution

$$y = \sin x + C_1 x + C_2.$$

The boundary conditions yield two equations to determine C_1 and C_2:

$$y(0) = C_2 = 0,$$
$$y(\pi) = C_1\pi + C_2 = 0,$$

from which we find $C_1 = C_2 = 0$, and we obtain the final equation of the extremal

$$y = \sin x.$$

II Generalizations of the Simplest Problem of Calculus of Variations

8. Problems with Variable Endpoints. General Formula for the Variations

The problem of seeking the minimum of the functional

$$J = \int_a^b F(x; y; y')\,dx$$

is called simplest in calculus of variations. Various generalizations of this simplest problem will be investigated in this chapter.

Thus, up to now problems were examined in which the extremum was sought among curves with fixed endpoints. Henceforth problems are encountered where the endpoints are not fixed. A formula for the variations of the functional which results both from the variations of the desired function, and from the variations of the endpoints, must be derived in order to solve them.

Let us examine Fig. 9, where $y(x)$ is the original function and $y(x)+h(x)$ the variation. The increment in the functional for the pas-

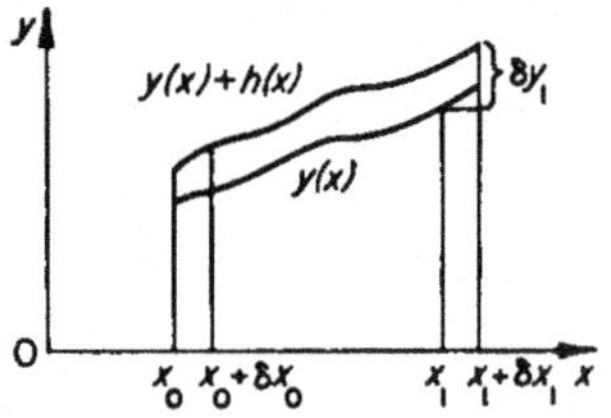

FIG. 9

sage from y to $y+h$ may be written as

$$\begin{aligned}\Delta J &= J(y+h) - J(y)\\ &= \int_{x_0+\delta x_0}^{x_1+\delta x_1} F(x;\, y+h;\, y'+h')\,dx - \int_{x_0}^{x_1} F(x;\, y;\, y')\,dx\\ &= \int_{x_0}^{x_1} [F(x;\, y+h;\, y'+h') - F(x;\, y;\, y')]\,dx\\ &\quad+ \int_{x_1}^{x_1+\delta x_1} F(x;\, y+h;\, y'+h')\,dx\\ &\quad- \int_{x_0}^{x_0+\delta x_0} F(x;\, y+h;\, y'+h')\,dx. \end{aligned} \tag{1}$$

Let us again isolate the main smooth, linear portion of the increment of the functional, its variation. We obtain

$$\delta J = \int_{x_0}^{x_1} [F_y h + F_{y'} h']\,dx + F|_{x=x_1}\delta x_1 - F|_{x=x_0}\delta x_0. \tag{2}$$

After the second member of the integrand has been integrated by parts, (2) becomes

$$\delta J = \int_{x_0}^{x_1} \left(F_y - \frac{d}{dx}F_{y'}\right) h\,dx + F_{y'}h\Big|_{x_0}^{x_1} + F\Big|_{x_1}\delta x_1 - F\Big|_{x_0}\delta x_0.$$

But since to the accuracy of higher order infinitesimals (as is seen from Fig. 9)

$$h(x_0) = \delta y_0 - y'\,\delta x_0; \qquad h(x_1) = \delta y_1 - y'\,\delta x_0,$$

we then obtain the final expression for the variation of the functional

$$\begin{aligned}\delta J &= \int_{x_0}^{x_1} \left(F_y - \frac{d}{dx}F_{y'}\right) h\,dx + F_{y'}|_{x=x_1}\delta y_1\\ &\quad+ (F - y'F_{y'})|_{x=x_1}\delta x_1 - F_{y'}|_{x=x_0}\delta y_0\\ &\quad- (F - y'F_{y'})|_{x=x_0}\delta x_0. \end{aligned} \tag{3}$$

Hence, the variation of the functional consists of an integral term resulting from the variation of $y(x)$ within the old range of integration, and terms outside the integrals due to the variations of the endpoints. By using (3) a number of new problems may be solved.

9. Transversality Conditions

Let it be necessary to find the extremum of a functional among curves $y(x)$ whose endpoints may slide along two certain lines: $y=\varphi(x)$ and $y=\psi(x)$. The problem of finding the shortest distance between two curves, particularly between two circles (Fig. 10), is an example of such

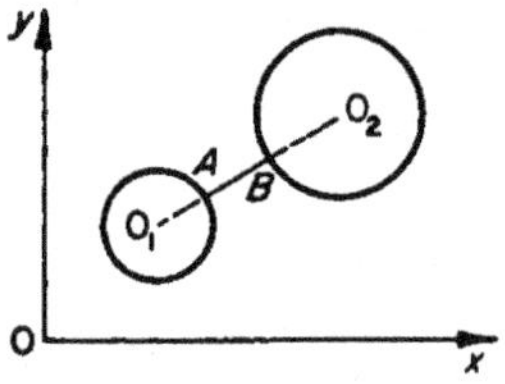

FIG. 10

a problem. To solve it, it is necessary to find not only the equation of the desired curve, but also the position of the points A and B which are not known beforehand.

Let us assume that the problem has been solved, i.e., a curve passing through the points A and B and yielding the minimum distance has been found. This curve may be only the extremal. In fact, if this curve is not the extremal, then another curve may be drawn between these same points A and B on which the value of the functional will be less. But the integral term in (3) vanishes for an extremal and

$$\delta J = F_{y'}|_{x=x_1}\,\delta y_1 + (F - y'F_{y'})|_{x=x_1}\,\delta x_1 - F_{y'}|_{x=x_0}\,\delta y_0 - (F - y'F_{y'})|_{x=x_0}\,\delta x_0\,.$$

Since to the accuracy of higher-order infinitesimals

$$\delta y_0 = \varphi'(x)\,\delta x_0\,; \qquad \delta y_1 = \psi'(x)\,\delta x_1\,,$$

the condition for the extremum $\delta J = 0$ may then be written as

$$\delta J = (F_{y'}\psi' + F - y'F_{y'})|_{x=x_1}\,\delta x_1 - (F_{y'}\varphi' + F - y'F_{y'})|_{x=x_0}\,\delta x_0\,. \tag{4}$$

Since δx_0 and δx_1 are mutually independent increments, it then follows from (4)

$$\begin{aligned} \psi'F_{y'} + F - y'F_{y'}|_{x=x_1} &= 0\,; \\ \varphi'F_{y'} + F - y'F_{y'}|_{x=x_0} &= 0\,. \end{aligned} \tag{5}$$

The conditions (5) are called the transversality conditions.

Let us recall that two arbitrary constants enter into the solution of the Euler equation. To determine them, it is necessary to have two equations. These equations are indeed the transversality conditions. Hence, the transversality conditions permit finding the position of the end points of the extremal.

The transversality conditions appear particularly simply for functionals of the form

$$J = \int_{x_1}^{x_2} f(x; y)(1 + y'^2)^{1/2}\, dx. \tag{6}$$

Indeed, in this case

$$F_{y'} = f(x; y)\frac{y'}{(1 + y'^2)^{1/2}} = \frac{Fy'}{1 + y'^2},$$

and the transversality condition becomes

$$\frac{F(1 + y'\psi')}{1 + y'^2} = 0,$$

from which it follows that $\psi' y' + 1 = 0$; $\psi' y' = -1$, i.e.,

$$y' = -1/\psi'. \tag{7}$$

Analogously at the second endpoint

$$y' = -1/\varphi'. \tag{8}$$

But conditions (7) and (8) mean that the extremal is orthogonal to the curves $\varphi(x)$ and $\psi(x)$, i.e., intersects them at a right angle. Transversality for the functionals (6) reduces to orthogonality.

In particular, among functionals of the form (6) is the length of a curve, i.e., the functional

$$S = \int_{x_1}^{x_2} (1 + y'^2)^{1/2}\, dx,$$

whose extremals are straight lines, as we established earlier.

Now, on the basis of the results of this section, we may assert that the shortest distance between two curves may only be a line perpendicular to both curves. Thus a line lying on the line of centers (Fig. 10) will be the shortest distance between two circles.

An example of an engineering problem for whose solution the transversality conditions must be used is presented in Section 21.

10. Extremals with Breaks. Weierstrass-Erdmann Conditions

The necessary condition for the existence of an extremum in the class of smooth curves was found in Section 6. Let us now consider a class of admissible curves and endpoints of piecewise-continous curves with a finite number of break points. In a number of cases the extremum may generally be achieved only on curves with breaks. Let us consider the functional

$$J = \int_0^2 y^2 (1 - y')^2 \, dx \tag{9}$$

with the boundary conditions: $y(0) = 0$; $y(2) = 1$. The functional (9) is not negative, its least value is zero and will only be achieved on the function $y = 0$ or the function $y = x + c$ (for which $1 - y' = 0$). However, neither of these functions will satisfy the boundary conditions and the minimum of the functional, which is zero, may only be achieved on a composite curve consisting of the pieces $y = 0$ and $y = x - 1$ with a break at the point $(y = 0; x = 1)$ (Fig. 11).

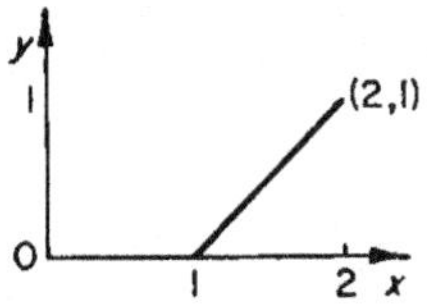

FIG. 11

In order to be able to seek the extremals with breaks, it is necessary to determine the conditions which must be satisfied at the break points. Let us turn to their derivation.

For simplicity, let us assume that the curve yielding the extremum of the integral

$$J = \int_a^b F(x; y; y') \, dx,$$

has one break at the point x_0 between a and b (Fig. 12).

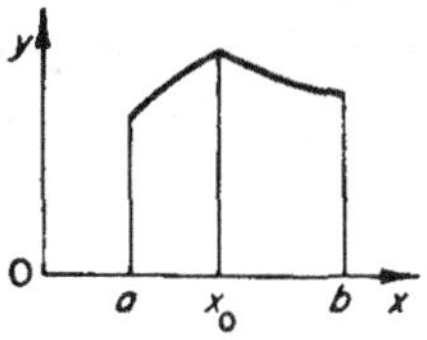

FIG. 12

Let us represent this integral as the sum of two integrals

$$J = \int_a^{x_0} F(x; y; y')\,dx + \int_{x_0}^{b} F(x; y; y')\,dx \tag{10}$$

and let us evaluate the variation of each separately. The curves $y(x)$ are extremals on each of the segments $[a; x_0]$ and $[x_0; b]$; therefore, the integral term in (3) vanishes, and

$$\begin{aligned} \delta J_1 &= F_{y'}\Big|_{x=x_0-0}\delta y_0 + (F - y'F_{y'})\Big|_{x=x_0-0}\delta x_0; \\ \delta J_2 &= F_{y'}\Big|_{x=x_0+0}\delta y_0 + (F - y'F_{y'})\Big|_{x=x_0+0}\delta x_1, \end{aligned} \tag{11}$$

where the symbol $x = x_0 - 0$ means that the derivatives are taken for x tending to x_0 from the left, and $x = x_0 + 0$ means that they are taken for x tending to x_0 from the right.

The necessary condition for the extremum is that the first variation equal zero, i.e.,

$$\delta J = \delta J_1 + \delta J_2 = 0.$$

Therefore

$$\left(F_{y'}\Big|_{x=x_0-0} - F_{y'}\Big|_{x=x_0+0}\right)\delta y_0 + \left[(F - y'F_{y'})\Big|_{x=x_0-0} - (F - y'F_{y'})\Big|_{x=x_0+0}\right]\delta x_0 = 0, \tag{12}$$

from which results, because of the arbitrariness of δx_0 and δy_0, that

$$\begin{aligned} F_{y'}\Big|_{x=x_0-0} &= F_{y'}\Big|_{x=x_0+0}; \\ (F - y'F_{y'})\Big|_{x=x_0-0} &= (F - y'F_{y'})\Big|_{x=x_0+0}. \end{aligned} \tag{13}$$

Conditions (13) are called the Weierstrass-Erdmann conditions. These conditions permit the determination of the missing arbitrary constants in the equations for the extremals. In fact, two arbitrary constants enter into the solution of the Euler equation on the section $[a; x_0]$ and the constants may be entirely different on the section $[x_0; b]$.

Four arbitrary constants in all must be determined, for which four equations are necessary. Two of them result from the boundary conditions $y(a) = A$; $y(b) = B$, and the missing two from the Weierstrass-Erdmann conditions (13).

Example. Let us consider the problem of seeking the curve passing through the points $x = 0$; $y = 0$ and $x = 2$; $y = 1$ and yielding the minimum of the functional

$$J = \int_0^2 (y^2 - 2y^2 y' + y^2 y'^2)\, dx. \tag{14}$$

In this case

$$F_{y'} = 2y^2 (y' - 1); \qquad F_{y'y'} = 2y^2.$$

Since the functional is explicitly independent of x, let us now write the first integral of the Euler equation

$$F - y' F_{y'} = C,$$

that is

$$y^2 (1 - y'^2) = C \tag{15}$$

from which it follows that either $y = 0$, or dividing Eq. (15) by $y \neq 0$ we obtain

$$y' = \pm \left(1 - \frac{C}{y^2}\right)^{1/2}. \tag{16}$$

Hence, the Euler equation has several solutions. There may be breaks on the horizontal axis, at which one solution of the Euler equation changes into the other.

From the Weierstrass-Erdmann conditions there results that $y' - 1 = 0$ should occur at the point of conjugation with the solution $y = 0$ for the extremals satisfying (16), i.e., $C = 0$ (actually, if $C \neq 0$, then to the right of the break point $F - y'F_{y'} = y^2(1 - y'^2) = C$ while to the left $F - y'F_{y'} = y^2(1 - y'^2) = 0$ since $y = 0$).

Thus, the minimum of the functional (14) is achieved on a curve with a break: we have $y = 0$ for $0 \leqslant x \leqslant 1$ and $y = x - 1$ for $1 \leqslant x \leqslant 2$. The solution becomes evident if the functional (14) is represented as

$$J = \int_0^2 y^2 (1 - y')^2 \, dx .$$

A curve composed of solutions to the Euler equation in such a way that the Weierstrass-Erdmann conditions are satisfied at the break points is called a broken-line extremal.

In particular, discontinuities (jumps) in the integrand $F(x; y; y')$ may be the reason for breaks in the extremals. An example of seeking the extremal for the case when $F(x; y; y')$ has discontinuities is presented in Section 19.

11. Functionals Dependent on Several Unknown Functions

Let us consider the curve $y = y(x)$; $z = z(x)$ in three-space. Its length

$$S = \int_{x_0}^{x_1} (1 + y'^2 + z'^2)^{1/2} \, dx \tag{17}$$

is an example of a functional dependent on two unknown functions. In order to find the shortest curve connecting two points in space, it is evidently necessary to find the two functions $y(x)$ and $z(x)$ yielding the minimum of the integral (17).

Let us consider the general expression for a functional dependent on n functions $y_i(x)$ $(i = 1, 2, \ldots, n)$:

$$J = \int_{x_0}^{x_1} F(x; y_1, \ldots, y_n; y_1', \ldots, y_n') \, dx . \tag{18}$$

Let us assume that the extremum exists and is achieved on the curve $y_1 = y_1(x); \ldots; y_n = y_n(x)$. Let us fix all functions except one, $y_1 = y_1(x)$, say, to which we shall assign the increment $\delta y_1(x)$. Then the variation of the functional (18) will depend only on one function, and exactly as in Section 5, the Euler equation for the function $y_1(x)$

$$\frac{\partial F}{\partial y_1} - \frac{d}{dx} \frac{\partial F}{\partial y_1'} = 0 .$$

will follow from the condition $\delta J = 0$.

But the very same reasoning may be repeated relative to any unknown function and we arrive at the final conclusion: For the curve $y_1 = y_1(x); \ldots; y_n = y_n(x)$ to yield the extremum of the functional (18), it is necessary that the functions $y_i(x)$ satisfy a system of differential equations, Euler equations:

$$F_{y_1} - \frac{d}{dx} F_{y_1'} = 0; \quad \vdots \quad F_{y_n} - \frac{d}{dx} F_{y_n'} = 0. \tag{19}$$

Example. The system of Euler equations for the functional (17) will be

$$\frac{y'}{(1 + y'^2 + z'^2)^{1/2}} = C_1; \qquad \frac{z'}{(1 + y'^2 + z'^2)^{1/2}} = C_3,$$

from which follows

$$y = C_1 x + C_2; \qquad z = C_3 x + C_4$$

i.e., straight lines in space are the extremals.

Legendre Condition

Let us present the Legendre condition (without the proof as given by Giunter [3]) for a functional dependent on several unknown functions.

In order for the minimum of a functional to be obtained at the extremals, it is necessary to satisfy the chain of inequalities:

$$F_{y_1'y_1'} \geqslant 0; \quad \begin{vmatrix} F_{y_1'y_1'} F_{y_1'y_2'} \\ F_{y_2'y_1'} F_{y_2'y_2'} \end{vmatrix} \geqslant 0; \quad \begin{vmatrix} F_{y_1'y_1'} \cdots F_{y_1'y_n'} \\ \cdots\cdots \\ F_{y_n'y_1'} \cdots F_{y_n'y_n'} \end{vmatrix} \geqslant 0. \tag{20}$$

The signs of the inequalities are reversed for a maximum.

If the functional depends on two unknown functions $y(x)$ and $z(x)$, then the two first members of the chain remain, and the Legendre condition becomes

$$F_{y'y'} \geqslant 0; \qquad F_{y'y'}F_{z'z'} - F_{y'z'}F_{z'y'} \geqslant 0. \tag{21}$$

Thus, for the problem we consider of the shortest distance between two points in space we have

$$F_{y'z'} = F_{z'y'} = \frac{y'z'}{(1 + y'^2 + z'^2)^{3/2}};$$

$$F_{y'y'} = \frac{1 + z'^2}{(1 + y'^2 + z'^2)^{3/2}}; \qquad F_{z'z'} = \frac{1 + y'^2}{(1 + y'^2 + z'^2)^{3/2}};$$

$$F_{y'y'}F_{z'z'} - F_{y'z'}F_{z'y'} = \frac{1}{(1 + y'^2 + z'^2)^{1/2}} > 0.$$

Hence, the minimum distance between two points in space can actually be achieved on extremals (straight lines).

12. Functionals Dependent on Higher-Order Derivatives

Functionals dependent not only on the first but also on the higher derivatives of the desired function are encountered in problems of the calculus of variations.

Let the functional be

$$J = \int_{x_0}^{x_1} F(x; y; y'; y''; \ldots; y^{(n)})\, dx. \tag{22}$$

Then the curve yielding the extremum should satisfy the Euler-Poisson equation

$$F_y - \frac{d}{dx} F_{y'} + \frac{d^2}{dx^2} F_{y''} - \cdots + (-1)^n \frac{d^n}{dx^n} F_{y^{(n)}} = 0. \tag{23}$$

Let us prove (23) by limiting ourselves, for simplicity, to a computation of the case of the second derivative, i.e.,

$$J = \int_{x_0}^{x_1} F(x; y; y'; y'')\, dx. \tag{24}$$

Let us add a variation δy to the function $y(x)$ such that both δy and $\delta y'$ would vanish at the endpoints, i.e., at $x = x_0$ and $x = x_1$.

The principal, linear part of the increment of the functional (the first variation) will be

$$\delta J = \int_{x_0}^{x_1} (F_y\, \delta y + F_{y'}\, \delta y' + F_{y''}\, \delta y'')\, dx. \tag{25}$$

Let us now convert the expression for the variations by using integration by parts:

$$\int_{x_0}^{x_1} F_{y'}\,\delta y'\,dx = F_{y'}\,\delta y\Big|_{x_0}^{x_1} - \int_{x_0}^{x_1} \frac{d}{dx} F_{y'}\,\delta y\,dx\,;$$

$$\int_{x_0}^{x_1} F_{y''}\,\delta y''\,dx = F_{y''}\,\delta y'\Big|_{x_0}^{x_1} - \int_{x_0}^{x_1} \frac{d}{dx} F_{y''}\,\delta y'\,dx \tag{26}$$

$$= F_{y''}\,\delta y'\Big|_{x_0}^{x_1} - \frac{d}{dx} F_{y''}\,\delta y\Big|_{x_0}^{x_1} + \int_{x_0}^{x_1} \frac{d^2}{dx^2} F_{y''}\,\delta y\,dx\,.$$

According to the conditions at the endpoints, all the nonintegral members vanish, and we obtain

$$\delta J = \int_{x_0}^{x_1} \left(F_y - \frac{d}{dx} F_{y'} + \frac{d^2}{dx^2} F_{y''} \right) \delta y\,dx\,. \tag{27}$$

Since a necessary condition of the extremum is that the first variation equal zero, and as δy is arbitrary, the Euler-Poisson equation (23) follows from the equality $\delta J = 0$, and in this case it is a fourth-order differential equation. The four arbitrary constants in the solution are determined from the boundary conditions. Thus, if values of the function $y(x)$ and its derivative $y'(x)$ are given at two points, this permits the formation of four equations for the determination of the four constants of integration.

Example. A homogeneous heavy beam is clamped at the ends at the points A and B (Fig. 13). We are required to determine the shape of

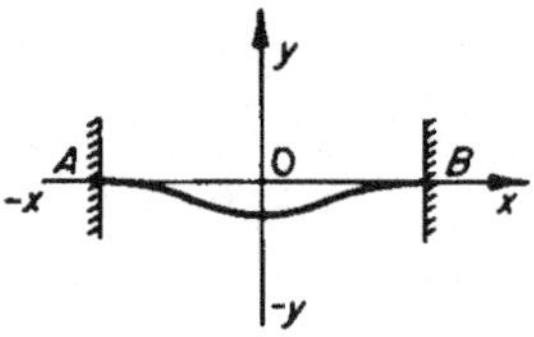

FIG. 13

the bent axis of the beam. For the solution we use the known principle: The potential energy of a beam achieves a minimum in a state of stable equilibrium.

Let us introduce a coordinate system such that the Ox axis connects the points of support, and the origin divides the segment AB in half (Fig. 13).

Let us choose $2l$ to be the distance between the supports, ρ to be the weight per unit length of the beam and ds to be an element of arc of the bent axis. Let $y(x)$ be the equation of the axis. The potential energy of the elastic forces, the bending moment, will equal

$$\tfrac{1}{2}\mu \int_0^L \left(\frac{d\varphi}{ds}\right)^2 ds. \tag{28}$$

where μ is a constant coefficient dependent on the elastic modulus of the material and the moment of inertia of the beam cross section, L is the length of the beam between the supports, and φ the angle formed by the tangent to the beam axis and the Ox axis.

The potential energy produced by gravity will be

$$\rho \int_0^L y\, ds. \tag{29}$$

The total potential energy of the beam, produced both by the elastic forces and the force of gravity, will be

$$E = \int_0^L \left[\tfrac{1}{2}\mu \left(\frac{d\varphi}{ds}\right)^2 + \rho y\right] ds. \tag{30}$$

Substituting the values

$$ds = (1 + y'^2)^{1/2}; \qquad \frac{d\varphi}{ds} = \frac{y''}{(1 + y'^2)^{3/2}}$$

(where $d\varphi/ds$ is the curvature of the beam axis) we obtain

$$E = \int_{-l}^{+l} \left[\tfrac{1}{2}\mu \frac{y''^2}{(1 + y'^2)^{5/2}} + \rho y (1 + y'^2)^{1/2}\right] dx. \tag{31}$$

Since E is a minimum at the stable equilibrium position, then $y(x)$ is an extremal of the functional (31). The exact equation of the extremal is awkward; hence, let us limit ourselves to an approximate solution, as we would in practice, by assuming that the beam deflection is small and that second degrees in y' may be neglected. We obtain

$$E = \int_{-l}^{+l} \left[\tfrac{1}{2}\mu y''^2 + \rho y\right] dx, \tag{32}$$

and the Euler-Poisson equation becomes

$$p + \mu \frac{d^2}{dx^2} y'' = 0. \tag{33}$$

Therefore

$$y^{\mathrm{IV}} = -p/\mu$$

and

$$y = -\frac{p}{24\mu} x^4 + C_3 x^3 + C_2 x^2 + C_1 x + C_0. \tag{34}$$

The four constants C_i are determined from the conditions at the endpoints. Because of symmetry $C_3 = C_1 = 0$. Furthermore, since

$$\begin{aligned} y(-l) = y(l) &= -\frac{p}{24\mu} l^4 + C_2 l^2 + C_0 = 0; \\ y'(-l) = y'(l) &= -\frac{p}{6\mu} l^3 + 2C_2 l = 0, \end{aligned} \tag{35}$$

we finally obtain by solving (35)

$$y = \frac{p}{24\mu}(-x^4 + 2l^2x^2 - l^4).$$

The greatest deflection $y_{\max} = -(p/24\mu)l^4$ will be at the middle of the beam, for $x = 0$.

If the ends are not clamped, then a more general formula is necessary for the variations, taking account of the variation of the ends. Analogously to formula (3) for the functional (24), it is possible to derive the following expression:

$$\begin{aligned} \delta J = &\int_{x_0}^{x_1} \left[F_y - \frac{d}{dx} F_{y'} + \frac{d^2}{dx^2} F_{y''} \right] dx \\ &+ \left[F - y'\left(F_{y'} - \frac{d}{dx} F_{y''} \right) + y' \frac{d}{dx} F_{y''} \right]\Bigg|_{x=x_1} \delta x_1 \\ &+ \left(F_{y'} - \frac{d}{dx} F_{y''} \right)\Bigg|_{x=x_1} \delta y_1 + F_{y''}\Big|_{x=x_1} \delta y_1', \end{aligned} \tag{36}$$

where δx_1 is the variation of the abscissa of the end, δy_1 the variation of the ordinate; $\delta y_1'$ the variation of the derivative at the endpoint.

Exactly as from (3) before, transversality conditions for functionals dependent on higher-order derivatives can be derived from (36).

Let us note an important particular case. Let the endpoints be fixed, but let the derivative of the extremal not be defined there. In this case $\delta x_0 = \delta x_1 = \delta y_0 = \delta y_1 = 0$ and

$$\delta J = F_{y''}\bigg|_{x=x_1} \delta y_1' - F_{y''}\bigg|_{x=x_0} \delta y_0 .$$

Hence, because of the arbitrariness of the variations δy_0 and δy_1, there follows from the condition $\delta J = 0$,

$$F_{y''}\bigg|_{x=x_0} = 0; \qquad F_{y''}\bigg|_{x=x_1} = 0. \tag{37}$$

In combination with the conditions $y(x_0) = y_0$ and $y(x_1) = y_1$, these two conditions yield four equations to determine the four constants of integration in the Euler-Poisson equations.

Example. Let us turn to the problem of determining the deflection mode of a heavy elastic beam, but let us assume this time that the ends of the beam are not fixed but are freely supported at A and B (Fig. 14). Such fixing does not predetermine the values of $y'(x)$ at A and B beforehand.

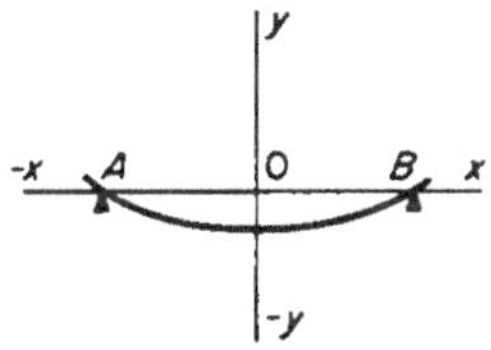

FIG. 14

The equation of the extremal $y(x)$ agrees with (34) of the preceding example. To determine the constants, let us use the conditions (37) just derived at the endpoints.

From symmetry conditions $C_3 = C_1 = 0$. Furthermore, we obtain $-(\rho/24\mu)\, l^4 + C_2 l^2 + C_0 = 0$ from $y(l) = y(-l) = 0$. From $F_{y''}(l) = \mu y''(l) = 0$ we have $-(\rho/2\mu)\, l^2 + 2C_2 = 0$; finally

$$y = -\frac{\rho}{24\mu} x^4 + \frac{\rho}{4\mu} l^2 x^2 - \frac{5\rho}{24\mu} l^4 .$$

The greatest deflection $y_{max} = -(5p/24\mu)\,l^4$ is fivefold greater than in the case of the clamped ends. This example illustrates the role of the boundary conditions.

Legendre Condition

In the simplest problem of the calculus of variations, the sign of the expression $F_{y'y'}$ permitted separation of the maximum from the minimum. The sign of the expression $F_{y^{(n)}y^{(n)}}$ plays the same part for a functional dependent on the higher derivatives.

There exists a theorem: If $y(x)$ yields the minimum of the functional (22) it is necessary that

$$F_{y^{(n)}y^{(n)}} \geqslant 0\,; \tag{38}$$

if $y(x)$ yields the maximum, then

$$F_{y^{(n)}y^{(n)}} \leqslant 0\,. \tag{38'}$$

This is indeed the Legendre condition for the functional dependent on the higher derivatives. The proof may be found in the work of Giunter [3] and Lavrent'ev and Liusternik [4].

If $F_{y^{(n)}y^{(n)}}$ is identically zero, this means the functional is degenerate. Degenerate functionals will be investigated separately.

Example. Let us investigate the problem, presented in this section, of the flexure of a heavy beam. The functional (32) depends on the second derivative. Therefore, the sign of the expression $F_{y''y''}$ must be determined. We have

$$F_{y''} = \mu y''; \qquad F_{y''y''} = \mu > 0\,.$$

Hence, the functional (32) is nondegenerate and a minimum of the potential energy of the beam may be achieved on the extremal (34).

13. Conditional Extremum

Variational problems such as when the functions yielding the extremum of the functional are themselves subject to some additional conditions (coupling equations) are encountered in engineering very frequently. Such problems are designated problems with a conditional extremum. A number of such examples are presented in Chapters III and VI. The problem of finding the shortest distance between two points, i.e., the minimum of the integral

$$S = \int_{x_0}^{x_1} (1 + y'^2 + z'^2)^{1/2} \, dx, \tag{39}$$

under the condition that the curve connecting these points lie on a certain surface, the sphere, e.g.,

$$z^2 + y^2 + x^2 - R^2 = 0 \tag{40}$$

is the simplest such example.

In principle, z may be expressed in terms of y and x from the coupling equation (40), be substituted into the integral (39), and the minimum of the usual functional of one variable might be sought.

However, such elimination of variables often leads to very complex computations, and it is more convenient to utilize another method of solution, such as the Lagrange method of undetermined multipliers.

The following simple mnemonic rule (theorem) exists: In order to find the extremum of the functional

$$J = \int_{x_0}^{x_1} F(x; y; y'; z; z') \, dx \tag{41}$$

under the condition

$$\varphi(x; y; z) = 0, \tag{42}$$

it is necessary to introduce an intermediate function

$$H = F + \lambda(x) \, \varphi(x; y; z), \tag{43}$$

where $\lambda(x)$ is a function of x as yet unknown, and to seek the extremum of the functional

$$J_1 = \int_{x_0}^{x_1} H \, dx \tag{44}$$

by customary methods.

In all we must determine three unknown functions: $y(x)$, $z(x)$, and $\lambda(x)$. We have three equations for their determination: the two Euler equations for the functional (44)

$$H_y - \frac{d}{dx} H_{y'} = F_y - \frac{d}{dx} F_{y'} + \varphi_y \lambda(x) = 0\,;$$
$$H_z - \frac{d}{dx} H_{z'} = F_z - \frac{d}{dx} F_{z'} + \varphi_z \lambda(x) = 0 \qquad (45)$$

and the coupling equation (42). From these equations we indeed find the desired functions. The function $\lambda(x)$ is designated the Lagrange multiplier.

Let us prove the validity of the mnemonic rule.

Let us assume that the extremum is achieved on the curve $y = y(x)$; $z = z(x)$; to $y(x)$ and $z(x)$ let us add the variations δy and δz, which differ from zero only in a small neighborhood of some point x_c (where $x_0 < x_c < x_1$), and let us use the notation

$$\sigma_1 = \int_{x_0}^{x_1} \delta y\, dx; \qquad \sigma_2 = \int_{x_0}^{x_1} \delta z\, dx\,.$$

Now, let us evaluate the variation of the functional for the passage from the curve $y = y(x)$; $z = z(x)$ to the curve $y + \delta y$; $z + \delta z$.

Executing the customary variational transformations, we obtain

$$\delta J = \int_{x_0}^{x_1} \left(F_y - \frac{d}{dx} F_{y'}\right) \delta y\, dx + \int_{x_0}^{x_1} \left(F_z - \frac{d}{dx} F_{z'}\right) \delta z\, dx$$
$$= \left(F_y - \frac{d}{dx} F_{y'}\right)\bigg|_{x = x_c} \sigma_1 + \left(F_z - \frac{d}{dx} F_{z'}\right)\bigg|_{x = x_c} \sigma_2\,. \qquad (46)$$

However, the curve which has been variated, $y = y(x) + \delta y$; $z = z(x) + \delta z$, should lie on the surface, i.e., should satisfy (42), just as the original does. Therefore

$$\int_{x_0}^{x_1} [\varphi(x; y + \delta y; z + \delta z) - \varphi(x; y; z)]\, dx$$
$$= \int_{x_0}^{x_1} (\varphi_y\, \delta y + \varphi_z\, \delta z)\, dx = \varphi_y\Big|_{x = x_c} \sigma_1 + \varphi_z\Big|_{x = x_c} \sigma_2 = 0.$$

Assuming at least one of the coefficients φ_y and φ_z to be nonzero, we have

$$\sigma_2 = \frac{\varphi_y}{\varphi_z} \sigma_1 \qquad (47)$$

and substituting (47) into (46), we reduce the expression for the variations (46) to

$$\delta J = \left[F_y - \frac{d}{dx} F_{y'} - \frac{\varphi_y}{\varphi_z}\left(F_z - \frac{d}{dx} F_{z'} \right) \right] \sigma_1 ,$$

from which it follows that

$$F_y - \frac{d}{dx} F_{y'} - \frac{\varphi_y}{\varphi_z}\left(F_z - \frac{d}{dx} F_{z'} \right) = 0$$

or

$$\frac{F_y - \dfrac{d}{dx} F_{y'}}{\varphi_y} = \frac{F_z - \dfrac{d}{dx} F_{z'}}{\varphi_z}. \tag{48}$$

The equality (48) is satisfied for any x within the range $x_0 \leqslant x \leqslant x_1$; hence, denoting the right- and left-hand sides of (48) by $\lambda(x)$, we obtain (45). The mnemonic rule has thereby been proved.

The same rule is extended to the case when several conditions of the type (42) are given. In this case the intermediate function has the form

$$H = F(x;\, y_i;\, y_i') + \sum_{j=1}^{n} \lambda_j \varphi_j(x;\, y_i). \tag{49}$$

The same rule is retained if the coupling equation contains derivatives of the desired functions, i.e., is a differential equation

$$\varphi(x;\, y;\, y';\, z;\, z') = 0. \tag{50}$$

This problem (when derivatives enter into the coupling equation) is called the general Lagrange problem.

The mnemonic rule is extended also to seeking the transversality conditions. They are written exactly as for the simplest problem except that the intermediate function $H = F + \lambda\varphi$ plays the part of the function F.

14. Isoperimetric Problem

The conditions to which the desired functions are subject in conditional extremum problems may be given in integral form. Thus, it is possible to seek the extremum of the functional

$$J_1 = \int_{x_0}^{x_1} F(x; y; y')\, dx \tag{51}$$

under the condition that another functional

$$J_2 = \int_{x_0}^{x_1} K(x; y; y')\, dx \tag{52}$$

retain a given value J_{20}.

This kind of problem is called isoperimetric according to the name of one of them—that of finding the curve bounding the greatest area among all curves of equal length (identical perimeter).

The isoperimetric problem may be reduced to the general Lagrange problem. In fact, using the notation

$$\psi(x) = \int_{x_0}^{x} K(x; y; y')\, dx \tag{53}$$

we obtain

$$\psi' = K(x; y; y'), \tag{54}$$

and we arrive at the following Lagrange problem: To find functions $y(x)$ and $\psi(x)$ yielding an extremum of the functional (51) in the presence of the coupling equation (54). According to the general rule of solving Lagrange problems, it is necessary to form the Euler equation for the intermediate function

$$H = F + \lambda(x)(\psi' - K).$$

The Euler equations are

$$H_y - \frac{d}{dx} H_{y'} = 0;$$

$$H_\psi - \frac{d}{dx} H_{\psi'} = -\frac{d}{dx}\lambda = 0.$$

From the second equation there follows that $\lambda = \text{const}$, i.e., the Lagrange multiplier becomes a constant for the isoperimetric problem. The presented proof is easily generalized for any number of conditions of the type (52), and we arrive at the following mnemonic rule: If a curve

$y(x)$ yields the extremum of the integral (51) in the presence of the n conditions

$$J_i = \int_{x_0}^{x_1} K_i(x; y; y')\,dx \qquad (i = 1, 2, \ldots, n),$$

then $y(x)$ satisfies the Euler equation

$$H_y - \frac{d}{dx} H_{y'} = 0$$

where

$$H = F + \lambda_{01}K_1 + \lambda_{02}K_2 + \cdots + \lambda_{0n}K_n,$$

and the λ_{0n} are constants.

Example. Among all curves of length l connecting two points A and B, find the curve bounding the greatest area in combination with the segment AB (Fig. 15).

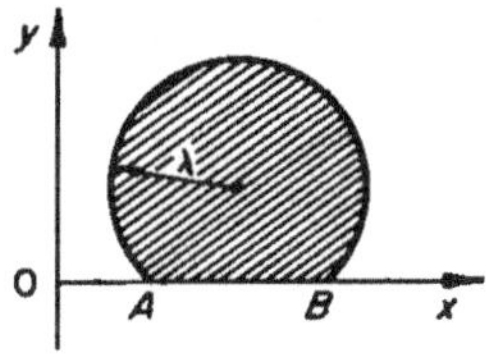

FIG. 15

Disposing the coordinate axes so that the Ox axis passes through the points A and B (Fig. 15), we calculate that the area bounded by the desired curve $y(x)$ will equal the integral

$$J = \int_a^b y\,dx. \tag{55}$$

It is necessary to find the function $y(x)$ yielding the maximum of the integral (55) under the condition

$$\int_a^b (1 + y'^2)^{1/2}\,dx = l$$

and the conditions $y(a) = y(b) = 0$ at the endpoints.

Applying the mnemonic rule, we form the intermediate function

$$H = y + \lambda_0(1 + y'^2).$$

Since H is explicitly independent of x, the first integral of the Euler equation may be written as

$$H - y'H_{y'} = C_1,$$

that is

$$y + \lambda_0(1 + y'^2)^{1/2} - \lambda_0[y'^2/(1 + y'^2)^{1/2}] = C_1,$$

from which

$$y = C_1 - [\lambda_0/(1 + y'^2)^{1/2}]$$

or

$$(y - C_1)^2 = \lambda_0^2/(1 + y'^2).$$

Integrating, we obtain

$$(x - C_2)^2 + (y - C_1)^2 = \lambda_0{}^2. \tag{56}$$

This is the equation of a circle of radius λ_0.

Hence, the curve bounding the greatest area will be part of a circle. The three unknown constants C_1, C_2, and λ_0 are determined from three conditions: that the circle pass through the point A, the point B, and that its length between A and B be l.

Reciprocity Principle

The equations for the extremals of the functional $J = \int_{x_0}^{x_1} H\, dx$ do not change if the function H is multiplied by a constant. Taking this into account we may write the intermediate function H in the symmetric form:

$$H = \lambda_{01}F + \lambda_{02}K. \tag{57}$$

This equality shows that the functions F and K in the expression for H are equivalent. If the cases $\lambda_{01} = 0$ and $\lambda_{02} = 0$ are eliminated, the equations of the extremals do not change, whether we seek the extremum of the integral J_1 under the condition of constant J_2, or the extremum of J_2 under the condition of constant J_1. This is indeed the reciprocity principle.

In the problem just considered, we found that a circle of given perimeter bounds the greatest area. According to the reciprocity principle, if we seek the curve of shortest length bounding a portion of the given area, the extremals will also be circles.

LEGENDRE CONDITION; TRANSVERSALITY CONDITIONS

The mnemonic rule is also extended to the transversality and Legendre conditions. In the expressions obtained for the simplest problem it is just necessary to substitute the intermediate function $H = F + \lambda_0 K$ in place of the function F.

The proof of the mnemonic rule for this case is given by Giunter [3] and Lavrent'ev and Liusternik [4].

Example. Let us return to the problem we just considered of a curve of given length bounding the greatest area, but let us assume that the end-points of the curve are not fixed but may move freely along the Ox axis.

The desired curve is an extremal, i.e., part of a circle. We just do not know how this circle is disposed relative to the Ox axis. The transversality conditions aid in answering this question. In the case we have under consideration

$$H + (\varphi' - y')\, H_{y'} = y + \lambda_0\,(1 + y'^2)^{1/2} - \lambda_0\,[y'^2/(1 + y'^2)^{1/2}] = 0$$

(since $\varphi' = 0$), and we have for $y = 0$

$$\lambda_0/(1 + y'^2)^{1/2} = 0\,. \tag{58}$$

The equality (58) may be satisfied only for $y' = \infty$, i.e., the desired curve is a semicircle with the Ox axis as the diameter (Fig. 16).

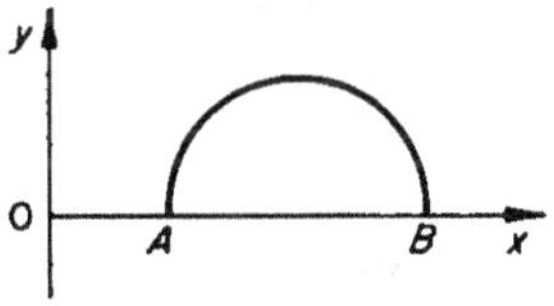

FIG. 16

15. General Lagrange Problem. Maier and Bolza Problems

As has already been mentioned, the problem of the conditional extremum is called the general Lagrange problem when differential equations enter among the conditions. It is the most general problem in the calculus of variations. Other problems are either particular cases of the Lagrange problem, or are equivalent. Thus, it has been shown in the previous section that the isoperimetric problem may be reduced to the Lagrange problem. Also, even the problem on the extremum of a functional dependent on the higher derivatives, say,

$$J = \int_{x_0}^{x_1} F(x; y; y'; y'')\, dx\,, \tag{59}$$

may be reduced to the Lagrange problem by putting $y' = z;\ y'' = z'$.

We then obtain the problem of the extremum of the functional

$$J = \int_{x_0}^{x_1} F(x; y; y'; z')\, dx \tag{60}$$

under the condition

$$y' - z = 0. \tag{61}$$

Hence, all the problems we considered earlier are included among the general Lagrange problems.

The following variational problem is called the Maier problem: Given a system of m equations (differential or finite) with n unknown functions $y(x)$

$$\begin{aligned} \varphi_1(x; y_1, \ldots, y_n; y_1', \ldots, y_n') &= 0; \\ &\vdots \\ \varphi_m(x; y_1, \ldots, y_n; y_1', \ldots, y_n') &= 0, \end{aligned} \tag{62}$$

in the interval $(a; b)$, where $n > m$, i.e., the number of equations is less than the number of unknown functions. If $n = m$ the system (62) with the appropriate boundary conditions then determines all the functions in it. Since $n > m$, the variation remains free, and we may seek $(n - m)$ such functions $y_i(x)$ as would yield the extremal value at one of the endpoints of the interval $(a; b)$. This is the Maier problem.

An example of the Maier problem is the problem of controlling an accelerating motor so that its velocity $v(T)$ would become a maximum at the time T.

The specificity of the Maier problem is that at first glance it seems to be necessary to seek the extremum of a functional which does not have the customary "standard" form

$$J = \int_a^b F(x; y; y')\, dx\,.$$

Thus, in the problem with the accelerating motor, it is necessary to find the extremum of the functional $v(T)$ (taking account of the coupling equations). But since

$$v(T) = \int_0^T v' \, dt,$$

this functional is then easily reduced to the customary, "standard" form (the problem of controlling an accelerating motor is considered in more detail in Section 41).

Even in the general case, the Maier problem is easily reduced to the Lagrange problem if $(n - m)$ new functions $u_i(x)$ connected to the old by means of the relationships $y_i' = u_i$ are introduced.

Then the Maier problem is reduced to the problem of the extremum of the functional

$$J = \int_a^b (u_1 + u_2 + \cdots + u_{n-m}) \, dx \tag{63}$$

with the coupling equations (62).

The converse is also possible; the Lagrange problem can be reduced to a Maier problem. Both problems are equivalent.

The problem of seeking the extremum of a functional of the form

$$I = \int_{x_0}^{x_1} F(x; y; y') \, dx + \Phi(x_0; y_0; x_1; y_1)\Big|_{x_0}^{x_1} \tag{64}$$

in the presence of coupling equations is called the Bolza (or mixed) problem.

The Bolza problem is also equivalent to the Lagrange problem, and may be reduced thereto by the introduction of the auxiliary variable

$$u = d\Phi/dx.$$

Hence, all three problems, the Lagrange, Maier and Bolza, possess an equal degree of generality.

16. Variational Problems in Parametric Form

A number of inconveniences occur in seeking extremals in the form $y = y(x)$. It must be assumed that $y(x)$ is a single-valued function, while the extremum is often achieved on curves where several values of y correspond to the same x (Fig. 15). For the extremals shown in Fig. 15, the reasoning of the previous sections is, strictly speaking, meaningless. However, these inconveniences and constraints can be avoided if we use a parametric representation of the curves, i.e., give the curve by means of the equations

$$x = x(t); \qquad y = y(t), \tag{65}$$

where t is a parameter, instead of by the equation $y = y(x)$.

Thus, the equation of a circle may be written as

$$x = a\cos t; \qquad y = a\sin t, \quad 0 \leqslant t \leqslant 2\pi. \tag{66}$$

The very same circle may be given by different parametric equations. Thus, transforming from the parameter t in (66) to the parameter u by means of the formula $\tan \frac{1}{2}t = u$, we obtain the following equation of a circle:

$$x = \frac{a(1-u^2)}{1+u^2}; \qquad y = \frac{2au}{1+u^2}, \qquad -\infty < u < \infty. \tag{67}$$

In investigating some functional

$$J = \int_{x_0}^{x_1} F(x; y; y')\, dx,$$

let it turn out to be more convenient to seek the solution in the parametric form $x = x(t)$; $y = y(t)$. Then the functional becomes

$$J = \int_{t_0}^{t_1} F\left(x; y; \frac{y'(t)}{x'(t)}\right) x'(t)\, dt = \int_{t_0}^{t_1} \Phi(x; y; x'; y')\, dt, \tag{68}$$

in which the integrand is a homogeneous function with respect to $x'(t)$ and $y'(t)$.

Two Euler equations,

$$\Phi_x - d/dt\, \Phi_{x'} = 0; \qquad \Phi_y - d/dt\, \Phi_{y'} = 0, \tag{69}$$

may be formed for the functional (68).

However, because of the homogeneity of the function Φ, Eqs. (69) are not independent; one is a consequence of the other. To find the extremal, it is necessary to take one of the Euler equations and to integrate it in combination with the equation determining the selection of the parameter.

17. Canonical Form of the Euler Equations

The Euler equation

$$F_y - d/dx\, F_{y'} = 0$$

may be written in another form by using a transformation of variables. Instead of x and y let us introduce the new variables

$$p = F_{y'} \tag{70}$$

$$H = F - y'F_{y'}. \tag{71}$$

Now, since $H = F - y'F_{y'}$ and $\partial H/\partial y = F_y$,

$$\frac{\partial H}{\partial y} = \frac{dp}{dx}; \tag{72}$$

$$\frac{\partial H}{\partial p} = -\,y' = -\frac{dy}{dx}. \tag{73}$$

then follow from (70) and (71).

The system of equations

$$\frac{\partial H}{\partial y} = \frac{dp}{dx}; \qquad \frac{\partial H}{\partial p} = -\frac{dy}{dx} \tag{74}$$

is called the Hamiltonian, or canonical, form of the Euler equations. It is equivalent to the second-order Euler equation with one unknown function. The variables H and p are called canonical variables.

The representation of the Euler equation in the form (74) is often convenient in theoretical investigations. Thus, the Weierstrass-Erdmann conditions become in the canonical variables

$$p_{x+0} = p_{x-0}; \qquad H_{x+0} = H_{x-0},$$

i.e., reduce to the condition that the canonical variables be continuous at the break point.

Analogously, for the general Lagrange problem the system of Euler equations

$$\Phi_{y_i} - \frac{d}{dx}\Phi_{y_i'} = 0 \qquad (i = 1, 2, \ldots, n) \tag{75}$$

for the intermediate function

$$\Phi = F + \sum_{i=1}^{n} \lambda_i \varphi_i \tag{76}$$

may be written as

$$\frac{\partial H}{\partial y_i} = \frac{dp_i}{dx}; \qquad \frac{\partial H}{\partial p_i} = -\frac{dy_i}{dx}, \tag{77}$$

where

$$H = \Phi - \sum_{i=1}^{n} y_i \Phi_{y_i'}; \qquad p_i = \Phi_{y_i'}. \tag{78}$$

18. Extremum of a Functional Dependent on a Function of Several Variables

Let us consider the functional, the double integral

$$J[z = f(x; y)] = \iint_D F\left(x; y; z; \frac{\partial z}{\partial x}; \frac{\partial z}{\partial y}\right) dx\, dy, \tag{79}$$

defined on some surface $z = f(x; y)$ in Fig. 17. Let $z = f(x; y)$ be given on

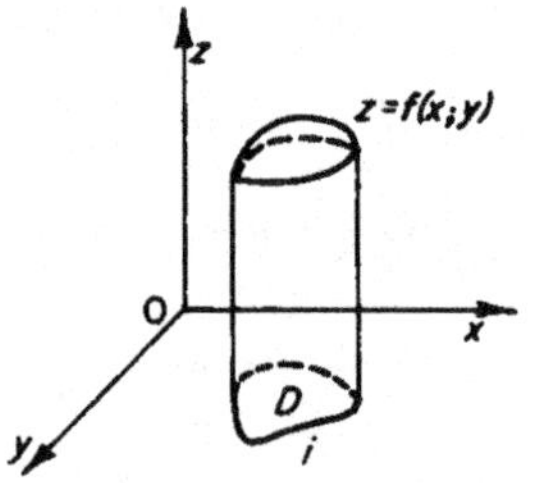

FIG. 17

the boundary of the domain D (i.e., the edges of the surface are fixed); let us pose the problem: Find that surface with fixed edges $z = f(x; y)$ on which the functional (79) would take the extremal value.

Let us derive the necessary condition for the extremum, the Euler-Ostrogradskii equation. Let the extremum of the functional (74) be achieved on some function $z = f(x; y)$. If we add the variation δz, an arbitrary function subject only to the condition that $\delta z = 0$ on the boundary of the domain D, to the function z, then the first variation of the functional (79) should vanish.

Using the notation

$$\frac{\partial z}{\partial x} = p; \qquad \frac{\partial z}{\partial y} = q$$

for brevity, we obtain

$$\delta J = \iint_D [F_z \, \delta z + F_p \, \delta p + F_q \, \delta q] \, dx \, dy. \tag{80}$$

Let us now use the Green's formula to transform (80)

$$\iint_D \left(\frac{\partial Q}{\partial x} - \frac{\partial P}{\partial y} \right) dx \, dy = \int_L P \, dx + Q \, dy, \tag{81}$$

where the integral on the right-hand side is taken over the curve L which is the contour of the domain D.

Since

$$\iint_D \left[F_p \, \delta\left(\frac{\partial z}{\partial x}\right) + F_q \, \delta\left(\frac{\partial z}{\partial y}\right) \right] dx \, dy$$

$$= \iint_D \left[\frac{\partial}{\partial x}(\delta z \, F_p) - \frac{\partial}{\partial y}(\delta z \, F_q) \right] dx \, dy$$

$$- \iint_D \delta z \left(\frac{\partial}{\partial x} F_p + \frac{\partial}{\partial y} F_q \right) dx \, dy,$$

by transforming the first term by means of the Green's formula, we obtain

$$\iint_D (F_p \, \delta p + F_q \, \delta q) \, dx \, dy = \int_L \delta z \, F_p \, dy$$

$$- \delta z \, F_q \, dx - \iint_D \delta z \left(\frac{\partial}{\partial x} F_p - \frac{\partial}{\partial y} F_q \right) dx \, dy.$$

Since δz vanishes on the contour of the domain D, the final expression for the first variation will be

$$\delta J = \iint_D \left(F_z - \frac{\partial}{\partial x} F_p - \frac{\partial}{\partial y} F_q \right) \delta z \, dx \, dy,$$

from which there follows, by virtue of the arbitrariness of δz, that for the variation to vanish it is necessary that the desired function $z(x; y)$ satisfy the following equation (the Euler-Ostrogradskii equation):

$$F_z - \frac{\partial}{\partial x} F_p - \frac{\partial}{\partial y} F_q = 0. \tag{82}$$

This equation is named in honor of the Russian mathematician M. V. Ostrogradskii who obtained the most general formula for the variations of multiple integrals in 1834. It is a partial differential equation.

For the complete solution of the variational problem it is necessary to find the solution of (82), which takes a prescribed value on the boundary of the domain. Hence, the solution of the variational problem reduces to the solution of a partial differential equation.

Example. Find the surface of least area "stretched" on a given contour.

The area of a surface given by the equation $z = z(x; y)$ equals the integral

$$J = \iint_D (1 + p^2 + q^2)^{1/2} \, dx \, dy. \tag{83}$$

Since

$$F_z = 0; \qquad F_p = \frac{p}{(1 + p^2 + q^2)^{1/2}}; \qquad F_q = \frac{q}{(1 + p^2 + q^2)^{1/2}},$$

the Euler-Ostrogradskii equation for the functional (83) is

$$\frac{\partial}{\partial x}\left(\frac{p}{(1 + p^2 + q^2)^{1/2}} \right) + \frac{\partial}{\partial y}\left(\frac{q}{(1 + p^2 + q^2)^{1/2}} \right) = 0, \tag{84}$$

or

$$p_x(1 + q^2) - 2p_y pq + q_y(1 + p^2) = 0. \tag{85}$$

In order to elucidate the physical meaning of (85), let us recall the formula for the mean curvature of a surface

$$H = \frac{1}{2}\left(\frac{1}{R_1} + \frac{1}{R_2} \right) = \frac{p_x(1 + p^2) - 2p_y pq + q_y(1 + p^2)}{2(1 + p^2 + q^2)^{3/2}}.$$

Since the numerator of the formula for H agrees with the left-hand side of the Euler-Ostrogradskii equation, the surface of least area should have a zero mean curvature. In this case we have used the Euler-Ostrogradskii equation to establish an important physical fact concerning the surface of least area, that its mean curvature equals zero, rather than to integrate it and obtain the equation of the desired surface as $z = z(x; y)$.

In general, it is always necessary to keep in mind that the value of the Euler equations is not only that they can be integrated to yield the expression for the extremals, but also that these equations permit a direct elucidation of those properties which the desired function should possess in order to yield the minimum of the functional.

An analysis of these properties is often no less important than seeking the extremals.

III Applying the Euler Equation to the Solution of Engineering Problems

19. Direct Current Electric Motor

The simplest necessary conditions for an extremum, the Euler and Legendre conditions, were considered in the previous two chapters. By using these two conditions a number of engineering problems could already be solved although an analysis of more complex sufficient conditions, to be studied in the fourth chapter, is needed for complete confidence in the result. Without analyzing the sufficient conditions, it may only be concluded that the curves found from the Euler equation are "suspect" at the extremum. However, a direct analysis of the physical meaning of the actual engineering problem often permits the deduction that the "suspect" curve actually realizes the extremum we seek.

As the first example of the application of methods of calculus of variations to the solution of specific engineering problems, let us consider the problem of seeking the best current and velocity diagram for a direct current electric motor.

Let us consider an electric motor which turns the platform of an excavator. The aim of the electric motor is to produce a definite angular displacement of the platform which would guarantee motion of the scoop between the excavation and the unloading of the ground. The angular velocity of the platform should be zero at the initial and terminal moments, while the rotations of the motor are arbitrary in the rest of the current-velocity diagram provided a possible rapid turning of the platform is assured and overheating of the motor would not simultaneously occur. It is natural to assume that there exist best (optimum) current-velocity diagrams satisfying the imposed conditions in greatest measure. Let us turn to seeking these.

Let us consider the case when the excavator platform is set in motion by a direct current electric motor, and let us write down the fundamental electric motor equation, the equilibrium equation for the moments on the shaft:

$$C_{\Phi} I \Phi_{\text{motor}} = J(d\omega/dt) + M_C, \tag{1}$$

where I is the armature current of the electric motor; Φ_{motor} the active resultant magnetic flux; C_{Φ} a constant; J the moment of inertia of the electric motor and the load; ω the angular rotation of the armature; and M_C the resistance moment.

It is convenient to transform to relative units by taking the nominal values as the units for the armature current, magnetic flux, velocity and moment, and the mechanical time constant

$$T_M = J\omega_H / M_H, \tag{2}$$

as the unit of time, which is numerically equal to the time to accelerate the motor from zero to the nominal angular velocity under the effect of a nominal torque. Since the flywheel moment GD^2 rather than the moment of inertia is usually presented in catalogs on electrical equipment, it is convenient to write (2) as:

$$T_M = \frac{GD^2 n_H}{375 M_H} \,[\text{sec}], \tag{3}$$

where the units are as follows: GD^2 is in kg·m^2; n_H is in rpm; and M_H is in kg·m. Formula (3) aids in the transformation from relative back to absolute units.

Introducing the new variables

$$i = \frac{I}{I_H}; \qquad \Phi = \frac{\Phi_{\text{motor}}}{\Phi_H}; \qquad \nu = \frac{\omega}{\omega_H}; \qquad \mu = \frac{M_C}{M_H}; \qquad \tau = \frac{t}{T_M},$$

let us write (1) as

$$i\Phi = (d\nu/d\tau) + \mu. \tag{4}$$

For motors with independent excitation, the magnetic flux may be considered nearly constant ($\Phi = 1$), and (4) becomes

$$i = v' + \mu . \tag{5}$$

If the angle traversed in the time $t = T_M$ at the nominal angular velocity is taken as the unit of the angle of rotation, then the angle of rotation α in relative units will be expressed by the integral

$$\alpha = \int_0^T v \, d\tau . \tag{6}$$

Let us note that if the electric motor does not perform rotations but progressive displacement of the load, then by taking the load displacement within the time $t = T_M$ at the nominal angular velocity of the motor, we show that the path traversed is expressed by the same integral (6). Hence, α may be either the displacement, or the angle of rotation in non-dimensional relative units in both cases.

Let us take the loss at the time $t = T_M$ at a current $I = I_0$ as the loss unit in the armature winding. Then in relative units the losses in the armature will be expressed by the integral

$$Q = \int_0^T i^2 \, d\tau . \tag{7}$$

In order that overheating of the armature winding should not occur, the magnitude of the integral Q should not exceed some limiting admissible quantity $Q_{\max}$. The value of $Q_{\max}$ depends on the relationship of the duration of the operating cycle and the duration of the pause, and on cooling conditions. Methods of determining $Q_{\max}$ are elucidated in handbooks on electric motors.

Now, it is possible to give the mathematical formulation of the problem of the best current-velocity diagrams which is to find the functions $i(\tau)$ and $v(\tau)$, interrelated by means of (5) and yielding a minimum of the integral (7) for a given value of the integral (6) and the boundary conditions $v(0) = v_1$; $v(T) = v_2$ (minimum loss formulation).

Another formulation of the problem is also possible, which is to find the current and velocity diagrams, i.e., the functions $i(\tau)$ and $v(\tau)$, assuring the least time of displacement of the scoop, i.e., the minimum of the integral

$$T = \int_0^T d\tau, \tag{8}$$

for given values of the integrals (6) and (7), the boundary conditions $v(0) = v_1$; $v(T) = v_2$ and the coupling equation (4) the formulation on the smallest time necessary to obtain the given velocity (highest speed formulation).

Finally, still a third formulation of the problem of the optimum diagrams is possible, which is to find the functions $i(\tau)$ and $v(\tau)$, yielding (under the same boundary conditions and coupling equations) a maximum of the integral (6) for a given value of the integral (7), i.e., the maximum displacement for given armature losses (maximum efficiency formulation).

Hence, the problem of the best current and velocity diagrams reduces to a Lagrange variational problem.

The determination of the optimum current and velocity diagrams is important not only for excavators, but also for many other electric motors. The main electric motors of reversing rolling mills, the electric motor of manipulators, expediters, ingot carriers, and other auxiliary mechaisms of rolling mill production, i.e., all the electric motors performing cyclic load displacements, reach their highest efficiency or fastest response in optimum current and velocity diagrams.

Expressing the variable i in terms of $v' + \mu$ on the basis of the coupling equation (5), we reduce the determination of the optimum velocity diagram to an isoperimetric problem. Thus, for the first formulation (minimum loss), it is sufficient to find the function $v(\tau)$, yielding a minimum of the integral

$$Q = \int_0^T (v' + \mu)^2 \, d\tau \tag{9}$$

for a given value of the integral

$$\alpha = \int_0^T v \, d\tau .$$

We have an isoperimetric problem with the intermediate function

$$H_1 = (v' + \mu)^2 + \lambda_0 v . \tag{10}$$

The intermediate function in the maximum quick-response formulation will be

$$H_2 = 1 + \lambda_1 (v' + \mu)^2 + \lambda_2 v. \tag{11}$$

and in the maximum efficiency formulation

$$H_3 = \lambda_3 (v' + \mu)^2 + v. \tag{12}$$

Let us determine the form of the optimum diagrams for the simplest particular case when the moment of the resistance on the shaft of the electric motor is constant, i.e., when $\mu = \mu_0 = \text{const}$. According to the reciprocity principle, the equations of the extremals do not change whether we solve the Euler equation for H_1, H_2, or H_3. In fact, the Euler equation for H_1 is

$$2v'' - \lambda_0 = 0, \tag{13}$$

for H_2

$$2\lambda_1 v'' - \lambda_2 = 0, \tag{14}$$

and for H_3

$$2\lambda_3 v'' - 1 = 0. \tag{15}$$

The solution of all three Eqs. (13), (14), and (15) is the same family of curves, namely, a parabola.

Hence, *the optimum velocity diagram is a parabola, and the optimum current diagram of the armature is linear* (Fig. 18).

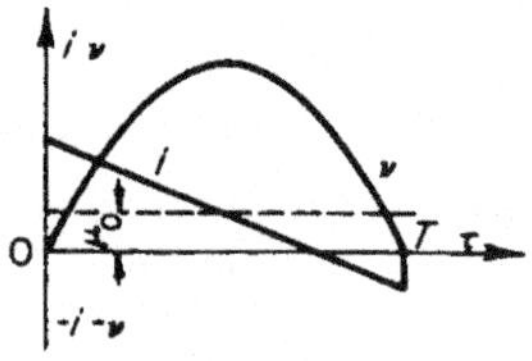

FIG. 18

Let us consider the first formulation, the minimum loss in the armature, in more detail. The solution of the Euler equation (13) is

$$v = C_1 + C_2 \tau + \frac{\lambda_0}{4} \tau^2, \tag{16}$$

in which three arbitrary constants enter. To determine them, we have three equations $v(0) = v_1$; $v(T) = v_2$; and $\int_0^T v \, d\tau = \alpha$.

It follows at once from the first equation that $C_1 = v_1$. Furthermore, from the system of the remaining two equations with two unknowns

$$v_2 = v_1 + C_2 T + \frac{\lambda_0}{4} T^2;$$

$$\alpha = v_1 T + \frac{C_2 T^2}{2} + \frac{\lambda_0 T^3}{12},$$

we find

$$C_2 = \frac{6\alpha - 4v_1 T - 2v_2 T}{T^2}; \qquad \lambda_0 = -\frac{24\alpha - 12(v_1 + v_2)T}{T}. \tag{17}$$

In particular, for the most widespread, zero boundary conditions, when $v_1 = v_2 = 0$, we have

$$v = \frac{6\alpha}{T^2}\left(\tau - \frac{\tau^2}{T}\right); \qquad i = \mu_0 + \frac{6\alpha}{T^2} - \frac{12\alpha}{T^3}\tau. \tag{18}$$

Integrating the square of the armature current, we obtain

$$Q = \frac{12\alpha^2}{T^3} + \mu_0{}^2 T. \tag{19}$$

Let us investigate the Legendre condition.

We have

$$H_{1v'v'} = 2 > 0. \tag{20}$$

Hence, a minimum Q may be achieved on the extremals.

Let us now compare a "rectangular" current diagram with those in Fig. 18 when the armature current is maintained constant during acceleration ($i = i_{max}$) and during deceleration ($i = -i_{max}$) of the load mechanism. This diagram was considered the best for many years. The quality of the system was estimated by the "coefficient of filling" of the current diagram, i.e., by the ratio of the area outlined by the current diagram (separately during acceleration for $i > 0$, and deceleration for $i < 0$), to the area of a rectangle with the same base and a height equal to the maximum ordinate on the current diagram. The "filling coefficient" is one for a "rectangular" diagram, and 0.5 for the optimum diagram (Fig. 18). Meanwhile, if the losses in the armature are evaluated for a "rectangular" diagram, we obtain

$$Q = 16(\alpha^2/T^3) + \mu_0{}^2 T. \tag{21}$$

Comparing (21) and (19), we see that for equal efficiency (i.e., equal α and T), the "rectangular" current diagram with the "filling coefficient" equal to 1 leads to an increase in losses in the armature (by 33% in particular, for $\mu_0 = 0$) as compared with the linear current diagram (Fig. 18) with an 0.5 "filling coefficient."

Hence, calculus of variations has established that the "filling coefficient" of the current diagram is unsuitable for estimates of control systems, and has also assisted in finding the actual optimum current diagram.

If the angular velocity passes through zero in the realization of the optimum control, the solution is then complicated by the fact that the static moment of the load customarily generated by frictional resistive load forces can no longer be considered constant. Indeed, the moment produced by the friction may be considered approximately constant in absolute value, but it changes sign with the change in sign of the velocity.

Such a case is encountered in studying nonzero boundary conditions, if $v(0) = v_1 < 0$, for example, and it is first necessary to decelerate the motion of the load, and then to communicate an opposite displacement to it. For $v < 0$ we have $i = v' - \mu_0$ (friction aids in decelerating the load mechanism), while $i = v' + \mu_0$ for $v > 0$ (friction hinders acceleration). Therefore, the intermediate function H_1 is a discontinuous function

$$H_1 = (v' + \mu_0 \operatorname{sign} v)^2 + \lambda_0 v,$$

where the symbol $\operatorname{sign} v$ denotes a function having a jump at $v = 0$; $\operatorname{sign} v = +1$ for $v > 0$, and $\operatorname{sign} v = -1$ for $v < 0$.

As already mentioned in Sections 6 and 10, in this case the extremals $v(\tau)$ may have a break at $v = 0$, but they must satisfy the Weierstrass-Erdmann conditions at the breakpoint. Since the ordinate of the possible breakpoint ($v = 0$) is fixed in the case we consider, and its variation δy is zero, we see by returning to formula (12) of the first chapter that the second Weierstrass-Erdmann condition should be satisfied here, i.e., the expression $H_1 - v'H_{1v'}$ to the left of the possible break point should be equal to the expression $H_1 - v'H_{1v'}$, evaluated to the right of the break point.

But to the left of the break point

$$H_1 - v'H_{1v'} = \mu_0{}^2 + \lambda_0 v - v'^2,$$

and to the right

$$H_1 - v'H_{1v'} = \mu_0{}^2 + \lambda_0 v - v'^2.$$

Equating these expressions, we see that the derivative of the extremal $v'(\tau)$ to the left of the possible break point equals the derivative to the right, i.e., there is actually no break point. In this case, the curve of the angular velocity $v(\tau)$ is a smooth function, and the armature current should experience a jump upon passage of the angular velocity through zero (Fig. 19).

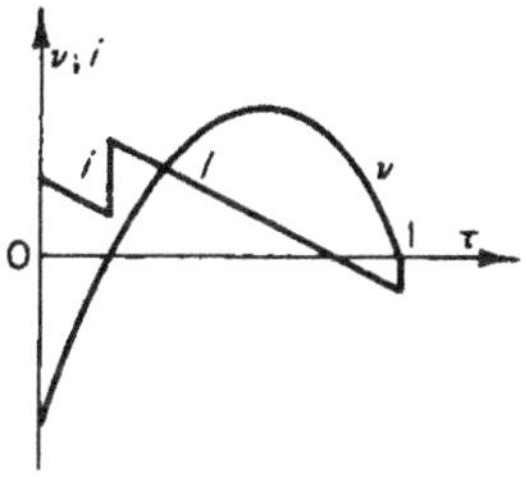

FIG. 19

The optimum current-velocity diagrams were analyzed in this section without taking account of constraints on commutation, on maximum velocity, etc. A complete analysis of the optimum control taking account of constraints will require additional mathematical apparatus, and will be given in Chapter 6.

20. Estimate of the Change in a Functional When the Actual Function Deviates from the Extremal

The linear current diagram (Fig. 18), and the "rectangular" diagram as well, is an ideal control law, and no real regulation system may realize it perfectly exactly. In particular, the optimum diagram demands that the current in the armature loop grow instantaneously from zero to $i_{\text{initial}} =$

$\mu_0 + (6\alpha/T^2)$ at $\tau = 0$, and drop instantaneously to zero as well at $\tau = T$. Such jumps in the current in an armature loop possessing finite inductance will require the application of infinite voltages and are not realizable. Any real control system may only assure the current diagram

$$i = i_{\text{opt}} + \varepsilon, \tag{22}$$

where i_{opt} is the optimum diagram's current, and ε is the error which is not identically zero, but may even achieve a large magnitude at certain times (Fig. 20).

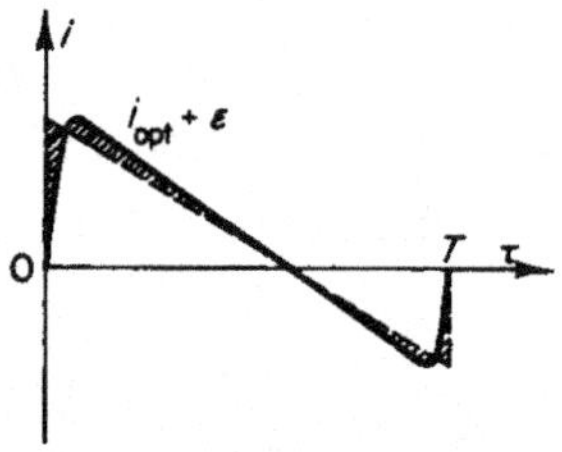

FIG. 20

Naturally, a very important question is to what degree does the existence of an error ε affect the indices of electric-motor operation, particularly heating of the armature. If the magnitude of the losses increases substantially for small ε then it is necessary to utilize a very accurate control system assuring optimality of the current diagram; if small deviations from optimality are not dangerous, then an essentially simpler control system may be used.

It is possible to estimate approximately the change in the functional for deviations of the desired function from the extremal by means of the magnitude of the second variation

$$\delta^2 J = \frac{1}{2}\int_0^T \left[\left(H_{vv} - \frac{d}{d\tau} H_{vv'}\right) \delta v^2 + H_{v'v'}\, \delta v'^2\right] d\tau .$$

In fact, in Section 5 we expanded the increment in the functional in a power series of the small parameter α, for deviations of the function from the extremal. Since the first variation vanishes on the extremal, and the third and even higher variations containing higher powers of α decrease more rapidly than the second variation, then the magnitude of the second variation may be utilized to estimate the change in the functional for small deviations of the actual function from the extremal.

In our case $H_{vv} = 0$; $H_{vv'} = 0$; $H_{v'v'} = 2$ and therefore

$$\delta^2 J = \int_0^T \delta v'^2 \, d\tau = \int_0^T \varepsilon^2 \, d\tau \tag{23}$$

(since $\delta v' = \varepsilon$).

Therefore, for small ε the increase in armature losses approximately equals the integral of the deviations squared.

Since the functional $\int_0^T H \, d\tau$ is quadratic, the third and all higher variations vanish (the derivatives H_{vvv}, $H_{vvv'}$, $H_{v'v'v'}$, etc., therein, equal zero in this case). Hence, the estimate in terms of the second variation is not approximate for quadratic functionals, but exact, i.e.,

$$\Delta Q = \int_0^T \varepsilon^2 \, d\tau , \tag{24}$$

and (24) is true not only for small but for any and all ε.

To confirm this, let us derive (24) directly without relying upon the second variation.

Let us consider two electric motors executing an identical displacement program. For the first motor $i = i_{\text{opt}}$ and for the second $i = i_{\text{opt}} + \varepsilon$.

For the first motor we have

$$v_1(\tau) = v_1(0) + \int_0^\tau (i_{\text{opt}} - \mu_0) \, d\tau ,$$

and for the second

$$v_2(\tau) = v_2(0) + \int_0^\tau (i_{\text{opt}} + \varepsilon - \mu_0) \, d\tau .$$

Since

$$v_1(0) = v_2(0) \qquad \text{and} \qquad v_1(T) = v_2(T),$$

then

$$\int_0^T \varepsilon \, d\tau = 0 . \tag{25}$$

Furthermore, for the first motor

$$\alpha_1(\tau) = \alpha_1(0) + v_1(0)\,\tau + \int_0^\tau d\tau \int_0^\tau (i_{\text{opt}} - \mu_0) \, d\tau ,$$

and for the second

$$\alpha_2(\tau) = \alpha_0(0) + v_2(0)\,\tau + \int_0^\tau d\tau \int_0^\tau (i_{\text{opt}} + \varepsilon - \mu_0)\, d\tau .$$

and since

$$\alpha_1(0) = \alpha_2(0) \qquad \text{and} \qquad \alpha_1(T) = \alpha_2(T),$$

then

$$\int_0^T d\tau \int_0^\tau \varepsilon\, d\tau = 0 . \tag{26}$$

Let us now calculate the difference in armature losses in the motors:

$$\Delta Q = \int_0^T (i_{\text{opt}} + \varepsilon)^2\, d\tau - \int_0^T i_{\text{opt}}^2\, d\tau = \int_0^T \varepsilon^2\, d\tau + 2\int_0^T i_{\text{opt}}\varepsilon\, d\tau .$$

Let us integrate the second integral by parts

$$\int_0^T i_{\text{opt}}\varepsilon\, d\tau = \int_0^T i_{\text{opt}}\, d\tau \int_0^\tau \varepsilon\, d\tau = i_{\text{opt}} \int_0^\tau \varepsilon\, d\tau \Big|_0^T - \int_0^T di_{\text{opt}} \int_0^\tau \varepsilon\, d\tau .$$

Since

$$i_{\text{opt}} = \mu_0 + \frac{6\alpha}{T^2} + \frac{12\alpha}{T^3}\,\tau ,$$

then

$$\int_0^T i_{\text{opt}}\varepsilon\, d\tau = i_{\text{opt}} \int_0^T \varepsilon\, d\tau + \frac{12\alpha}{T^3} \int_0^T d\tau \int_0^\tau \varepsilon\, d\tau ,$$

from which follows if (25) and (26) are taken into account

$$\Delta Q = \int_0^T \varepsilon^2\, d\tau ,$$

i.e., we again obtain formula (24).

This formula yields a simple estimate of the deviation of the functional. Thus, if the deviations of the true current diagram from the optimum diagram do not exceed 10% of the mean-square current, it may then be guaranteed that the losses will grow less than 1%.

Similar computations show that in designing the control system for an electric motor there is no necessity to attempt a very exact execution of the optimum current diagram. It is sufficient just that ε not be large, i.e., that the general character of the current diagram should not deviate too much from the optimum.

Furthermore, since the quantity ΔQ is proportional to the integral of ε^2, large deviations from the optimum diagram will not even be dangerous (the neighborhoods of the points $\tau = 0$ and $\tau = T$ in Fig. 20), if they last a short time.

The example we have considered is typical of extremals of any functionals; since the principal, linear portion of the increment in the functional vanishes on the extremal, then degradation of the quality index of the process is not great for small deviations, inevitable in practice, of the true course of the process from the optimum.

This property of extremals plays an important part in the practical application of variational methods.

21. Reciprocity Principle; Its Boundedness

Let us examine the second and third formulations of the problem of the best current diagram in more detail. The problem in the second formulation (i.e., on the maximum fast-response) reduces to a problem with a free right endpoint. Thus, if the boundary conditions are zero, i.e., $v(0) = 0$; $v(T) = 0$, this means that the right endpoint of the extremal $v(\tau)$ slides along the line $v = 0$.

For the functional

$$\int_0^T H_2 \, d\tau = \int_0^T [1 + \lambda_1 (v' + \mu_0) + \lambda_2 v] \, d\tau \tag{27}$$

the parabolas

$$v = C_1 \tau + \frac{\lambda_2}{4\lambda_1} \tau^2 \tag{28}$$

are extremals [$C_2 = 0$ from the condition $v(0) = 0$].

The transversality condition

$$H_2 - v' H_{2v'} = 0, \tag{29}$$

is satisfied at the right endpoint, but

$$\begin{aligned} H_2 - v' H_{2v'} &= 1 + \lambda_1 (v' + \mu_0)^2 + \lambda_2 v - 2\lambda_1 v' (v' + \mu_0) \\ &= 1 - \lambda_1 v'^2 + \lambda_1 \mu_0^2 - \lambda_2 v, \end{aligned}$$

from which, taking into account that $v(T) = 0$, we have

$$1 + \lambda_1 \mu_0^2 - \lambda_1 v'^2 (T) = 0 \tag{30}$$

or

$$\lambda_1 = (v'^2(T) - \mu_0^2)^{-1}. \tag{31}$$

Finding the parameters C_1, λ_1, λ_2 and T from the boundary conditions, we see that they are not defined uniquely. Indeed, the relationship (19) will be satisfied for the extremal parabolas with boundary conditions $v(0) = v(T) = 0$. For given Q and α it will transform into a fourth degree equation for the determination of T

$$\mu_0^2 T^4 - QT^3 + 12\alpha^2 = 0, \tag{32}$$

which will have two positive roots according to Descartes' rule.

Hence, two extremals and their corresponding current diagrams (Fig. 21)

$$i = \mu_0 + i_0 - \frac{2i_0}{T}\tau, \tag{33}$$

exist for the same values of Q and α with the same boundary conditions, where in one $i_0 > \mu_0$ (solid line), and $i_0 < \mu_0$ (dashed line) in the other diagram.

Let us verify the Legendre condition. We have

$$H_{2v'v'} = 2\lambda_1. \tag{34}$$

In order for a minimum time to be reached on the extremal, it is necessary that $\lambda_1 \geqslant 0$. But taking (31) into account, $v'(T) \geqslant \mu_0^2$ follows from $\lambda_1 \geqslant 0$, and since $v' = i + \mu_0$, then $v'(T) = -i_0$ and the inequality $\lambda_1 \geqslant 0$ is equivalent to the inequality $i_0 \geqslant \mu_0$. Hence, the minimum in the displacement time may not be reached on the extremal shown dashed in Fig. 21 (the inequality $i \geqslant \mu_0$ will be violated).

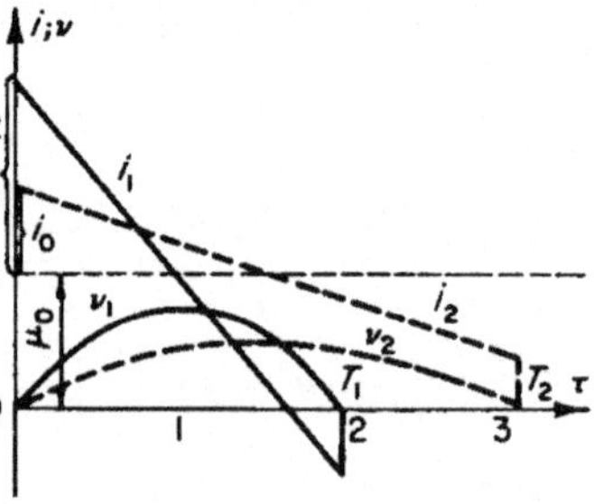

FIG. 21

Let us turn to the third formulation of the problem of the optimum current diagram; the formulation for the highest efficiency under constraints given on the heating.

The extremum of the functional

$$\int_0^T H_3\, d\tau \tag{34'}$$

is reached on the parabolas

$$v = C_2 + C_1\tau + \frac{1}{4\lambda_3}\tau^2 . \tag{35}$$

Determining the parameters C_1, C_2 and λ_3 from the conditions

$$\int_0^T (v' + \mu_0)^2\, d\tau = Q; \quad v(0) = v_1; \quad v(T) = v_2 ,$$

we obtain

$$\begin{aligned} C_1 &= \frac{v_2 - v_1}{T} \mp T\left(3\left[\frac{Q}{T^3} - \frac{1}{T^2}\left(\frac{v_2 - v_1}{T} + \mu_0\right)^2\right]\right)^{1/2} \\ C_2 &= v_1 \\ \lambda_3 &= \pm 4\left(3\left[\frac{Q}{T^3} - \frac{1}{T^2}\left(\frac{v_2 - v_1}{T} + \mu_0\right)^2\right]\right)^{-1/2} . \end{aligned} \tag{36}$$

Hence, the constants C_1 and λ_3 are not determined uniquely.

Let us verify the Legendre condition. We have

$$H_{3v'v'} = 2\lambda_3 . \tag{37}$$

Therefore, the maximum displacement may be reached only for $\lambda_3 \leqslant 0$, i.e., for a negative sign in front of the radical in (36), which corresponds to a decrease in armature current with time. For $\lambda_3 > 0$, i.e., for an increasing current diagram, the maximum displacement is not assured.

Two extremals with the same boundary conditions and equal values of Q are shown in Fig. 22. The maximum α is reached on the solid curve, but the maximum is not achieved on the dashed curve which does not satisfy the Legendre condition. However, the lower extremal yields a minimum Q for a given value of α (appropriate to this extremal).

It is therefore necessary to recall that the reciprocity principle is of limited value: although the equations of the extremals remain the same whether we seek minimum Q for given α or maximum α for given Q,

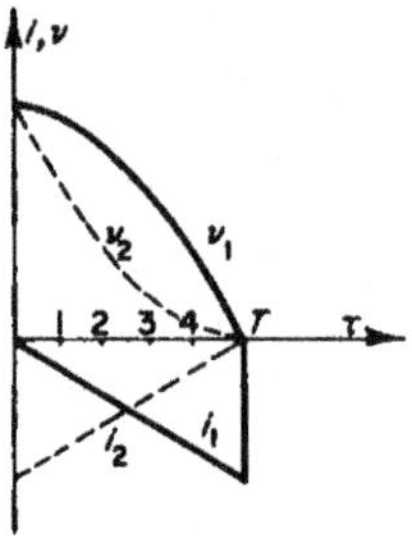

FIG. 22

yet not every extremal yielding minimum Q will yield a maximum to the integral α. The reciprocity principle does not extend to the Legendre condition.

Let us turn to an estimate of the gain in fast-response and efficiency of an electric motor which will be achieved by the transition to optimum current and velocity diagrams. Let us consider an arbitrary velocity diagram for zero boundary conditions and zero resistance moment.

In this case

$$Q_{\mu=0} = \int_0^T i^2\, d\tau = \int_0^T v'^2\, d\tau = \int_0^T (d^2\alpha/d\tau^2)^2\, d\tau, \tag{38}$$

where α is the moving value of the displacement of the load, namely $\alpha = \int_0^\tau v\, d\tau$.

It follows from (38) that the losses in the armature will grow n^2-fold, with an n-fold increase in the displacement angle α when the functions $\alpha(\tau)$ remain similar (similarity in the boundary conditions is assured by $v(0) = 0$ and $v(T) = 0$), and will decrease n^3-fold for an n-fold increase in the time T, i.e., the formula

$$Q_{\mu=0} = A\,\frac{\alpha^2}{T^3}, \tag{39}$$

is valid, where A is a number dependent only on the form of the velocity diagram. For an optimum parabolic diagram $A = 12$, for any other diagram $A > 12$.

When a constant resistance moment is present, we have

$$Q = \int_0^T (v' + \mu_0)^2\, d\tau = \int_0^T v'^2\, d\tau + 2\mu_0 \int_0^T v'\, d\tau + \mu_0{}^2 \int_0^T d\tau, \tag{40}$$

and since

$$\int_0^T v'\,d\tau = v(T) - v(0) = 0,$$

then

$$Q = A(\alpha^2/T^3) + \mu_0{}^2 T. \tag{41}$$

Hence, the losses in the armature are composed of the loss due to the static load $\mu_0{}^2T$ and the loss in accelerating and decelerating $A\,\alpha^2/T^3$. Various velocity diagrams may be compared according to the value of the coefficient A. The difference in the diagrams may be canceled for a significant static load, and is manifest most acutely for small μ, when the fundamental portion of the motor power goes into acceleration and deceleration of the inertial masses of the performance mechanism which are set into motion.

Let us compare the optimum current diagram with the "rectangular" diagram with a unity "filling factor," and $A = 16$. For α and T equal, i.e., for equal efficiency, the losses in the armature for $\mu = 0$ and the "rectangular" diagram increase by $(\frac{16}{12} - 1)\cdot 100 = 33\%$.

For equal armature losses and equal T, the efficiency of the load mechanism (the value of α) under optimum control will increase by $(\frac{16}{12} - 1)^{1/2}\cdot 100 = 15\%$ as compared to the "rectangular" diagram.

Finally, for equal α and Q, the fast-response of an electric motor under optimum control will increase by $(\frac{16}{12} - 1)^{1/3}\cdot 100 = 11\%$ as compared with the "rectangular" diagram.

The advantages of the optimum current and velocity diagrams become even more significant if the gear ratio is selected at the same time as the diagram.

22. Selection of the Optimum Gear Ratio. Extremals with a Parameter

In the previous section, we saw that the optimum current diagrams assure an essential reduction in the losses and a rise in efficiency and fast-response of the electric motor.

The material in the present section shows that the advantages of optimum diagrams are still greater if they are selected simultaneously with the selection of the optimum gear ratio. However, we will encounter here the singular problem of the calculus of variations when it is necessary to find not only the extremal but also a constant (a parameter) characteristic of this extremal, which, in conjunction with the extremal, will assure an extremum of the functional. Following V. G. Boltianskii we shall designate such problems as problems of an extremum with a parameter.

Let us consider the electric motor of a repeated start-stop operating regime which assures (through a gear) cyclic displacement of a load. Let us introduce the assumptions that, (1) we neglect energy losses in the gear; and (2) we neglect the gear moment of inertia.

Taking account of these assumptions, we may write the following equilibrium equation for the moments on the shaft of the load mechanism;

$$jM_{\text{motor}} = \frac{GD_M{}^2}{375}\frac{dn_M}{dt} + j^2\frac{GD^2_{\text{motor}}}{375}\frac{dn_M}{dt} + M_C, \tag{42}$$

where M_{motor} is the torque of the motor (kg·m), GD^2_{motor} and $GD_M{}^2$ are the flywheel moments of the motor and load, respectively (kg·m^2), n_M is the shaft rpm for the load, j the gear ratio, and M_C the resistance moment.

Let us introduce relative units which differ somewhat from the units in the previous sections. Let us consider α_M, the angle of rotation of the load shaft (in complete turns), and t_0 the time to execute a displacement cycle, to be given quantities. As the unit of velocity let us take

$$n_{\text{mean}} = 60(\alpha_M/t_0) \quad \text{rpm}, \tag{43}$$

and as the unit of the moment

$$M_0 = \frac{GD_M{}^2}{375}\frac{n_{\text{mean}}}{t_0} \quad \text{kg·m}. \tag{44}$$

Dividing all members of the equality (42) by jM_0, we obtain

$$M = \frac{\mu_1}{j} + \left(\frac{1}{j} + \frac{j}{n_0}\right)\frac{dv_1}{d\tau_1}, \tag{45}$$

where

$$M = \frac{M_{\text{motor}}}{M_0}; \qquad \mu_1 = \frac{M_C}{M_0}; \qquad n_0 = \frac{GD_M{}^2}{GD^2_{\text{motor}}}; \qquad v_1 = \frac{n_M}{n_{\text{mean}}}; \qquad \tau = \frac{t}{t_0}.$$

The mean-square moment of the motor will equal (in relative units)

$$M_{\text{mean quad.}} = \left(\frac{t_0}{t_0 + kt_n}\right)^{1/2} \left\{\frac{\mu_1^{\ 2}}{j^2} + \left(\frac{1}{j} + \frac{j}{n_0}\right)\int_0^1 \left(\frac{dv_1}{d\tau_1}\right)^2 d\tau_1\right\}^{1/2} \tag{46}$$

(we assume that $v_1(0) = v_1(1) = 0$), where t_n is the time of pause between displacement cycles of the load mechanism, and k is a coefficient taking account of degradation of the conditions of cooling during this interval. When the motor is cooled by a separate fan $k = 1$.

Since $\int_0^1 v_1 \, d\tau_1 = 1$, then $\int_0^1 v_1'^2 \, d\tau = A$. The value of the coefficient A was determined in the preceding section.

Hence

$$M_{\text{mean quad.}} = \left(\frac{t_0}{t_0 + kt_n}\right)^{1/2} \left\{\frac{\mu_1^{\ 2}}{j^2} + A\left(\frac{1}{j} + \frac{j}{n_0}\right)\right\}^{1/2}. \tag{47}$$

If the load drive-motor is given, and only the gear ratio is chosen, then n_0 is a constant, and differentiating (47) with respect to j, we obtain the value of the optimum gear ratio corresponding to the mean-square moment of the motor:

$$j_{\text{opt}} = \left\{n_0\left(1 + \frac{\mu_1^{\ 2}}{A}\right)\right\}^{1/2}. \tag{48}$$

This formula shows that for a given motor the optimum gear ratio depends on the velocity diagram. In particular, the greatest ratio corresponds to the optimum diagram, i.e., $A = 12$. Formula (48) takes on a particularly simple form for $\mu_1 = 0$. In this case

$$j_{\text{opt}} = \sqrt{n_0}, \tag{49}$$

and substituting (49) into (45), we obtain that for $j = j_{\text{opt}}$, the motor torque is divided into two equal parts: half goes into accelerating and decelerating the load mechanism, and half into accelerating and decelerating the armature of the electric motor. For $j = j_{\text{opt}}$, the motor torque required to execute a given displacement program is a minimum:

$$M_{\text{mean quad. min.}} = \left(\frac{t_0}{t_0 + kt_n} \cdot A \cdot \frac{1}{n_0}\right)^{1/2}. \tag{50}$$

These results are valid for a motor chosen in advance; they may be utilized in a checking analysis, for example.

Of much greater practical value, however, is another problem, that of simultaneously selecting the gear ratio and the minimum size motor which would be capable of performing a given program of displacing the load mechanism. In such a formulation of the problem, it should be taken into account that the quantity n_0 in (48) depends on $M_{\text{mean quad.}}$ since the flywheel moment of the motor, dependent on its size, i.e. on $M_{\text{mean quad.}}$, enters that equation.

The solution of the problem is complicated even more by the fact that, for commercial electric motors, the relationship between the motor torque and its flywheel moment cannot be expressed analytically. Data is presented in Table I for the *П* series of Soviet dc motors thus. The quotient *a*, resulting from division of the nominal motor torque by its mean-square moment, of dimension m^{-1}, is given in the last column of the table. On the whole, the value of *a* depends unexpectedly on M_H. However, the approximate constancy of *a* is striking: as the torque changes 690-fold (for *П*-11 to *П*-112 motors), the quantity *a* changes

TABLE I. Soviet Direct Current Electric Motors of the *П* Series

Motor type	M_H (kg·m)	n_H (rpm)	P_H (kW)	GD^2 (kg·m²)	M_H/GD (m⁻¹)
П-11	0.177	1650	0.3	0.012	14.6
П-12	0.25	1700	0.45	0.015	16.6
П-21	0.4	1700	0.7	0.045	8.9
П-22	0.57	2700	1	0.055	10.4
П-31	0.82	1800	1.5	0.085	9.7
П-32	1.15	1700	2.2	0.105	11
П-41	1.95	1600	3.2	0.15	13
П-42	2.4	1800	4.5	0.18	13.3
П-51	3.5	1650	6	0.35	10
П-52	4.4	1750	8	0.4	11
П-61	6.2	1700	11	0.56	11.1
П-62	7.6	1800	14	0.65	11.7
П-71	12.4	1770	19	1	12.4
П-72	16.3	1760	25	1.2	13.6
П-81	20.8	1760	32	2.8	7.5
П-82	27.3	1770	42	3.2	8.5
П-91	31.2	1180	32	5.9	5.3
П-92	40.9	1180	42	7	5.8
П-101	58.5	1240	55	10.3	5.2
П-102	73	1250	75	12	6.1
П-111	97.5	1300	100	20,4	4.8
П-112	122	1300	125	23	5.3

only 2.75-fold. As is easy to verify, the same approximate constancy of the ratio M_H/GD^2 is also observed for other series of electric motors.

This permits a to be assumed constant in the first stage of the analysis ($a = 10\ \mathrm{m}^{-1}$ for the Π series), and to be refined later in subsequent stages of the analysis. For constant a,

$$n_0 = \frac{GD_M{}^2}{GD^2_{\text{motor}}} = \frac{GD_M{}^2 a}{M_0} \cdot \frac{1}{M_H}. \tag{51}$$

When a motor is chosen according to heating up, its mean-square moment equals the nominal, $M_H = M_{\text{mean quad.}}$; using the notation

$$\frac{GD_M{}^2 a}{M_0} = b \tag{52}$$

and substituting into (46), we obtain

$$M_{\text{mean quad.}} = \left(\frac{t_0}{t_0 + kt_n}\right)\left\{\frac{\mu_1{}^2}{j^2} + A\left(\frac{1}{j} + \frac{jM_{\text{mean quad.}}}{b}\right)^2\right\}^{1/2}$$

or squaring both sides of this equality, we will have

$$L = \frac{t_0 + kt_n}{t_0} M_{\text{mean quad.}} - \frac{\mu_1{}^2}{j^2} - A\left(\frac{1}{j} + \frac{jM_{\text{mean quad.}}}{b}\right)^2 = 0. \tag{53}$$

Taking the partial derivative $\partial L/\partial j$ and solving the system of two equations $\partial L/\partial j = 0$ and $L = 0$ with the two unknowns $M_{\text{mean quad.}}$ and j, we obtain the following formulas for the optimum transfer number and the least mean-square moment of the motor:

$$\begin{aligned} j_{\text{opt}} &= \left(\frac{t_0 + kt_n}{t_0}\right)^{1/2} \cdot \frac{b}{(2A)^{1/2}}\left[\left(1 + \frac{\mu_1{}^2}{A}\right)^{1/2} \Big/ 1 + \left(1 + \frac{\mu_1{}^2}{A}\right)^{1/2}\right]^{1/2} \\ M_{\text{mean quad.}} &= \frac{t_0}{t_0 + kt_n} \cdot \frac{2A}{b}\left[1 + \left(1 + \frac{\mu_1{}^2}{A}\right)^{1/2}\right]. \end{aligned} \tag{54}$$

On the whole, the calculation of the motor and the gear is performed as follows:

(1) We determine n_{mean} according to the given quantities α_M, t_0 and

$GD_M{}^2$ and we establish the unit of torque

$$M_0 = \frac{GD_M^2}{375} \frac{n_{\text{mean}}}{t_0}.$$

(2) Having been given the mean value $a = M_H/GD^2$ for the series of motors being used, we calculate the values of b and $M_{\text{mean quad.}}$.

(3) Using Table 1 (or analogous tables for other series of motors), we refine the value of the coefficient a by means of the value found for $M_{\text{mean quad.}}$.

(4) Using the refined value of a, we refine the values of j_{opt} and $M_{\text{mean quad.}}$ by means of (54).

Such a computation method permits bypassing the difficulties associated with the nonanalytic dependence of GD^2 on M_H.

Formulas (54) are simplified substantially if the static resistance moment is small as compared to the dynamic resistance moment resulting from acceleration and deceleration of the inertial masses of the motor and the load. In this case it is convenient to write (54) at once in absolute, rather than in relative, units:

$$j_{\text{opt}} = \frac{3.12}{\sqrt{A}}\left(\frac{t_0 + kt_n}{t_0}\right)^{1/2} \cdot \frac{at_0{}^2}{\alpha_M}$$
$$M_{\text{motor}} = 0.102 \frac{t_0}{t_0 + kt_n} GD_M{}^2 \frac{A}{a} \cdot \frac{\alpha_M^2}{t_0^4} \quad [\text{kg}\cdot\text{m}], \tag{55}$$

where the units are as follows: a is in m^{-1}; GD^2 in kg·m²; α_M in complete revolutions; t_0 in seconds; M_{motor} in kg/m.

Formulas (55) permit a number of important deductions.

First, the optimum transfer number depends on such factors, not taken into account customarily, as the motor running time, the parameter a of the series of motors being used, and the parameter A of the velocity diagram.

Second, the motor torque, which is needed to perform the assigned program of displacing the load, turns out to be proportional to the first power, rather than the square root of the coefficient A when the optimum transfer number and motor are simultaneously selected. In particular, for equivalent efficiency and fast-response, the required motor torque increases by 33% upon transfer from the optimum to a "rectangular" current diagram with a unit filling factor.

It should be taken into account, however, that (55) may only be used when the maximum angular velocity of the motor at $j = j_{opt}$ does not exceed the admissible limit for this kind of motor. Thus, for a parabolic velocity diagram

$$n_{max} = \left(\frac{t_0 + kt_n}{t_0}\right)^{1/2} 81at_0 \quad [\text{rpm}]. \tag{56}$$

Otherwise, formulas (55) must be rejected and the transfer number should be selected according to the condition of the limiting motor velocity.

Example. A mechanical load with a 200 kg·m^2 flywheel moment must be rotated 180° in two seconds. The time of pause between rotations is 1 sec. We are to determine the gear ratio and the required motor power if the motor is chosen from the *П* series.

Being given the average value $a = 10$ m^{-1} for the *П* series, we determine the approximate value of the maximum rotational velocity from (56):

$$n_{max} = 81\left(\frac{2+1}{2}\right)^{1/2} 10\cdot 2 = 2 = 1970 \quad [\text{rpm}]$$

(motors of the *П* series are provided with a separate fan for motor cooling, hence, we may put $k = 1$). Since n_{max} does not exceed the admissible limits, (55) may be used. For optimum control when $A = 12$, we have

$$M_{motor\,1} = 0.102 \frac{2}{2+1} \cdot \frac{12}{10} 200 \frac{0.5^2}{2^4} = 0.256 \quad [\text{kg}\cdot\text{m}].$$

We establish by means of Table 1 that the *П*-21 motor for which $a = 8.9$, will correspond to this value. Refining the value of M_{motor} we obtain

$$M_{motor\,2} = M_{motor\,1} \frac{10}{8.9} = 0.29 \quad [\text{kg}\cdot\text{m}].$$

Since $M_{motor\,2}$ is less than M_H of the *П*-21 (and greater than the M_H for the next motor *П*-12 in the *П* series), we finally select the *П*-21 motor for which

$$M_H = 0.4 \quad \text{kg}\cdot\text{m}; \qquad GD^2 = 0.045 \quad \text{kg}\cdot\text{m}^2$$

$$n_0 = \frac{GD_M^2}{GD_{\text{motor}}^2} = \frac{200}{0.045} = 4450; \qquad j_{\text{opt}} = \sqrt{n_0} = 67.$$

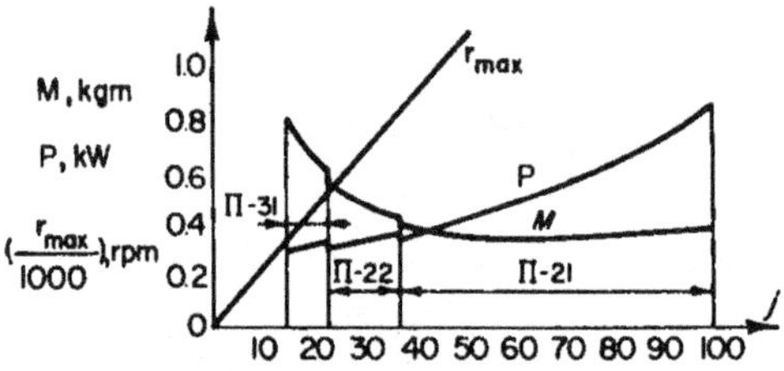

FIG. 23

Shown in Fig. 23 is the required motor torque as a function of the gear ratio. Small deviations from $j = j_{\text{opt}}$ are admissible, but motors of greater and greater power (*П*-22, *П*-31, etc.) are needed for a large deviation from j_{opt}.

23. Electric Load Driver with Time-Dependent Resistance Moment. Boundary Conditions at Infinity

Electric motors for which the resistance moment of the load is some function of time will be investigated in this section. Rockcrushers, fiber separators, paddle motors, etc., are examples of such loads. By studying them we meet a new type of boundary conditions – boundary conditions at infinity.

Let us consider an electric drive with a dc motor with independent excitation and let us pose the problem of selecting the current (and velocity) diagram which would guarantee minimum armature losses for a given efficiency, i.e., for a given value of the integral

$$\alpha = \int_0^T \nu \, d\tau. \tag{57}$$

The armature losses may be expressed by the integral

$$Q = \int_0^T (\nu' + \mu)^2 \, d\tau, \tag{58}$$

and our problem reduces to an isoperimetric one: To find the function $v(\tau)$ (and thereby also $i(\tau) = v' + \mu$), achieving the minimum of the integral (58), where $\mu = \mu(\tau)$, for a given value of the integral (57).

The intermediate function H will be

$$H = (v' + \mu)^2 + \lambda_0 v;$$

and the Euler equation for H

$$2\left(v'' + \frac{d\mu}{d\tau}\right) - \lambda_0 = 0$$

has the first integral

$$v' + \mu = C_1 + \frac{\lambda_0}{2}\tau,$$

from which we obtain the following equations for the optimum diagrams:

$$i = C_1 + \tfrac{1}{2}\lambda_0\,\tau; \qquad v = C_2 + C_1\tau + \tfrac{1}{4}\lambda_0\,\tau^2 - \int_0^\tau \mu\,d\tau. \tag{59}$$

If the boundary conditions $v(0) = v_1$ and $v(T) = v_2$ are given, then with the aid of (57) the arbitrary constants C_1, C_2, and λ_0 may be found from (59). Let us note that it is necessary to know the magnitude of the integral

$$\int_0^T \mu\,d\tau$$

in order to determine them, i.e., in order to be able to form the optimum current diagram, it is necessary to have information on the resistance moment in the whole interval $(0, T)$ "in advance," at the initial instant $\tau = 0$, itself.

However, another formulation of the problem, when it is required only that the angular velocity remain bounded during a long time period and the mean efficiency retain a given value, is more common for mechanisms of the considered class. In other words, it is necessary that a given value of the mean rotational velocity

$$v_{\text{mean}} = \frac{1}{T}\int_0^T v\,d\tau,$$

be retained, and that the mean value of the losses in the armature winding

$$p_{mean} = \frac{1}{T}\int_0^T (v' + \mu)^2 \, d\tau$$

be a minimum.

Since formulas (59) are valid for any T, the minimum losses will be reached on the extremals (59) in any case, and the conditions at infinity will now play the part of boundary conditions: the rotational velocity

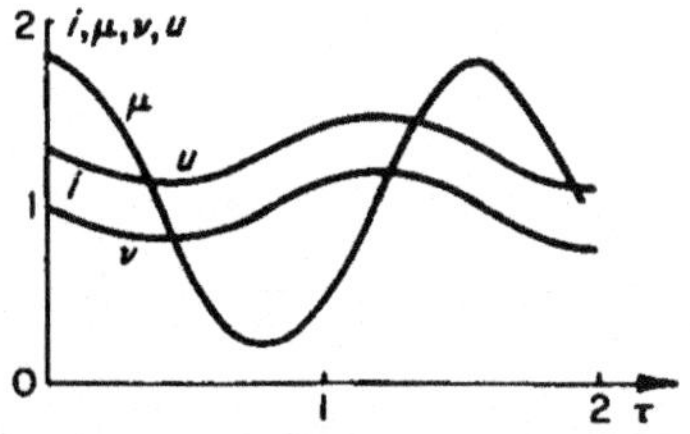

FIG. 24

should remain bounded as $\tau \to \infty$. From this condition it follows that $\lambda_0 = 0$; $C_1 = \mu_{mean}$ and hence

$$i = \mu_{mean} = \text{const};$$

$$v = v(0) + \int_0^\tau (\mu_{mean} - \mu)\, d\tau. \tag{60}$$

Therefore, to achieve minimum losses in the armature winding and by its heating, it is necessary to regulate the input voltage so that the armature current remains constant, and the rotational velocity will fluctuate around a mean value. Shown in Fig. 24 is an example of such control for $\mu = 1 + 0.8\cos 4\tau$.

Let us now compare the optimum mode of motor operation ($i = \text{const}$) with the mode when the voltage on the armature terminals is kept constant. If the voltage drop in the armature winding may be neglected in comparison with the counter emf, then we will have $i = \mu$ for constant voltage at the terminals, and therefore

$$p_{mean} = \lim_{T \to \infty} \frac{1}{T}\int_0^T \mu^2 \, d\tau,$$

i.e., the losses grow substantially as compared to the optimum regime, particularly for a suddenly varying loading. Thus if the load variation is periodic $\mu = 4$ for $0 \leqslant \tau \leqslant 0.25$ and $\mu = 0$ for $0.25 \leqslant \tau \leqslant 1$, then $p_{\text{mean}} = 1$ in the optimum regime, and $p_{\text{mean}} = 4$ for a constant voltage on the terminals, i.e., is four times greater.

Hence, optimum control permits a very substantial reduction in armature losses and heat losses, where, in contrast to control in a finite time segment, detailed information on the resistance moment is not required for accomplishment of the optimum regime. It is sufficient to know just the mean value.

However, it must be recalled that the fluctuations in the motor's rotational velocity should not exceed admissible limits, i.e., the inequality

$$\nu_{\text{min}} \leqslant \nu \leqslant \nu_{\text{max}} \tag{61}$$

should be satisfied.

If the inequality (61) is violated in the optimum regime, it is necessary to go over to a more complex control. Taking account of a constraint such as (61) will be examined in Chapter V.

24. More General Problems of Optimum Control. Electric Drive with a Resistance Moment Dependent on the Velocity, and a Magnetic Flux Dependent on the Armature Current

We shall study herein optimum control laws not associated with the assumptions used in Sections 19–23 on constancy of the resistance moment and the magnetic flux of the motor, for more general classes of electric drive.

The examples to be examined permit solution of the important general problem of whether it is possible to replace the exact functionals by their approximate expressions, and to estimate the error associated with such replacement.

Let us consider a motor with constant magnetic flux operating on a load with a resistance moment dependent on the velocity, and let us find the armature-current diagram and the rotational velocity assuring mini mum armature losses during execution of the given program of displacements of the performing mechanism. As has already been mentioned in Section 19, this problem reduces to finding the minimum of the functional

$$\int_0^T H_1\,d\tau = \int_0^T [(v' + \mu)^2 + \lambda_0 v]\,d\tau, \tag{62}$$

where $\mu = \mu(v)$.

The Euler equation becomes

$$v'' - \mu\frac{d\mu}{dv} - \frac{\lambda_0}{2} = 0. \tag{63}$$

In practice, the velocity dependence of the resistance moment can ordinarily be approximated with a good degree of accuracy by the linear function

$$\mu = \mu_0 + kv, \tag{64}$$

and if greater accuracy is needed, by the quadratic function

$$\mu = \mu_0 + kv + k_1 v^2. \tag{65}$$

For a linear velocity-dependence of the resistance moment, (63) is an equation with constant coefficients

$$v'' - k^2 v - \mu_0 k - \frac{\lambda_0}{2} = 0,$$

which is easily integrated in elementary functions:

$$\begin{aligned} y &= b + C_1 e^{k\tau} + C_2 e^{-k\tau} \\ i &= \mu_0 + kb + 2kC_1 e^{k\tau}, \end{aligned} \tag{66}$$

where

$$b = -\left(\frac{\mu_0}{k} + \frac{\lambda_0}{2k^2}\right).$$

Hence, the optimum velocity diagram is a catenary.

For zero boundary conditions $v(0) = v(T) = 0$ the catenary is symmetric relative to the middle of the $0; T$ interval, and in this case

$$C_1 = -\frac{b}{e^{kT} + 1}; \qquad C_2 = -\frac{be^{kT}}{e^{kT} + 1}. \tag{67}$$

Integrating the rotational velocity and the square of the armature current, we obtain

$$b = \frac{k\alpha}{[kT]}; \qquad Q = \frac{k^3\alpha^2}{[kT]} + 2k\mu_0\alpha + \mu_0{}^2 T, \tag{68}$$

where for brevity of writing we have used the notation

$$[kT] = kT - 2\frac{e^{kT} - 1}{e^{kT} + 1}. \tag{69}$$

Example. Find the optimum current and velocity diagrams for an electric drive operating on a load with resistance moment $\mu = 0.4 + 0.8v$ which assures a displacement angle $\alpha = 1$ within the time $T = 2$.

We evaluate $[kT] = 0.272$; $e^{kT} = 4.593$ for given k and T, and substituting into (66) and (68), we obtain the equations for the optimum diagrams:

$$v = 2.94(1 - 0.168e^{0.8\tau} - 0.832e^{-0.8\tau}); \qquad i = 2.75 - 0.79e^{0.8\tau}$$

and the armature losses $Q = 2.84$.

The optimum diagrams for this example are shown in Fig. 25.

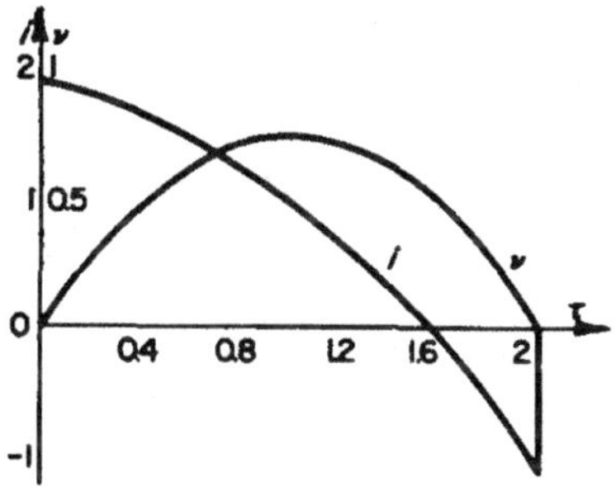

FIG. 25

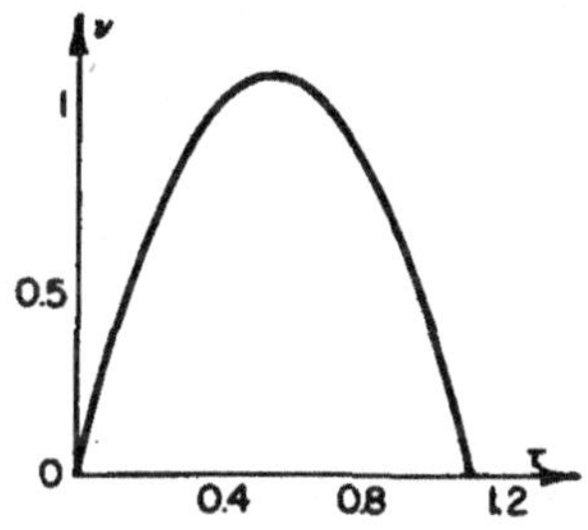

FIG. 26

The Euler equation is not integrated in elementary functions for a resistance moment dependent on the square of the velocity. The inverse dependence of τ on v, may reduce to the elliptic integral

$$\tau = \int_{v_1}^{v} \pm\left(\frac{C + v}{\lambda_0} + (\mu_0 + kv + k_1 v^2)^2\right)^{-1/2} dv. \tag{70}$$

The optimum velocity diagram constructed by means of (70) for the values $C = -1$; $\lambda_0 = -\frac{1}{16}$; $\mu_0 = 0$; $k = 0$; $k_1 = 1$ is shown in Fig. 26.

Now, let us apply an approximate method to the computation of optimum diagrams. Namely, let us put $k = k_1 = 0$ in the computation of the velocity diagram, i.e., let us consider the optimum parabolic diagram, and let the armature current be the sum of two components; the optimum current at $\mu = 0$, and the load current $i = \mu$.

The error associated with the approximation used is easily estimated for the resistance moment $\mu = \mu_0 + kv$. By integrating we see that the parabolic velocity diagram leads to the armature losses

$$Q_{\text{approx}} = \frac{12\alpha^2}{T^3}(1 + 0.1k^2T^2) + 2\mu_0 k\alpha + \mu_0{}^2 T. \tag{71}$$

Comparing (71) with the expression for the losses under optimum control (68), we see that for all values of k and T encountered in practice the quantity Q_{approx} differs very slightly from Q. Thus, for the example we have already considered of $\alpha = 1$; $T = 2$; $\mu = 0.4 + 0.8v$ we have $Q_{\text{approx}} =$ 2.85, for the parabolic velocity diagram, i.e., Q_{approx} is only 0.35% greater than under optimum control.

Let us now consider the same problem of selecting the optimum current and velocity diagrams for a motor with the magnetic flux dependent on the armature current. For simplicity, let us limit ourselves to the case of constant resistance moment. Strictly speaking, the magnetic flux depends on the armature current in any dc motor (even with independent excitation) because of the armature reactance. This dependence is particularly obvious in series motors.

Let us solve the problem in general form by assuming that the magnetic flux Φ in the equilibrium equation for moments on the shaft

$$i\Phi = v' + \mu_0 \tag{72}$$

is a certain function of the current $\Phi = \Phi(i)$. The optimum current diagram shows that the armature losses

$$Q = \int_0^T i^2 \, d\tau$$

is a minimum for a given value of the displacement of the performance mechanism $\alpha = \int_0^T v \, d\tau$ and the coupling equation (72).

The intermediate function H is

$$H = i^2 + \lambda_0 v + \lambda(v' + \mu_0 - i\Phi), \tag{73}$$

where λ_0 is a constant and λ is a function of τ.

Let us form two Euler equations, one related to the function $i(\tau)$,

$$2i - \lambda\left(\Phi + i\frac{d\Phi}{di}\right) = 0, \tag{74}$$

and the other for $v(\tau)$,

$$\lambda_0 - \frac{d\lambda}{d\tau} = 0. \tag{75}$$

It follows from (75) that $\lambda = C + \lambda_0 \tau$; substituting this into (74) we obtain the following expression for the optimum current diagram

$$2i\bigg/\left(\Phi + i\frac{d\Phi}{di}\right) = C + \lambda_0 \tau. \tag{76}$$

A linear current diagram is obtained from (76) for $\Phi = \text{const}$.

Let us verify compliance with the Legendre condition.

We assume that by using the coupling equation (72) we have expressed i^2 as some function of v and v', i.e., $i^2 = f(v; v')$. Then the problem we consider will reduce to an isoperimetric problem with the intermediate function

$$H = i^2 + \lambda_0 v = f(v; v') + \lambda_0 v,$$

and verification of the Legendre condition to verification of the sign of the second partial derivative with respect to v'. But

$$\frac{\partial^2 H}{\partial v'^2} = \frac{\partial^2 H}{\partial (v' + \mu_0)^2} = \frac{\partial^2 i^2}{\partial (i\Phi)^2}.$$

Now, taking the derivative, we finally establish

$$H_{v'v'} = \frac{\Phi - i\Phi_i - i^2 \Phi_{ii}}{(i\Phi_i + \Phi)^3}. \tag{77}$$

Using (76) and (77), the problem we have posed can be solved in general form. Substituting specific values of $\Phi(i)$ therein, we obtain the possibility of investigating different classes of electric motors. Thus, for motors with independent excitation the transverse reactance of the armature may be taken approximately into account by means of the formula

$$\Phi = \Phi_0(1 - bi^2). \tag{78}$$

Substituting (78) into (76), we find the optimum current diagram

$$i = \frac{\left(1 + 12b\left(C + \frac{\lambda_0}{2}\tau\right)^2\right)^{1/2} - 1}{6b\left(C + \frac{\lambda_0}{2}\tau\right)}, \tag{79}$$

and substituting into (77), we obtain

$$H_{v'v'} = 2\,\frac{1 + 5bi^2}{1 - 3bi^2}. \tag{80}$$

It follows from (80) that $H_{v'v'} > 0$ for all values of b and i to be encountered in practice and the optimum diagram assures minimum losses in the armature. The constants C and λ_0 in (79) are determined from the boundary conditions. Presented in Fig. 27 are optimum current and velocity diagrams for the following example: $b = 0.05$; $T = 4$; $v(0) = v(T) = 0$.

The armature losses under optimum control are $Q = 9.38$, and the displacement angle of the load $\alpha = 5.77$.

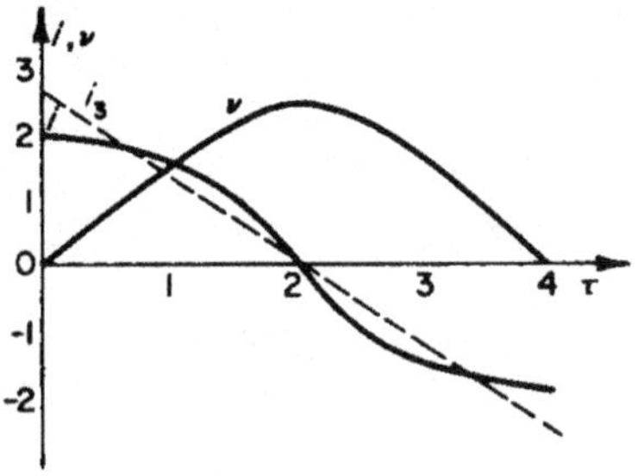

FIG. 27

The dashed line in Fig. 27 shows the current diagram for $\Phi=1$ (linear diagram), and which is equivalent with respect to heat losses to the optimum. In the case of a linear current diagram the displacement angle of the load is $\alpha=5.69$, i.e., 1.4% less than for the optimum diagram.

This example, just as the example considered earlier about the computation of the optimum control for a velocity-dependent moment, when the assumption $\mu=0$ also leads to a very small degradation (by 0.35%) in the value of the functional, reflects the general regularity of extremum problems. They may be solved heuristically without danger of great error by using approximate coupling equations. In fact, let the extremum of the functional

$$J=\int_{x_0}^{x_1} F(x;y;y')\,dx$$

be reached in the curve $y=y(x)$ by using the exact coupling equations. Replacing the exact by the approximate coupling equations, and solving the Euler equation, we find some function $y_1(x)$. If our approximations are acceptable, then

$$y_1(x)=y(x)+\eta(x),$$

where $\eta(x)$ is small compared to $y(x)$.

Now, let us compare the true extremal value of the functional J_{ex} on the extremal $y(x)$ with its value J_{approx} on the curve $y_1(x)=y+\eta$, which we found from the approximate equation. Expanding the difference

$$\Delta J=J_{\text{approx}}-J_{\text{ex}}=\int_{x_0}^{x_1}[F(x;y+\eta;y'+\eta')-F(x;y;y')]\,dx$$

in a variational series

$$\Delta J=\int_{x_0}^{x_1}\left(F_y-\frac{d}{dx}F_{y'}\right)\eta\,dx+\frac{1}{2}\int_{x_0}^{x_1}\left(F_{yy}-\frac{d}{dx}F_{yy'}\right)\eta^2\,dx$$
$$+\frac{1}{2}\int_{x_0}^{x_1}F_{y'y'}\eta'^2\,dx,$$

we see that, since the first variation in the extremum vanishes, the error in the value of the functional will, in any case, be a higher-order quantity compared to the error in determining the extremum (and its derivative). Returning to Fig. 27, we see that although the error in the value of the derivative of the extremal ($i = v'$) reaches 42.5% with respect to its mean square value (at the points $\tau = 0$ and $\tau = 4$, and much less at the remaining points) because of the assumption $\Phi = 1$, the error in the functional as a whole is only 1.4%.

This property of functionals plays an exceptionally important part in practical applications of the calculus of variations. Indeed, the coupling equations need be known only approximately, with some error as a rule, in actual engineering problems. If these small errors were to lead to large deviations in the values of the functionals, the solutions of variational problems would have no practical meaning. Actually, the situation is much more favorable. Since the principal, linear member of the increment in the functional vanishes on the extremal, changes in the functional for small deviations from the extremal will not only be small but even of higher order of smallness as compared with the deviations of the actual functions from the extremal.

IV Field Theory. Sufficient Conditions for an Extremum

25. Field of Extremals

The study of the sufficient conditions for an extremum requires a more complex theoretical structure than the investigation of the necessary conditions. In particular, we shall not now consider extremals taken individually, but families of extremals.

The solutions of the Euler equation for the simplest functional

$$J=\int_a^b F(x; y; y')\,dx \tag{1}$$

generate a family of curves $y=y(x; C_1; C_2)$ dependent on two parameters, the integration constants C_1 and C_2. These constants are sought from the condition that the curve passes through two given points A and B. If only one constant is determined, say from the condition that the extremal passes through the point A, then we obtain a pencil of extremals issuing from the point A (Fig. 28). Among them will be the extremal passing through the point B.

Let us now introduce the concept of a "field," which is important for

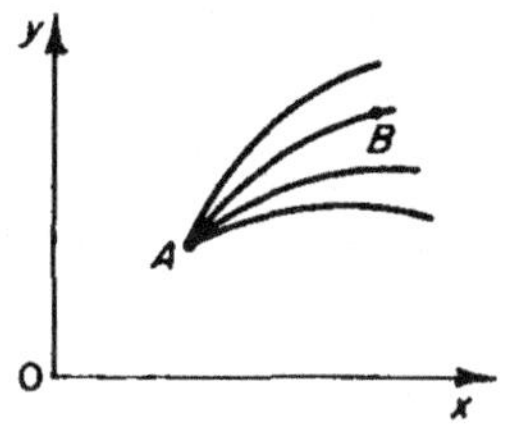

FIG. 28

the subsequent exposition. If a family of curves dependent only on one parameter is disposed in some domain D in such a way that one and only one curve of the family will pass through each point of the domain, then it is said that this family generates a field (more exactly, a proper field) in the domain D.

Let us consider a family of parallel lines $y = x + C$. They generate a field at any part of the plane (Fig. 29) .On the other hand, the family of parabolas $y = (x + C)^2$ (Fig. 30) does not generate a field in the upper half-plane; two curves of the family pass through each point.

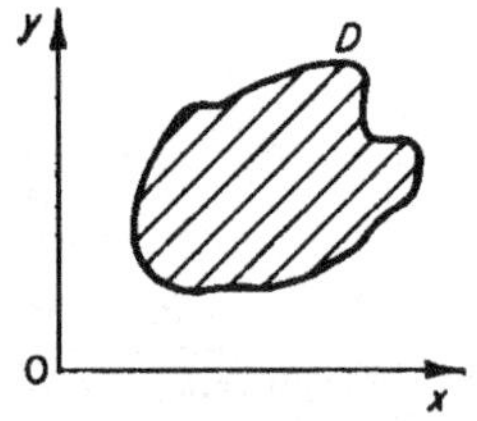

FIG. 29

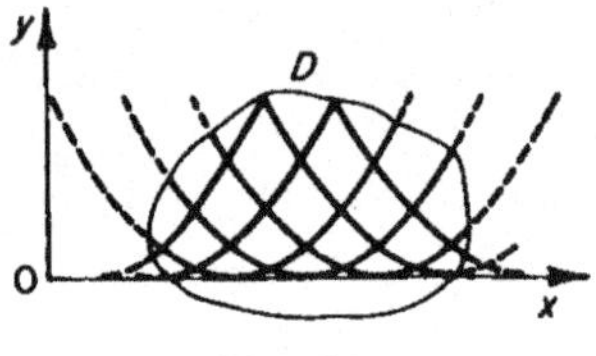

FIG. 30

Let it be necessary to find the minimum distance between two points A and B. The straight lines $y = C_1x + C_2$ are the extremals. If the point A (say, $x = 0$; $y = 0$) is fixed, we then obtain a family of lines issuing from the single point $y = C_1x$. This family forms a field since one curve of the family passes through each point of the plane (with the exception of the center of the field, the point $x = 0$; $y = 0$). In contrast to the proper field, such a field is called central.

The extremals of the functional

$$J = \int_a^b (y^2 - y'^2)\, dx$$

are the sinusoids

$$y = C_1 \sin x + C_2 \cos x .$$

The pencil of extremals passing through the origin ($y = C_1 \sin x$) generates a field (central) if $-\pi < x < \pi$ (Fig. 31), and does not generate a

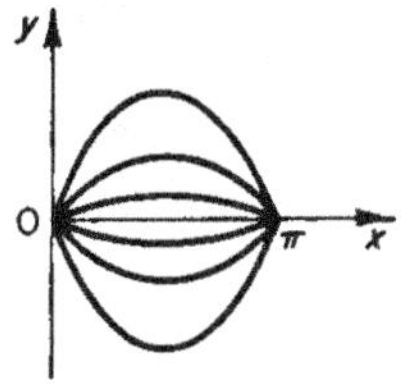

FIG. 31

field if $x \geqslant \pi$ or $x \leqslant -\pi$. The extremals intersect at the points $x = \pi$ or $x = -\pi$.

The envelope of the family plays a special part in the study of families of curves. Thus, the horizontal axis is the envelope for the family of parabolas $y = (x + C)^2$ pictured in Fig. 30. Two infinitely nearby curves of the family intersect on the envelope. Thus, if the family of parabolas pictured in Fig. 30 is examined, it is easy to see that the closer two parabolas are to each other, the more does their intersection approach the horizontal axis. In the limit two infinitely close parabolas will intersect on the Ox axis, the envelope of the family.

Since curves intersect at the envelope, it is evident that if the domain D under consideration includes the envelope of the family also, the curves then do not generate a field in this domain.

26. Jacobi and Legendre Conditions

Let us turn to a study of the sufficient conditions, where we start with the investigation of a weak extremum when both δy and $\delta y'$ are small. In this case, the sign of the increment in the functional will agree with the sign of the second variation when going from one extremal to another adjacent curve (since the first variation vanishes on the extremal).

It has been shown in Section 7 that the condition

$$F_{y'y'} \leqslant 0 \tag{2}$$

is necessary for the second variation to be nonpositive (Legendre condition). Legendre tried to prove that compliance with the strict inequality

$$F_{y'y'} < 0 \tag{3}$$

is sufficient for the second variation to be negative.

Legendre reasoned as follows. Since we have $\eta(a) = \eta(b) = 0$ in the expression for the second variation obtained in Section 7

$$\delta^2 J = \int_a^b (P\eta^2 + R\eta'^2)\, dx, \tag{4}$$

then for any differentiable function $\omega(x)$ we will have

$$\int_a^b (\eta^2\omega' + 2\eta\eta'\omega)\, dx = \int_a^b (d/dx)(\eta^2\omega) = 0. \tag{5}$$

Hence, by attaching the expression (5), which equals zero, to (4), we will obtain

$$\delta^2 J = \int_a^b [R\eta'^2 + 2\eta\eta'\omega + (P + \omega')\eta^2]\, dx. \tag{6}$$

Now, let us choose the function $\omega(x)$ so that the expression in the square brackets will become a perfect square. To do this, the function $\omega(x)$ should satisfy the differential equation

$$R(P + \omega') = \omega^2. \tag{7}$$

Substituting (7) into (6), we obtain

$$\delta^2 J = \int_a^b \left[R\eta'^2 + 2\eta\eta'\omega + \frac{\eta^2\omega^2}{R}\right] dx = \int_a^b R\left[\eta'^2 + \frac{\eta\omega}{R}\right]^2 dx,$$

i.e., apparently the sign of the second variation will actually agree with the sign of R, i.e., with the sign of $F_{y'y'}$.

However, the Legendre proof had a defect which Lagrange pointed out. The equation (7) may not even have a solution in a sufficiently large interval $(a; b)$. Thus, if $R = -1$ and $P = 1$, we then obtain the equation $\omega' + 1 + \omega^2 = 0$, from which $\omega = \tan(C - x)$, and no solution exists at the points $x = C + \frac{1}{2}(2k + 1)\pi$.

By a change of variable, (7) may be reduced to a form more convenient for investigation. Setting

$$\omega = -(u'/u)R,$$

where u is a new unknown function, we obtain a linear second-order differential equation

$$-\frac{d}{dx}(Ru') + Pu = 0. \tag{8}$$

If the solution $u(x)$ of (8) does not vanish on the segment $(a; b)$, a solution of (7) then also exists. The points where $u = 0$ are designated conjugate points to the center of the field. Equation (8) is called the Jacobi equation and the condition that its solution does not vanish on the whole segment $(a; b)$ is the Jacobi condition.

The Jacobi condition (in conjunction with the strengthened Legendre condition: $F_{y'y'} > 0$ for a minimum and $F_{y'y'} < 0$ for a maximum) is the sufficient condition for the extremal $y(x)$ to achieve a weak relative extremum of the functional (1) on the segment $(a; b)$.

It can be proved that the Jacobi condition is also necessary, i.e., an extremum may not generally be reached when it is violated.

In contrast to the Euler and Legendre conditions, which refer to each point of an extremal (local conditions), the Jacobi condition characterizes the behavior of the extremal as a whole, on the whole segment $(a; b)$.

The importance of the Jacobi condition is that no set of local conditions may be sufficient for an extremum to be reached absolutely on the desired curve.

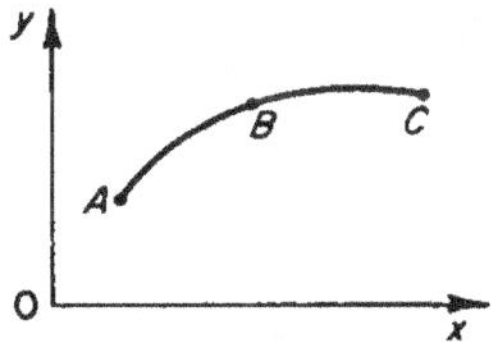

FIG. 32

In fact, for example, if each of the two arcs AB and BC (Fig. 32) satisfies the Euler equation (local condition), then the curve AC composed from these two arcs will also satisfy it. Meanwhile, from the fact that two parts of a curve separately reach an extremum of a functional does not at once follow that the whole curve will also reach the extremum.

Let us consider the shortest distance between two points A and B on a sphere. Arcs of a great circle are the extremums. If the arc AB is less than half the circumference, the minimum distance is then actually achieved on the extremal. If the arc AB equals half the circumference (the points A and B are poles, say), then there is no extremum. Actually all the meridians on a sphere are equal; there is no shortest one.

Hence, no set of local conditions may be sufficient for an extremum; it is necessary to investigate the field of extremals.

The investigation of (8), the Jacobi equation, is often quite difficult. Another method for investigating the Jacobi condition may be proposed.

Let $h(x)$ denote the difference in ordinates between two infinitely nearby extremals $y(x)$ and $y(x)+h(x)$. Since $y(x)+h(x)$ satisfies the Euler equation, then

$$F_y(x;\, y+h;\, y'+h') - \frac{d}{dx} F_{y'}(x;\, y+h;\, y'+h') = 0 .$$

Utilizing the Taylor formula, and retaining only first order of smallness terms in h (i.e., neglecting terms containing h^2, h^3, etc.) we obtain

$$F_{yy}h + F_{yy'}h - \frac{d}{dx}(F_{y'y'}h' + F_{y'y}h) = 0$$

or, combining similar terms we will have

$$Ph - \frac{d}{dx}(Rh') = 0,$$

which is indeed the Jacobi equation.

Two infinitely nearby extremals from the same initial point A intersect at the point where the solution of the Jacobi equation vanishes (in fact, the distance between the curves vanishes at the intersection point); the point where $h = 0$ is called the conjugate point of A.

Hence, two methods exist for verifying compliance with the Jacobi condition.

The first method is to construct the field of extremals. If the desired extremal which passes through the assigned points A and B does not intersect the infinitely nearby extremals (such an intersection is possible on the envelope of the field, in particular), the Jacobi condition is then satisfied.

The other method is analytic and tries to find the solution of the Jacobi equation (8). If this solution (with the initial conditions $u = 0$; $u' = 1$) does not vanish between the points A and B, then the Jacobi condition is satisfied. (Since (8) is linear, the point where its solution vanishes is independent of the initial condition for u'; for convenience, $u' = 1$ is selected.)

Example 1. Find the extremum of the functional

$$J = \int_0^1 y/y'^2 \, dx$$

for the boundary conditions $y(0) = 1$; $y(1) = 0.25$.

Since F does not depend explicitly on x, we have

$$F - y'F_{y'} = \frac{y}{y'^2} + y'\frac{2y}{y'^3} = \frac{3y}{y'^2} = C.$$

Integrating, we obtain the equation of the family of extremals

$$y = (C_1 x + C_2)^2.$$

We find $C_2 = 1$ from the condition $y(0) = 1$. The pencil of extremals $y = (C_1 x + 1)^2$ has the envelope $y = 0$ (Fig. 33). Two extremals pass through the point B (1; 0.25): one has a point of tangency with the envelope (conjugate point), and the other has no conjugate point (Fig. 33).

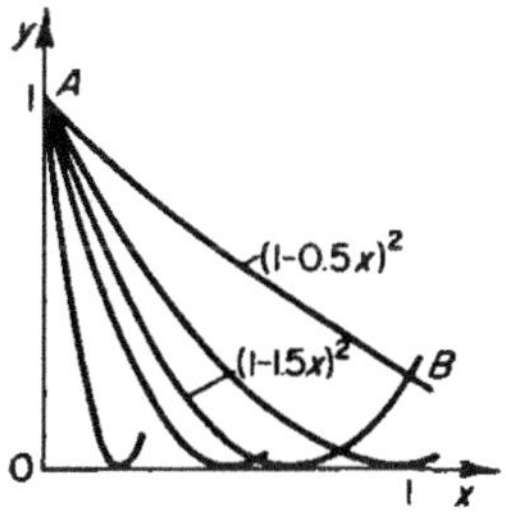

FIG. 33

The equation of the first extremal is $y = (1 - 1.5x)^2$ and of the second is $y = (1 - 0.5x)^2$. The Jacobi condition is not satisfied on the first extremal.

A weak minimum is achieved on the second extremal since

$$F_{y'y'} = \frac{6y}{y'^4} > 0 .$$

Example 2. Let us investigate the extremum of the integral

$$J = \int_0^a (y^2 - y'^2)\, dx$$

for the boundary conditions $y(0) = 0;\ y(a) = 1$.

Since

$$F_{y'y'} = -2 < 0 ,$$

a maximum may be achieved on the extremals.

The Euler equation $2y + 2y'' = 0$ has the solution

$$y = C_1 \sin x + C_2 \cos x .$$

We find $C_2 = 0$ from the condition $y(0) = 0$.

The family of extremals $y_1 = C_1 \sin x$ generates a field on the segment $(0; a)$ if $a < \pi$, but does not form a field for $a \geqslant \pi$, since all the extremals intersect at $a = \pi$. We arrive at this same conclusion on the basis of an investigation of the Jacobi equation which is $u'' + u = 0$. Its solution corresponding to the initial conditions $u(0) = 0;\ u'(0) = 1$ will be $u = \sin x$, which vanishes at $x = \pi$.

Hence, a maximum may be achieved on the extremals for $a < \pi$ but the extremum is not reached for $a \geqslant \pi$.

Calculating the value of the functional on the extremals, we see easily that when $a \to \pi$, the values of the functional increase more and more, tending to infinity. If $a \geqslant \pi$, the curve $y = C_1 \sin x$ from $x = 0$ to $x = a_1$, where $a_1 < \pi$, and $y = 1$ from $x = a_1$ to $x = a$, may be taken as a comparison curve. If a_1 is chosen very close to π, the value of the functional on the given curve may become as large as desired. Therefore, if $a \geqslant \pi$, there does not generally exist a maximum of the functional.

27. Strong Extremum. Weierstrass Condition

To seek the condition of the strong extremum, it is again necessary to examine the difference

$$\Delta J = \int_L F(x; y; y')\, dx - \int_{\text{extr}} F(x; y; y')\, dx , \tag{9}$$

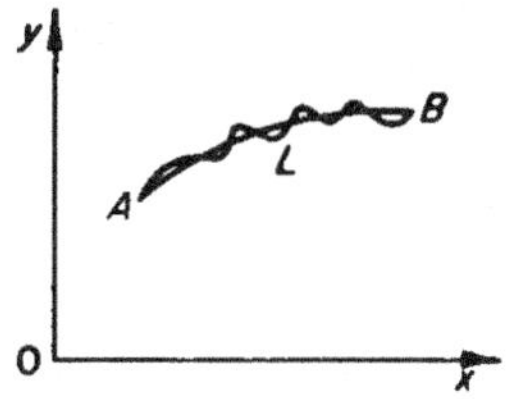

FIG. 34

where the symbol $\int_{\text{extr}} F(x; y; y')\,dx$ means that the extremal passing through the points A and B is taken as the function $y(x)$ (Fig. 34), and the symbol $\int_L F(x; y; y')\,dx$ that another curve which connects A and B and is situated from the extremal in zero order closeness, is taken as $y(x)$.

It is not possible to use the old method of a series expansion in the variations to study the sign of the difference ΔJ, since the variation $\delta y'$ is not small. Let us apply another method.

Let the Jacobi condition be satisfied on the extremals and let it be encircled by a field of extremals (Fig. 35), at each point of which the function of the slope of the field $p = p(x; y)$ is defined (the derivative of that extremal which passes through a point $x; y$ is called the function of

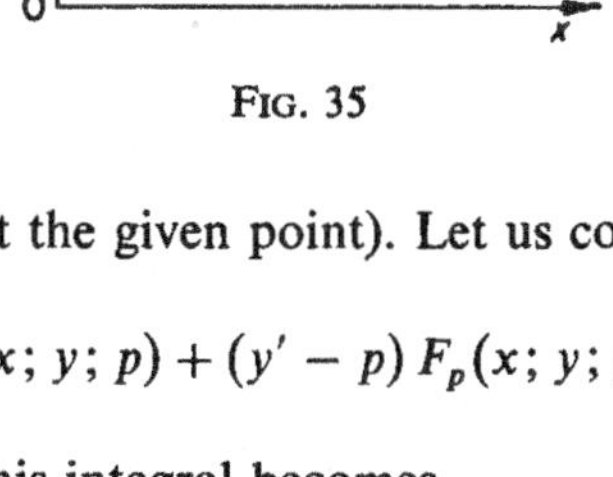

FIG. 35

the slope of the field at the given point). Let us consider the integral

$$\int_{x_0}^{x_1} [F(x; y; p) + (y' - p)\, F_p(x; y; p)]\, dx; \tag{10}$$

on the extremal $y(x)$ this integral becomes

$$\int_{x_0}^{x_1} F(x; y; y')\, dx,$$

since $p = y'$ on the extremal.

On the other hand, the integral (10), which may be represented as

$$\int_{A(x_0;y_0)}^{B(x_1;y_1)} [F(x;y;p) - pF_p(x;y;p)]\,dx + F_p(x;y;p)\,dy,$$

is independent of the path of integration since it is an integral of a total differential. In fact, from (3) of Chapter II it follows that

$$dJ = (F - y'F_{y'})\,dx + F_{y'}\,dy \tag{11}$$

and hence

$$\int_{A(x_0;y_0)}^{B(x_1;y_1)} [F - (y' - p)\,F_p]\,dx = \int dJ = J(x_1;y_1) - J(x_0;y_0). \tag{12}$$

Remarking that

$$F_p(y' - p) = 0$$

on the extremal where $y' = p$, we transform the difference (9) to

$$\Delta J = \int_L [F(x;y;y')\,dx - \int_{\text{extr}} [F(x;y;p) + F_p(y' - p)]\,dx. \tag{13}$$

But the integral in the subtraction is independent of the path of integration and therefore

$$\Delta J = \int_L [F(x;y;y') - F(x;y;p) - (y' - p)\,F_p]\,dx \tag{14}$$

or

$$\Delta J = \int_L E\,dx, \tag{15}$$

where the function

$$E(x;y;y';p) = F(x;y;y') - F(x;y;p) - (y' - p)\,F_p \tag{16}$$

is called the Weierstrass function.

We now obtain a simple sufficient condition for the extremum: In order for the function $y(x)$ to achieve a strong minimum of the functional

$$J = \int_{x_0}^{x_1} F(x;y;y')\,dx,$$

it is sufficient that for any y' the inequality

$$E \geqslant 0 \tag{17}$$

be satisfied in addition to the Jacobi condition in the neighborhood of the extremal.

The inequality of opposite sign

$$E \leqslant 0. \tag{18}$$

is sufficient for the strong maximum.

This condition is called the Weierstrass condition.

It may be shown that the Weierstrass condition is also necessary. Namely, if we have $E < 0$, for certain y' on the extremals, then there is known not to be a strong minimum; if $E > 0$, then there may not be a strong maximum.

If the Weierstrass condition is satisfied and the Jacobi condition is not, then a local extremum is reached on the extremal in any case; sufficiently small segments of the extremal will admit a strong extremum while an extremum may not be achieved on the extremal as a whole.

Simplified Weierstrass Condition

The Weierstrass function is difficult to investigate because of its awkwardness. It is more convenient to utilize a simplified Weierstrass criterion. Assuming that the function $F(x; y; y')$ is thrice differentiable with respect to y', we obtain on the basis of the Taylor formula

$$F(x; y; y') = F(x; y; p) + (y' - p)\, F_p + \frac{(y' - p)^2}{2!}\, F_{y'y'}(x; y; q)$$

where q is included between p and y'.

Replacing $F(x; y; y')$ by its Taylor series expansion, we have

$$E = \frac{(y' - p)^2}{2!}\, F_{y'y'}(x; y; q). \tag{19}$$

Now, the following simplified Weierstrass condition may be formulated: in order for $y(x)$ to achieve a strong minimum, it is sufficient that the inequality

$$F_{y'y'} \geqslant 0 \tag{20}$$

be satisfied as well as the Jacobi condition for all y', not only at the points of the extremal itself, but also in its neighborhood. Compliance with an inequality of opposite sign is sufficient for a strong maximum.

Let us note the difference between conditions (17) and (20) and the Legendre condition for a weak minimum: In verifying the Legendre condition we calculate $F_{y'y'}$ by taking y' equal to its value on the extremal; in verifying the Weierstrass condition we check the sign of $F_{y'y'}$ for any y', not only on the extremal itself, but also in its neighborhood.

Example 1. Let us investigate the functional

$$\int_{x=0;\, y=0}^{x=1;\, y=1} y'^3\, dx. \tag{21}$$

The extremal is the line $y = x$. The Jacobi condition is known to be satisfied (a central field). At points of the extremal we have

$$F_{y'y'} = 6y' = 6 > 0.$$

A weak minimum is achieved, equal to one, on the extremal AC (Fig. 36). At the same time there is no strong minimum because the function $F_{y'y'}$ may take any sign for arbitrary y'.

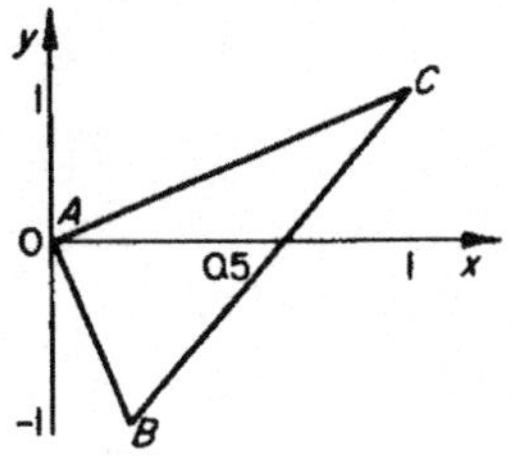

FIG. 36

Let us calculate the value of the functional on the broken line ABC (Fig. 36).

On the AB portion

$$y' = -5 \quad \text{and} \quad \int_0^{0.2} y'^3\, dx = -25.$$

On the BC portion

$$y' = 1.6 \quad \text{and} \quad \int_{0.2}^{1} y'^3\, dx = 3.28,$$

i.e., the value

$$\int_0^1 y'^3\, dx = -21.72$$

is somewhat less on the broken line ABC than on the extremal.

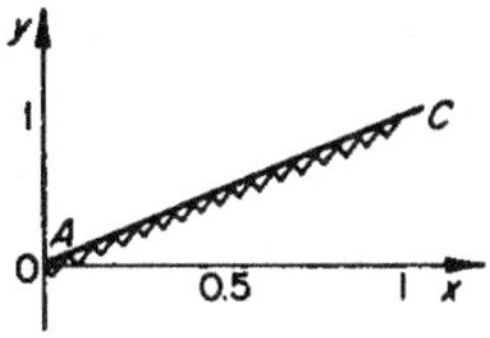

FIG. 37

It can be seen by a direct calculation that the sawtooth curve (Fig. 37) with steep "inclines" and shallower "rises" also gives the integral (21) a negative value, and it may simultaneously be in zero order closeness to the extremal for a sufficiently large number of breaks.

Example 2. Let us investigate the functional

$$\int_{x=0;\,y=0}^{x=1;\,y=1} (1 + y'^2)^{1/2}\,dx$$

i.e., the distance between the points 0; 0 and 1; 1.

The equation of the family of extremals passing through the point (0, 0) is

$$y = Cx.$$

The (central) field exists on the whole plane, the Jacobi condition is satisfied and

$$F_{y'y'} = [(1 + y'^2)^{1/2}]^{3/2} \tag{22}$$

Since (22) is greater than zero for any x, y and y', a strong minimum is reached on the extremal.

Example 3. Let us investigate the functional

$$J = \int_{x=0;\,y=0.}^{x=1;\,y=0} (y'^2 - yy'^3)\,dx.$$

The line $y = 0$ passing through the given points satisfies the Euler equation

$$2y'^3 - (2 - 6yy')\,y'' = 0.$$

On the extremal $J = 0$; evaluating $F_{y'y'}$ we obtain

$$F_{y'y'} = 2 - 6yy'.$$

We have $F_{y'y'} = 2 > 0$ on the extremals for $y = 0$, i.e., a weak minimum is reached on the extremals. However, there is no strong minimum since the function $F_{y'y'}$ may change sign in the neighborhood of the extremals for $y \neq 0$. Indeed, it may be proven that on a curve given by the equations

$$y = (2/\sqrt{\alpha})\, x \quad \text{for} \quad 0 \leqslant x \leqslant \alpha \quad \text{and}$$

$$y = \frac{2\sqrt{\alpha}(1-x)}{1-\alpha} \quad \text{for} \quad \alpha \leqslant x \leqslant 1,$$

we will have

$$J = -4 + \frac{4}{1-\alpha}\left(1 + \frac{2\alpha}{1-\alpha}\right),$$

and the value of the functional will be negative for sufficiently small α. This example (the Hadamard example) shows the importance of investigating the sign of $F_{y'y'}$ not only on the extremal itself but also in its neighborhood.

Example 4. Let us investigate the functional

$$J = \int_0^1 y/y'^2\, dx,$$

considered earlier in Section 25. We have $F_{y'y'} = 6y/y'^4$; in the neighborhood of the extremal $y = (1-0.5x)^2$ we will have $F_{y'y'} > 0$ for all y'. However, it is impossible herefrom to make any conclusion on the presence of a strong minimum since the function y/y'^2 is not differentiable at $y' = 0$ and a Taylor series expansion is impossible. Forming the Weierstrass function, we find that the expression

$$E = \frac{y}{y'^2} - \frac{y}{p^2} + \frac{2y}{p^3}(y' - p) = \frac{y(y'-p)^2(2y'+p)}{y'^2 p^3}$$

may have any sign for arbitrary y'.

The Weierstrass condition is not satisfied; there is no strong minimum.

28. Summary of Necessary and Sufficient Conditions for an Extremum

Necessary Conditions

In order for $y(x)$ to achieve a weak minimum of the functional

$$J = \int_{x_0}^{x_1} F(x; y; y')\, dx$$

among all the piecewise-smooth curves connecting the points $A(x_0; y_0)$ and $B(x_1; y_1)$, it is necessary that

(1) $y(x)$ be an extremal, i.e., should satisfy the Euler equation

$$F_y - \frac{d}{dx} F_{y'} = 0;$$

(2) the Legendre condition

$$F_{y'y'} \geqslant 0$$

be satisfied along $y(x)$;

(3) the Jacobi condition be satisfied, i.e., the curve $y(x)$ should not have points conjugate to x_0, or analytically: the solution of the Jacobi equation

$$-\frac{d}{dx}(ru') + Pu = 0$$

with the initial conditions $u(x_0) = 0$; $u'(x_0) = 1$ should not vanish for $x_0 < x < x_1$.

Moreover, in order for $y(x)$ to achieve a strong minimum a fourth condition is necessary:

(4) along the extremal

$$E(x; y; y'; p) \geqslant 0$$

for any y'.

SUFFICIENT CONDITIONS

For the function $y(x)$ to achieve a weak minimum it is sufficient that:

(1) $y(x)$ be an extremal;

(2) The strengthened Legendre condition

$$F_{y'y'} > 0$$

be satisfied along $y(x)$;

(3) The strengthened Jacobi condition be satisfied: the solution of the Jacobi equation should not vanish for $x_0 < x \leqslant x_1$.

For a strong minimum it is sufficient that the additional condition

(4) for any y' in the neighborhood of the extremal $y(x)$

$$E(x; y; y'; p) \geqslant 0$$

be satisfied.

The signs of all the inequalities are reversed in the conditions for the maximum.

Sufficient Conditions for Conditional Extremum Problems

A mnemonic rule may be used and the functional $\int H\,dx = \int (F + K)\,dx$ investigated in the isoperimetric problem to investigate the sufficient conditions. The proof of the mnemonic rule for the sufficient conditions for an extremum may be found in [4]. In the Lagrange problem it is more convenient to solve the coupling equation and to investigate the sufficient conditions for an absolute extremum in the problem hence obtained.

Practical Recommendations

It is difficult to investigate the sufficient conditions for an extremum, especially in the case of complex functionals or for the Lagrange problem. In engineering practice, it is customary to be restricted to the necessary conditions, the Euler equation and the Legendre condition, without investigating the sufficient conditions. Hence, let us analyze in more detail what an investigation of some necessary conditions will yield.

If the minimum of a functional in a given class of functions exists and the extremal is unique, it may then be asserted without any analysis of the sufficient conditions, that this minimum is reached on the extremal found. Similarly, for a maximum, this assertion is valid.

The case when several extremals satisfy the boundary conditions under consideration is somewhat more complicated. But even here, it is possible to dispense with the analysis of the sufficient conditions and to calculate directly the values of the functional at each of the extremals and to select that one on which the function reaches the minimum.

To give a foundation for the existence of an extremum in a selected class of functions is most complicated. Here, boundedness of the functional is not sufficient. The functional may be essentially positive, with a lower bound (zero, say), but nevertheless the minimum may not be achieved on the extremals. The reason might be that the minimum is achieved outside the limits of the class of piecewise-smooth functions. The functional

$$J = \int_0^1 y^2/y'^2\,dx$$

with the boundary conditions $y(0) = 1$; $y(1) = e = 2.718$ is an example of this.

The first integral of the Euler equation for this functional is

$$F - y'F_{y'} = \frac{y^2}{y'^2} + \frac{2y^2}{y'^2} = \frac{3y^2}{y'^2} = C$$

from which we find the equation of the extremals

$$y = C_2 e^{C_1 x}.$$

The single extremal

$$y = e^x$$

satisfies the assigned boundary conditions.

The value of the functional is one on the extremal. The functional is positive and has the lower bound zero. The minimum is known to exist, however, it is achieved outside the limits of the class of piecewise-smooth functions. The minimum of the functional, zero, is achieved on a discontinuous function, as will be shown in Section 30 (see Fig. 43). In this connection, the work of Krotov [5, 6] is of great value (see Section 30).

Krotov found a simple criterion which permits establishment of the absence of discontinuities in functions yielding an extremum. Upon compliance with the Krotov criterion, a conclusion relative to the existence of an extremum in the class of piecewise-smooth functions may be made on the basis of boundedness of the functional.

29. Degenerate Functionals

All the preceding theory refers only to functionals for which the function $F_{y'y'}$ is not identically zero. Functionals for which $F_{y'y'} \equiv 0$ have special properties. They are called degenerate functionals, and are hardly considered in textbooks on calculus of variations. Meanwhile, degenerate functionals are encountered quite frequently in practice, and hence, they merit a more detailed study.

If the function $F_{y'y'}$ equals zero identically, this then means that the functional has the form

$$J = \int_a^b [M(x; y) + N(x; y)\, y']\, dx, \tag{23}$$

i.e., depends linearly on y' (the functional is not at all dependent on y' in the special case when $N = 0$).

The Euler equation

$$F_y - \frac{d}{dx} F_{y'} = \frac{\partial M}{\partial y} + \frac{\partial N}{\partial y} y' - \frac{\partial N}{\partial y} y' - \frac{\partial N}{\partial x}$$
$$= \frac{\partial M}{\partial y} - \frac{\partial N}{\partial x} = 0 \tag{24}$$

for such functionals is not a differential, but a finite equation without any derivatives of the unknown function.

There may be two cases.

(1) The relationship (24) is satisfied identically for any y. But for

$$\frac{\partial M}{\partial y} = \frac{\partial N}{\partial x}$$

the functional (23), which may always be written as

$$J = \int_a^b M\,dx + N\,dy \tag{25}$$

(since $y'\,dx = dy$), is transformed into the integral of a total differential. The magnitude of the functional is independent of the path of integration, but depends only on the initial and final points. For any $y(x)$ the functional (23) retains the same value in this case, all the $y(x)$ are equivalent.

(2) If the relationship (24) is not satisfied identically, it then defines one (or several) curve (extremal) on which the extremum may be achieved.

Example 1. Find the extremum of the integral

$$J = \int_0^1 [y' \sin \alpha y - (x + y)^2]\,dx. \tag{26}$$

The Euler equation is

$$-2(x + y) = 0.$$

The extremum may be reached on the line $y = -x$.

Example 2. Find the extremum of the functional

$$J = \int_1^2 \sin y\,dx.$$

From the Euler equation $\cos y = 0$, we obtain that the extremum may be achieved on the lines $y = (2n+1)\,\pi/2$ $(n = 0;\ \pm 1;\ \pm 2;\ \pm 3;\ldots)$.

Example 3. Find the extremum of the functional

$$J = \int_{x=0;\, y=0}^{x=1;\, y=1} (y + xy')\, dx\,.$$

The Euler equation becomes the identity $1 = 1$, the integral is independent of the path of integration.

Indeed

$$\int (y + xy')\, dx = \int y\, dx + x\, dy = \int d(xy) = xy\Big|_{x=0;\, y=0}^{x=1;\, y=1} = 1\,;$$

no matter what the curve connecting the points $(0;\, 0)$ and $(1;\, 1)$ has been taken, the value of the functional will be the same.

Since the solution of (24) contains no arbitrary constants, only in exceptional cases may the extremal pass through two given points. Hence, it is necessary to change the formulation of the problem. Thus, for the particular case when $F(x;\, y;\, y')$ is entirely independent of y', it is necessary to pose the problem of a curve $y(x)$ achieving the extremum of the functional

$$J = \int_{x_0}^{x_1} F(x;\, y)\, dx$$

for given endpoint abscissas $x = x_0$ and $x = x_1$. The endpoint ordinates are not given, and therefore, we seek the desired curve among the curves having their endpoints on the vertical segments $x = x_0$ and $x = x_1$.

The sufficient condition for the minimum is compliance with the inequality $F_{yy} > 0$, and for the maximum, with $F_{yy} < 0$.

Returning to Example 2, we obtain

$$F_{yy} = -\sin y$$

and therefore, a maximum of the functional, equal to one, is reached on the lines $y = \pi/2$, $y = 2\pi + \pi/2$ (generally of the form $(4n+1)\,(\pi/2)$ for $n = 1;\, 2;\, 3$); and a minimum of the functional, equal to minus one, is reached on the lines $y = (4n-1)\,(\pi/2)$ (Fig. 38).

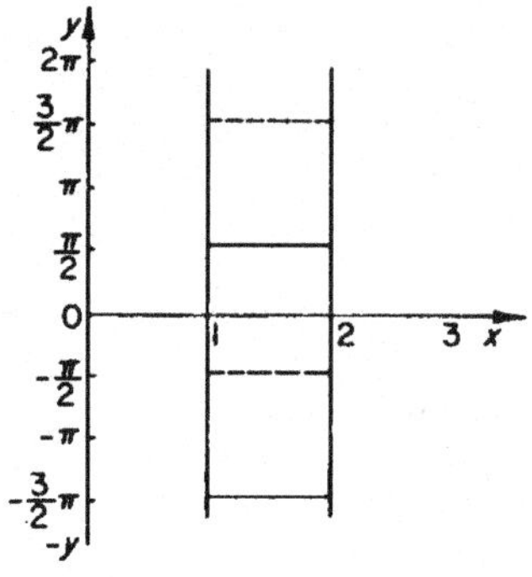

FIG. 38

For a functional of the form

$$J = \int_a^b (M + Ny')\, dx\,,$$

where $N \neq 0$, the extremum should be sought in a class of curves passing through two given points. But vertical segments (Fig. 39) may be portions

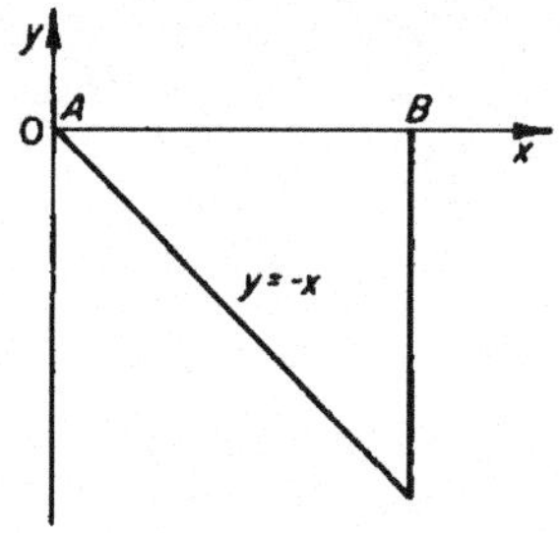

FIG. 39

of such curves. On the vertical segment we have $x = x_0$ and

$$J = \int_{y_1}^{y_2} N(x_0; y)\, dy\,.$$

Thus, the functional (26) we considered earlier with the boundary conditions $y(0) = 0$ and $y(1) = 0$ reaches an extremum on a composite curve (Fig. 39): on the extremal $y = -x$ for $0 < x < 1$, and on the vertical segment between $y = -1$ and $y = 0$ for $x = 1$.

The functional takes the value zero on this curve, thus reaching its minimum, as we see later. It has been shown by Lavrent'ev and Liusternik that the functional (26) achieves neither a maximum nor a minimum on the smooth extremal $y = -x$ which has endpoints on the vertical lines $x = 0$ and $x = -1$. Hence, the problem of the extremum of functionals such as

$$\int_a^b [M(x; y) + N(x; y)\, y']\, dx$$

with $N \neq 0$ has a solution only in the class of curves with vertical segments. This class of curves will be examined in more detail in the next section which is devoted to the work of Krotov.

Let us consider degenerate functionals which depend on the higher derivatives. We shall designate functionals for which $F_{y^{(n)}y^{(n)}} = 0$ identically as degenerate, where $y^{(n)}$ is the highest derivative in the given functional. The expression $F_{y^{(n)}y^{(n)}}$ can vanish identically when the functional depends linearly on the highest derivative. Thus, if the functional depends on the second derivative, it then follows from $F_{y''y''} = 0$ that

$$J = \int_a^b [A(x; y; y') + B(x; y; y')\, y'']\, dx. \tag{27}$$

After transformation, the Euler-Poisson equation becomes

$$A_y - A_{xy'} + B_{xx} + (B_{xy} - A_{yy'})\, y' - A_{y'y'} y'' = 0, \tag{28}$$

i.e., is a second-order differential equation, while it is a fourth-order equation in the general case for a nondegenerate functional depending on the second derivative. Hence, the order of the Euler-Poisson equation is reduced by two for a degenerate functional. The number of boundary conditions which the extremal should satisfy should be reduced correspondingly also.

30. The Work of V. F. Krotov

In the preceding exposition, we considered extremums in the class of piecewise-smooth functions. However, examples of functionals for which the extremum is not achieved in this class, do exist. Let us consider the functional

$$J = \int_{-1}^{+1} x^2 y'^2\, dx \tag{29}$$

with the boundary conditions $y(1) = 1;\ y(-1) = -1$.

The Euler equation is

$$2x^2y' = C;$$

its solutions are the hyperbolas

$$y = \frac{C_1}{x} + C_2 \tag{30}$$

however, no continuous extremal will pass through the points $x = -1$; $y = -1$ and $x = 1$; $y = 1$.

Meanwhile, the minimum of the integral (29) exists, and is zero. The integral (29) will equal zero on the composite curve (Fig. 40) consisting of the lines $y = -1$ for $-1 \leqslant x \leqslant 0$ ($y' = 0$ on these lines, and hence, $x^2y' = 0$) and the vertical segment which is the ordinate axis between $y = -1$ and $y = 1$ for $0 < x \leqslant 1$ ($x = 0$ on this segment). Any smooth curve

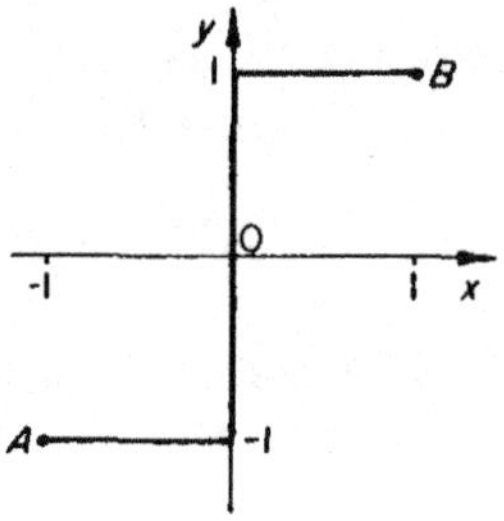

FIG. 40

connecting the points $(-1;\ -1)$ and $(1;\ 1)$ cannot yield the minimum of the integral (29) since there will be portions of this curve on which $x \neq 0$ or $y' \neq 0$; therefore, the integral (29) will be greater than zero (Fig. 40).

This example (the Weierstrass example) shows that an extremum may not be reached on piecewise-smooth functions and the class of admissible functions should be broadened for a complete solution of variational problems.

Let us seek the extremum of the functional

$$J = \int_a^b F(x;\ y;\ y')\,dx \tag{31}$$

in the class of piecewise-continuous functions $y(x)$, i.e., functions which may have as large a quantity of discontinuities of the first kind (jumps) as desired in the segment $(a; b)$ (see Fig. 4). The functions $y(x)$ are continuous between the points of the jump.

The function

$$y = \arctan 1/x$$

is an example of a piecewise-continuous function (its graph is pictured in Fig. 41a).

When x tends to zero from the left, y tends to $-\pi/2$, when x tends to zero from the right, y tends to $+\pi/2$. The function is not defined at $x = 0$,

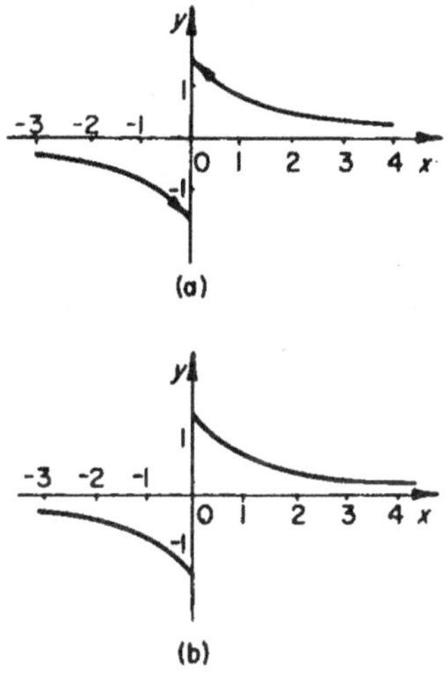

FIG. 41

and it may provisionally be supplemented by the vertical segment between $y = -\pi/2$ and $y = +\pi/2$ (Fig. 41b).

Let us proceed in such a manner in the general case also, by supplementing the function $y(x)$ with vertical segments at the points of discontinuity, and let us seek the extremum of the functional in the class of lines with vertical segments. Krotov [5, 6] investigated the extremum in this class of lines. The Krotov proofs involve utilization of the Lebesgue integral, whose analysis is beyond the scope of this book. Hence, let us briefly elucidate the Krotov fundamental results, without proofs.

The character of the extremals is determined by the behavior of the function

$$W(x; y) = \lim_{y' \to \pm\infty} F(x; y; y') \frac{1}{y'}, \tag{32}$$

wherein we shall designate $\lim_{y' \to +\infty} F(x; y; y')(1/y')$ as the right limit, and the limit as $y' \to -\infty$ as the left limit.

Five fundamental cases are possible.

(1) Let there not be a right nor a left finite limit. For example,

$$\lim_{y' \to +\infty} (y^2 + y'^2) \frac{1}{y'} = +\infty,$$

and

$$\lim_{y' \to -\infty} (y^2 + y'^2) \frac{1}{y'} = -\infty,$$

for the functional $\int_0^1 (y^2 + y'^2)\, dx$.

(2) Right and left limits exist and are equal at a finite number of points in the interval $(a; b)$. For example, the function

$$W(x; y) = 0 \qquad \text{for} \qquad x = 0$$

for the functional $\int_{-1}^{+1} x^2 y'^2\, dx$ but does not exist at all other points.

(3) Right and left limits exist and are equal everywhere in the interval $(a; b)$. Thus for any linear functional in y'

$$J = \int_a^b [M(x; y) + N(x; y)\, y']\, dx,$$

the equality

$$W(x; y) = N(x; y)$$

is valid.

(4) Right and left limits exist and are not equal at a finite number of points.

(5) Right and left limits exist and are not equal everywhere in the interval $(a; b)$.

The functional

$$\int_a^b y(1 + y'^2)^{1/2}\, dx,$$

for which

$$\lim_{y' \to +\infty} F(x; y; y') \frac{1}{y'} = + y, \quad \text{and} \quad \lim_{y' \to -\infty} F(x; y; y') \frac{1}{y'} = - y$$

might be an example.

First Kind of Functionals

The simplest (and at the same time most important) case is the first. If the finite limit (32) does not exist, the extremals in the class of piecewise-continuous functions coincide with the extremals in the class of piecewise-smooth functions. This is extremely important since, if there is no limit (32) (and this is established quite easily), then there may not be any vertical segments on the extremals and the piecewise-smooth extremals we found in previous sections will yield the extremums even among all piecewise-continuous functions.

Second Kind of Functionals

Functionals for which the limits (32) exist and are equal at a finite number of points belong to the second kind.

As an example, let us take the case when the limit (32) exists only at the single point with abscissa $x = x_0$.

Krotov showed that the functional (31) may be represented in this case as the sum

$$J = J_1 + J_2 + J_3 = \int_a^{x_0} F(x; y; y')\, dx + \int_{y_1}^{y_2} W(x_0; y)\, dy + \int_{x_0}^{b} F(x; y; y')\, dx.$$

Indeed, the value of the functional on the vertical segment may be considered as the limit of its value on the inclined segment (Fig. 42), either inclined to the right (then the slope will be y') or inclined to the left (then the slope will be $-y'$).

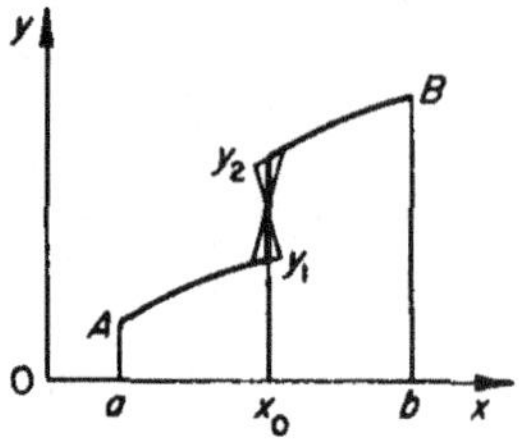

FIG. 42

The value of the functional on the vertical segment will be

$$J_2 = \lim_{y' \to \pm\infty} \int_{x_1}^{x_2} F(x; y; y')\, dx = \lim_{y' \to \pm\infty} \int_{y_1}^{y_2} F(x; y; y') \frac{1}{y'}\, dy$$
$$= \int_{y_1}^{y_2} W(x_0; y)\, dy. \qquad (33)$$

The validity of the passages to the limit is given a foundation by Krotov [5]. It follows from (33) that the functional (31) decomposes into two independent functionals:

$$J_{11} = \int_a^{x_0} F(x; y; y')\, dx - \int_c^{y_1} W(x_0; y)\, dy$$

and

$$J_{22} = \int_{x_0}^{b} F(x; y; y')\, dx + \int_c^{y_2} W(x_0; y)\, dy,$$

where c is an arbitrary point between y_1 and y_2.

Therefore, the extremal curve may consist of two continuous pieces, the extremals of the functionals J_{11} and J_{22}, and a vertical segment connecting their endpoints.

We must still find the points where the extremals join the vertical segment. The condition

$$F_{y'}(x_0; y_0; y_0') - W(x_0; y_0) = 0$$

is satisfied at the juncture point y_0.

This condition permits determination of y_0.

Example. Find the minimum of the functional

$$J = \int_{-1}^{+1} x^2 y'^2\, dx$$

we considered at the beginning of the section when $y(-1) = -1$; $y(1) = 1$.

Let us evaluate

$$\lim_{y' \to \pm\infty} x^2 y'^2 (1/y') = \lim_{y' \to \pm\infty} x^2 y' .$$

This limit exists and equals zero at $x=0$, but does not exist at the remaining points in the interval $(-1;\ +1)$. Therefore, the extremum may be reached on a curve containing the vertical segment $x=0$. The equations of the extremals were found earlier (see (30)). The extremals will have endpoints on the vertical segment if we put $C_1=0$. Since $F_{y'}$ $(x=0;\ y;\ y')=0$ and $W(x=0;\ y)=0$, the boundary conditions are satisfied in any case. By determining the constant C_2 from the condition that the curve passes through given points, we finally obtain that the extremum is achieved on a curve composed of the extremal $y=-1$ for $-1 \leqslant x < 0$, the extremal $y=1$ for $0 < x \leqslant 1$ and the vertical segment $x=0$ between $y=-1$ and $y=+1$.

It is important to note that the extremals are independent of the position of the right end in the left part of the interval up to the point x_0, and independent of the position of the left endpoint in the right part of the interval after x_0.

Third Kind of Functionals

The right and left limits (32) exist and are equal at any point of the interval $(a;\ b)$ for the third kind of functionals. Linear functionals in y' are an important example of functionals of the third kind.

In fact if

$$F(x;\ y;\ y') = M(x;\ y) + N(x;\ y)\, y'$$

then

$$W(x;\ y) = N(x;\ y),$$

i.e., the limits exist and equal $N(x;\ y)$ at any point.

As Krotov showed, the problem of the extremum of the functional (31) reduces, for functionals of the third kind, to the investigation of the extremum of the function

$$S(x;\ y;\ z) = F(x;\ y;\ z) - W(x;\ y)\, z - \int_c^y W_x(x;\ y)\, dy .$$

For the functional to have an extremum, either relative or absolute, it is necessary and sufficient that the function have the appropriate extremum.

Example 1. Find the extremum of the functional (analyzed earlier in section 28)

$$J = \int_0^1 y^2/y'^2 \, dx$$

for the boundary conditions $y(0)=1$; $y(1)=e$.

We have

$$\lim_{y \to \pm\infty} \frac{y^2}{y'^2} \frac{1}{y'} = 0\,;$$

the functional is of the third kind.

The function $S(x; y; z) = y^2/z^2$ has a minimum at either $y=0$ or as $z \to \pm\infty$, which corresponds to vertical segments. Hence, the functional achieves the absolute minimum, zero, on a composite curve consisting of the segment $y=0$ and the vertical segments at $x=0$ and $x=1$ (Fig. 43).

Example 2. Find the minimum of the functional

$$J = \int_0^1 \sin y' \, dx$$

under the boundary conditions $y(0)=0$; $y(1)=0$.

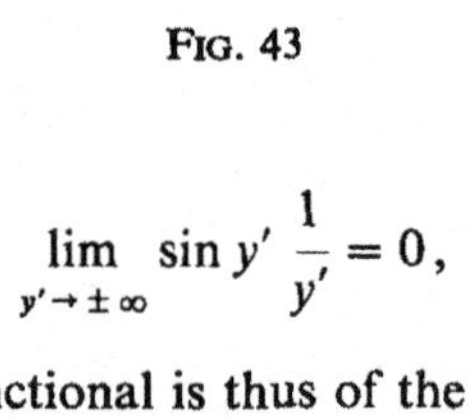

FIG. 43

We have

$$\lim_{y' \to \pm\infty} \sin y' \frac{1}{y'} = 0,$$

for each y and y'; the functional is thus of the third kind.

The function $S(x; y; z) = \sin z$ achieves a maximum at $z = \pi/2 + 2k\pi$ and a minimum at $z = -\pi/2 + 2k\pi$.

Therefore, the extremum may be achieved on the lines $y = (2k+1)\frac{1}{2}\pi x + C_2$, and composite curves consisting of lines and vertical segments. Evidently an infinite quantity of minimal curves, each of which may have any quantity of points of discontinuity, exists in this case. Various minimal curves are pictured in Figs. 44a, b, c. The functional achieves its minimum value $J = -1$ on each.

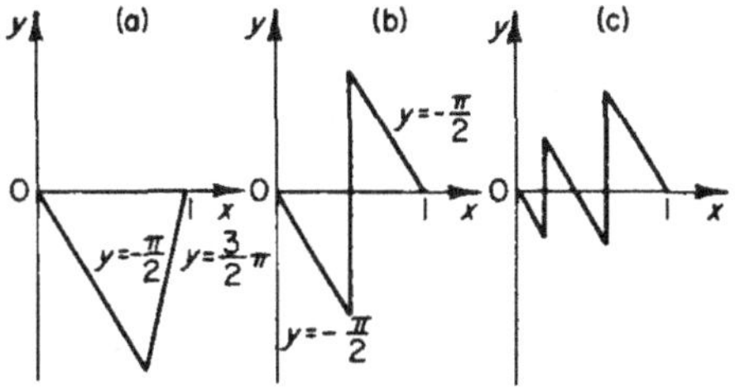

FIG. 44

In general, extremals of functionals of the third kind may have a very quaint character. Thus, an example might be presented of a functional whose extremum is achieved only on a curve with an infinity of discontinuous points.

Example 3. Find the minimum of the functional

$$J = \int_0^1 (y^2 + \sin y')\, dx$$

under the boundary conditions $y(0) = 0$; $y(1) = 0$. We have

$$\lim_{y' \to \pm\infty} \frac{y^2 + \sin y'}{y'} = 0.$$

The function $S(x; y; z) = y^2 + \sin z$ achieves a minimum at $y = 0$; $z = -\pi/2 + 2k\pi$.

Indeed, the second member of the functional $\int_0^1 \sin y'\, dx$ will retain its minimum value, -1, on any saw-tooth curve (Fig. 44) with any quantity of "teeth," and the first member of the functional $\int_0^1 y^2\, dx$ will be smaller, the greater the number of "teeth" in the sawtooth curve. The minimum of the functional, -1, will be achieved on a curve of the kind shown in Fig. 45, but with an infinite number of "teeth." Naturally, such a curve cannot even be pictured.

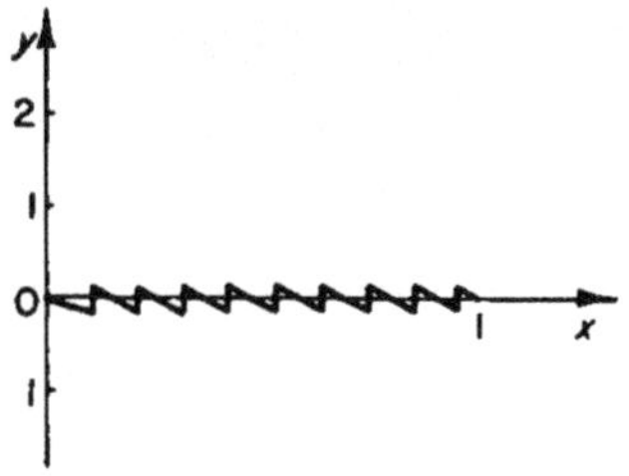

FIG. 45

Of all the functionals of the third kind, linear functionals in the first derivative

$$J = \int_a^b [M(x; y) + N(x; y)\, y']\, dx$$

are of the greatest practical value.

In this case

$$S(x; y; z) = M(x; y) - \int_0^y \frac{\partial N}{\partial x}\, dy. \tag{34}$$

The necessary condition for the extremum will be

$$S_y = \frac{\partial M}{\partial y} - \frac{\partial N}{\partial x} = 0. \tag{35}$$

The sufficient condition is the inequality $S_{yy} > 0$, while the sufficient condition for the maximum is the opposite inequality $S_{yy} < 0$. The extremum is reached on a composite curve consisting of extremals $y(x)$ satisfying (35), and vertical segments $x = a$ and $x = b$. The composite curve is unique, except in those cases when (35) becomes an identity or has several solutions. The absolute extremum is achieved there.

Let us note the following important property of extremal curves of functionals of the third kind. Up to now we have considered extremals which are solutions of the Euler equations, a second-order differential equation. Each infinitesimal element of such extremals depends on the position of adjacent elements and all together they seem to form a chain, whose position and shape is determined by the position of the endpoints. Extremal curves of functionals of the third kind are independent of the boundary conditions; each infinitesimal portion is "self-sufficient," i.e., is independent of the position of the remaining parts.

This property is of quite important practical value. In fact, if each portion of an extremal is connected to adjacent portions, and depends on the boundary conditions, then forces acting on the object in the whole control range, i.e., even in the "future," should be taken into account for the practical realization of the extremal of the control system. Thus, when examining the problem of selecting the optimum armature current diagram for dc electric drives in Chapter III, we saw that this diagram depends on the resistance moment of the performance mechanism in the whole control-time interval. Naturally, this circumstance makes construction of optimum automatic control systems difficult.

If the criterion of the quality is a functional of the third kind, the problem is simplified greatly. In this case it is sufficient to have information only for the given, current time in order to realize the optimum control. Information on the future is not necessary.

Fourth and Fifth Kinds of Functionals

The limits

$$\lim_{y' \to -\infty} F(x; y; y') \frac{1}{y'} \qquad \text{and} \qquad \lim_{y' \to +\infty} F(x; y; y') \frac{1}{y'}$$

exist for functionals of the fourth kind, but they are not equal at individual points of the interval $(a; b)$; they exist for functionals of the fifth kind but are not equal everywhere in the interval $(a; b)$.

As V. F. Krotov showed, both the customary extremals which do not contain vertical segments and depend on the position of the endpoints, and extremal curves with vertical segments can exist for such functionals.

An example is the well-known problem of a curve passing through two given points which generates a surface of revolution of least area when rotated around the abscissa axis. The problem reduces to seeking the function $y(x)$ yielding the minimum of the functional

$$\int_a^b y(1 + y'^2)^{1/2}\, dx, \tag{36}$$

for which

$$\lim_{y' \to +\infty} y(1 + y'^2)^{1/2} \frac{1}{y'} = + y \qquad \text{and} \qquad \lim_{y' \to -\infty} y(1 + y'^2)^{1/2} \frac{1}{y'} = - y.$$

Depending on the distance between the points a and b, the minimum of the functional (36) is achieved either on a smooth curve (hyperbolic cosine) passing through the points a and b, or on a composite curve composed of the abscissa axis and vertical segments at $x = a$ and $x = b$ [3, 4].

V Extremum Problem with Constraints

31. Problems with Constraints in Classical Calculus of Variations

In this chapter, we shall consider a problem of greatest practical value, the problem of seeking the extremum of a functional when certain constraints are imposed on the functions admissible for comparison. Precisely this problem is encountered in practice in the majority of cases since we should be concerned with the boundedness of the forces and stresses in structural elements, the boundedness of the power sources of control actions, etc., in real apparatus. From the mathematical viewpoint, this means that functions admissible for comparison should satisfy some system of inequalities

$$\varphi_k(x; y_i; y_i') \leqslant 0 \qquad (k = 1, 2, \ldots, n; i = 1, 2, \ldots, m). \tag{1}$$

Both the classical variational methods and the methods developed by mathematicians in recent years, the "maximum principle" and dynamic programming, may be utilized to solve such problems.

We start with the study of classical methods and we first consider the simplest problem: Find the extremum of the functional

$$J = \int_a^b F(x; y; y')\, dx \tag{2}$$

under the condition

$$y(x) \geqslant \varphi(x). \tag{3}$$

The equality $y = \varphi(x)$ defines the boundary of the admissible domain within which the function achieving the extremum may only be found

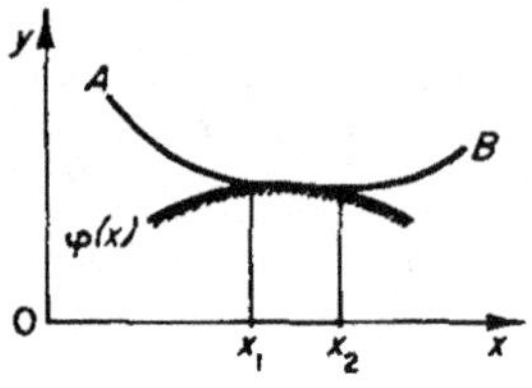

FIG. 46

(Fig. 46). The bounded domain together with its boundary is called a closed region. In the presence of constraints the extremum must be sought in the closed domain.

The fundamental necessary condition for an extremum, the Euler equation, was derived in Chapter I under the assumption of freedom of the variations, i.e., it was considered that if $y(x)$ is an extremal, then $y + \delta y$, where $\delta y > 0$, and $y - \delta y$ are also admissible functions and values of the functional (2) on the extremal $y(x)$ may be compared with its value on the functions $y + \delta y$ and $y - \delta y$.

The Euler equation was indeed derived on the basis of this comparison. Such a comparison is not always possible for a closed domain. Thus, if $y(x)$ passes through the boundary, the function $y - \delta y$, where $\delta y > 0$, will already emerge beyond the limits of the admissible domain. A variation on only one side, a one-sided variation, is admissible on the domain boundary.

Hence, the deduction of the Euler equation is meaningless for a closed domain, the extremum may even be achieved, but not on the extremals.

In order to bypass this difficulty, let us make a change of variables according to the equation

$$z^2 = y - \varphi(x). \tag{4}$$

It follows from (4) that $2zz' = y' - \varphi'(x)$, i.e., $y' = 2zz' + \varphi'(x)$, and the functional (2) becomes in the new variables

$$J = \int_a^b F[x; z^2 + \varphi(x); 2zz' + \varphi'(x)]\, dx. \tag{5}$$

No restrictions have been imposed on the new variable $z(x)$, the value $z = 0$ simply corresponds to the domain boundary.

The extremum of the functional (5) may be sought by the customary method which is valid for an open domain, i.e., the desired function

$z(x)$ should satisfy the Euler equation

$$F_z - \frac{d}{dx} F_{z'} = 0 \tag{6}$$

But

$$\frac{\partial F}{\partial z} = \frac{\partial F}{\partial y}\frac{\partial y}{\partial z} + \frac{\partial F}{\partial y'}\frac{\partial y'}{\partial z} = F_y 2z + F_{y'} 2z',$$

and

$$F_{z'} = \frac{\partial F}{\partial y'}\frac{\partial y'}{\partial z'} = F_{y'} 2z ;$$

therefore

$$\frac{d}{dx} F_{z'} = \frac{d}{dx}(F_{y'} 2z) = 2z' F_{y'} + 2z \frac{d}{dx} F_{y'},$$

i.e., finally

$$F_z - \frac{d}{dx} F_{z'} = 2z F_y - 2z \frac{d}{dx} F_{y'}.$$

Hence, equation (6) becomes

$$2z\left(F_y - \frac{d}{dx} F_{y'}\right) = 0 \tag{7}$$

and actually decomposes into two equations: $z = 0$, which the function $y = \varphi(x)$ satisfies, i.e., the boundary of the admissible domain, and the Euler equation for the original functional

$$F_y - \frac{d}{dx} F_{y'} = 0.$$

Now, the final result may be formulated: In the presence of the constraint (3), the extremum of the functional (2) may be achieved only on curves composed of pieces of the extremals and pieces of the boundary of the admissible domain (in particular cases the length of the pieces of the extremals or of the pieces of the domain boundary may vanish).

For the complete solution it is still necessary to find the condition at the point of passage from the extremal to the domain boundary and conversely.

Let the extremum of the functional (2) be achieved on a composite curve, where the passage from the extremum to the boundary of the domain $y = \varphi(x)$ occurs at the point x_0, therefore

$$J = \int_a^{x_0} F(x; y; y')\,dx + \int_{x_0}^{b} F[x; \varphi(x); \varphi'(x)]\,dx. \tag{8}$$

Let us take a variation of the transition point, i.e., let us go from the point x_0 to the point $x_0 + \delta x_0$, and let us evaluate the variation of the functional for such a change in the desired function. The variation of the functional will consist of two parts: the variation of the functional on the extremal

$$\delta J_1 = \int_a^{x_0+\delta x_0} F(x; y; y')\,dx - \int_a^{x_0} F(x; y; y')\,dx \tag{9}$$

and the variations of the functional on the boundary curve

$$\delta J_2 = \int_{x_0-\delta x_0}^{b} F[x; \varphi(x); \varphi'(x)]\,dx - \int_{x_0}^{b} F[x; \varphi(x); \varphi'(x)]\,dx. \tag{10}$$

The variation of the functional on the extremal is evaluated by the customary formula for the variation of a functional with a free right endpoint moving along a curve $y = \varphi(x)$:

$$\delta J_1 = [F + (\varphi' - y')\,F_{y'}]|_{x=x_0}\,\delta x_0. \tag{11}$$

The variation of the functional on the boundary curve is

$$\delta J_2 = F[x; \varphi(x); \varphi'(x)]|_{x=x_0}\,\delta x_0. \tag{12}$$

Since the extremum is achieved, by assumption, on the composite curve, the sum of the variations $\delta J_1 + \delta J_2$ should then equal zero; from which because of the arbitrariness of δx_0

$$F(x; y; y') - F(x; y; \varphi') - (y' - \varphi')\,F_{y'}|_{x=x_0} = 0 \tag{13}$$

follows, since $\varphi(x_0) = y(x_0)$.

We now transform the difference $F(x; y; y') - F(x; y; \varphi')$ by utilizing the Lagrange theorem of the mean

$$f(a) - f(b) = (a - b)\,f(c),$$

where c lies between a and b.

On the basis of this theorem we have

$$F(x; y; y') - F(x; y; \varphi') = (y' - \varphi')\, F_{y'}(x; y; q'),$$

where q' is a value intermediate between φ' and y'.

Formula (13) becomes

$$(y' - \varphi')\,[F_{y'}(x; y; q') - F_{y'}(x; y; y')] = 0. \tag{14}$$

Again applying the Lagrange theorem of the mean, we reduce (14) to

$$(y' - \varphi')\,(q' - y')\, F_{y'y'}(x; y; q_1')|_{x=x_0} = 0, \tag{15}$$

where q_1' is a value intermediate between q' and $y'(x_0)$.

It follows from (15) that if $F_{y'y'}$ is not zero at the point $x = x_0$, then indeed $y' = \varphi'$ ($q' = y'$ only for $y' = \varphi'$, since q' is the value intermediate between y' and φ').

Hence, we obtain the following important deduction: Tangents to the extremal and the boundary curve at the junction points should coincide. This condition may be violated only for $F_{y'y'} = 0$, i.e., either at singular points of the functional (break points) or for degenerate functionals for which $F_{y'y'} = 0$ identically. The condition of continuity of the tangent yields the additional equations needed for the determination of the constants of integration in the formulas for the extremals.

Thus, if the problem of finding a function $y(x)$ yielding the extremum of a functional (2) passing through two given points A and B and including one section of the boundary of the domain $y = \varphi(x)$ (Fig. 46) is posed, then after the equations of the extremals have been found it is necessary to determine:

(1) Two constants of integration in the equation of the left portion of the extremal;

(2) Two constants of integration for the right portion of the extremal;

(3) The abscissas of the points (x_1 and x_2) of transition from the extremal to the boundary and conversely.

In all we have six constants, for whose determination six equations must be composed. We obtain two equations from the boundary conditions (the extremals should pass through the given points A and B); two equations from the condition that the ordinates of the extremal at the junction points should equal the ordinates of the boundary curve, i.e., $y(x_1) = \varphi(x_1)$

and $y(x_2) = \varphi(x_2)$, and two equations from the condition that the derivatives of the extremal at the junction points should equal the derivatives of the domain boundary, i.e., $y'(x_1) = \varphi'(x_1)$; $y'(x_2) = \varphi'(x_2)$. We obtain six equations in all.

Let us consider an example. Find the shortest dry-land path between the points A (1; 0.5) and B (3.5; 3) without going into a circular lake of radius

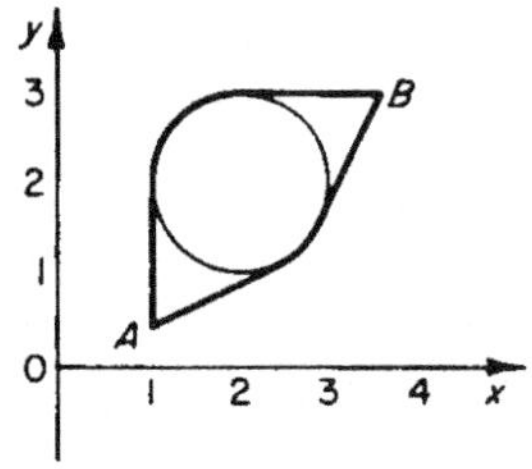

FIG. 47

1 with center at the point (2; 2), as in Fig. 47. In other words, to find the extremum of the integral

$$J = \int_1^{3.5} (1 + y'^2)^{1/2}\, dx; \qquad y(1) = 0.5; \quad y(3.5) = 3 \tag{16}$$

under the constraint $(x-2)^2 + (y-2)^2 \geqslant 1$.

Extremals of the integral (16) are straight lines. The extremal connecting the given points passes outside the boundary of the admissible domain; therefore, the extremum is achieved on composite curves including portions of the domain boundary. Since

$$F_{y'y'} = (1 - y'^2)^{-3/2} > 0,$$

the tangents are then continuous at junction points, and we obtain a simple method of constructing the curve on which the extremum is achieved: we draw a tangent to the circle $(x-2)^2 + (y-2)^2 = 1$ from the given initial point (1; 0.5) and then we move along the circle, emerging on its tangent passing through the second given point (3.5; 3). In this case two curves achieving the extremum exist (Fig. 47). An absolute minimum distance is achieved on the lower, and a relative minimum on the upper curve.

Todhunter solved the considered problem in 1871.

The constraining inequalities may not be assigned explicitly, but may follow from the physical sense of the problem under consideration.

Thus, let us consider the problem: Find the body of greatest volume among all bodies of revolution generated by the rotation of a curve $y(x)$ passing through two given points A and B and having a given surface, around the axis AB,

Let us select the coordinate system so that the axis AB coincides with the horizontal axis and the point A with the origin. Then the surface of the body of revolution will be expressed by the integral

$$S_{BP} = 2\pi \int_a^b y(1 + y'^2)^{1/2}\, dx, \tag{17}$$

and its volume by

$$V_{BP} = \pi \int_a^b y^2\, dx, \tag{18}$$

and the problem reduces to seeking the function $y(x)$ yielding the maximum of the integral (18) for a given value of the integral (17).

Let us form the intermediate function

$$H = \pi y^2 + \lambda_0 y(1 + y'^2)^{1/2}$$

and let us evaluate

$$H_{y'y'} = \frac{\lambda_0 y}{(1 + y'^2)^{3/2}}.$$

The inequality $H_{y'y'} \leqslant 0$ is possible on the curve $y(x)$ only if $y(x)$ does not intersect the horizontal axis. Hence, the maximum problem has meaning only for curves satisfying the inequality $y \geq 0$.

The first integral of the Euler equation

$$H - y'H_{y'} = C$$

is

$$\pi y^2 - \lambda_0 \frac{y}{(1 + y'^2)^{1/2}} = C. \tag{19}$$

Since $y = 0$ for $x = 0$, then $C = 0$ and (19) decomposes into the two equations

$$y = 0 \quad \text{and} \quad y = \lambda_0/(1 + y'^2)^{1/2};$$

where the solution of the second is

$$y^2 + (x - C_1)^2 = \lambda_0{}^2. \tag{20}$$

This is the equation of a circle with center on the horizontal axis and with radius λ_0, determined from (17):

$$\lambda_0 = (S_{BP}/4\pi)^{1/2}.$$

But, in the general case, such a circle does not pass through the two given points; the extremum is achieved on a composite curve formed from the domain boundary $y=0$ and the extremal (20). Since $H_{y'y'}=0$ for $y=0$, we then have the singular case when the tangents to the extremal and to the domain boundary do not coincide (Fig. 48).

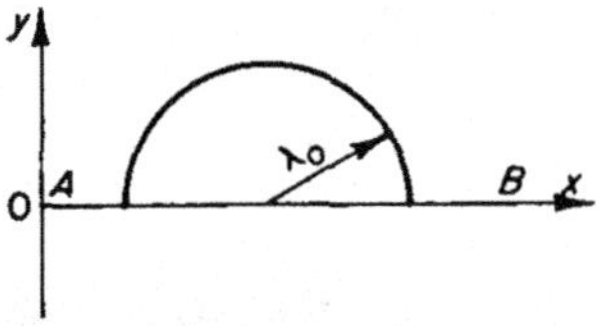

FIG. 48

Airey solved this problem in 1861.

The sufficient conditions for an extremum should be satisfied for the extremal, i.e., in order for the extremum actually to be achieved on the composite curve it is sufficient that Jacobi and Weierstrass conditions be satisfied on portions of the extremal.

Now, let us examine the condition which must be satisfied for the curve yielding the extremum on the portion coincident with the domain boundary. Let $y(x)$ yield the minimum of the functional (2) under the condition (3). Let us append the variation δy on the portion of the boundary where $y=\varphi(x)$ to $y(x)$. In order for the inequality (3) not to be violated, we should have $\delta y > 0$. The variation of the functional (2) may be reduced upon going from $\varphi(x)$ to $\varphi + \delta y$, as we have already done in Chapter I, to

$$\delta J = \int_a^b \left(F_\varphi - \frac{d}{dx} F_{\varphi'}\right) \delta y \, dx.$$

In order for the function $y(x)$ to yield the minimum, compliance with the inequality

$$\delta J \geqslant 0 \tag{21}$$

is necessary, but since $\delta y > 0$ now, it is impossible to deduce from (21), as before, that

$$F_\varphi - \frac{d}{dx} F_{\varphi'} = 0, \tag{22}$$

and it can just be asserted that

$$F_\varphi - \frac{d}{dx} F_{\varphi'} \geqslant 0. \tag{23}$$

Hence, in order for the function $y(x)$ to yield the minimum of the functional (2) under the condition (3), it is necessary that the Euler equation be satisfied on the extremal portions of the composite curve, and the Euler inequality (23) on the portions of the domain boundary.

An important corollary results from the Euler inequality. Let us draw an extremal y_M tangent to the domain boundary $\varphi(x)$ (so that $y_M' = \varphi_M'$) through a point M on the portion of the boundary at the curve yielding the extremum. Since

$$F_y - \frac{d}{dx} F_{y'} = F_y - F_{xy'} - F_{yy'} y' - F_{y'y'} y'' = 0 \tag{24}$$

then subtracting (24) from the inequality (23) which is satisfied on the extremal, we obtain

$$F_{y'y'}(y_M'' - \varphi_M'') \geqslant 0 \tag{25}$$

(since $y_M' = \varphi_M'$). If $F_{y'y'} > 0$, then condition (25) reduces to

$$y_M'' - \varphi_M'' \geqslant 0 \tag{26}$$

or, equivalently, to

$$\frac{y_M''}{(1 + y_M')^{3/2}} \geqslant \frac{\varphi_M''}{(1 + \varphi_M')^{3/2}}, \tag{27}$$

i.e., the curvature of the extremal drawn tangent to the domain boundary is greater than the curvature of the boundary at the point of tangency. This condition aids in finding extremal curves in the case of complex domain boundaries.

Let us consider this problem: Find the shortest dry-land path between two points in the presence of a lake with complex boundaries (Fig. 49). The extremals in this problem are straight lines whose curvature is zero.

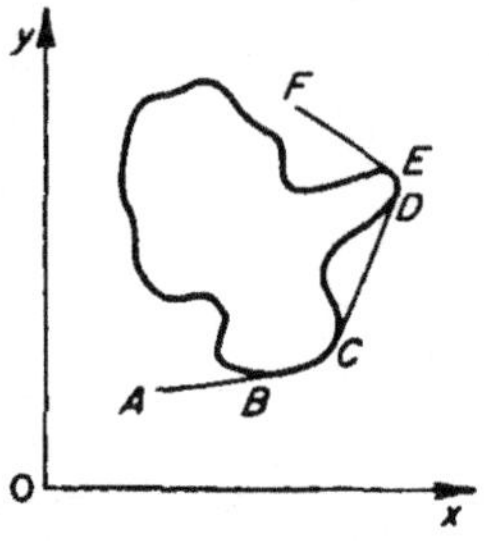

FIG. 49

Hence, the shortest path may pass along the shore of the lake on the convex portions BC but can not along the concave CD.

The results we have obtained may be extended to the case of more complicated constraints than the inequality (3). First of all, the constraints may be imposed not only on the function itself but also on its derivative, i.e., when we have the following differential inequality

$$y' \leqslant \psi(x; y) \tag{28}$$

instead of the inequality (3).

Assuming that the equation of the domain boundary

$$y' = \psi(x; y) \tag{29}$$

has been integrated and the solution

$$y = \varphi(x; C) \tag{30}$$

has been found, where C is a constant of integration, by using the substitution

$$z^2 = y - \varphi(x; C) \tag{31}$$

we arrive at the case we already examined. As before, the extremum is achieved on a composite curve consisting of segments of the extremals and pieces of the domain boundary.

Let us examine a problem solved first by Markov in 1889. To find the shortest line $y(x)$ between two points A (0; 0) and B (2; 4) under the conditions: (1) the radius of curvature of the desired line should not be less than one; and (2) the tangent to $y(x)$ at the point A should coincide with the horizontal axis.

We must therefore find the minimum of the integral

$$J = \int_0^2 (1 + y'^2)^{1/2} \, dx \tag{32}$$

in the presence of the second-order differential inequality

$$\left| \frac{(1 + y'^2)^{3/2}}{y''} \right| \geqslant 1$$

and the additional condition $y'(0) = 0$.

The extremals of the integral (32) are straight lines. No extremal with $y'(0) = 0$ and passing through the point B exists. The extremum may be achieved on composite curves. Let us integrate the equation of the domain boundary

$$\frac{(1 + y'^2)^{3/2}}{y''} = \pm 1 .$$

Its solutions are circles of radius 1:

$$(x - C_1)^2 + (y - C_2)^2 = 1 . \tag{33}$$

Through the point A (0; 0) let us draw circles corresponding to (33) and with $y'(0) = 0$. There will be two such circles (Fig. 50); they outline the domain. The extremals should be beyond this domain. The minimum

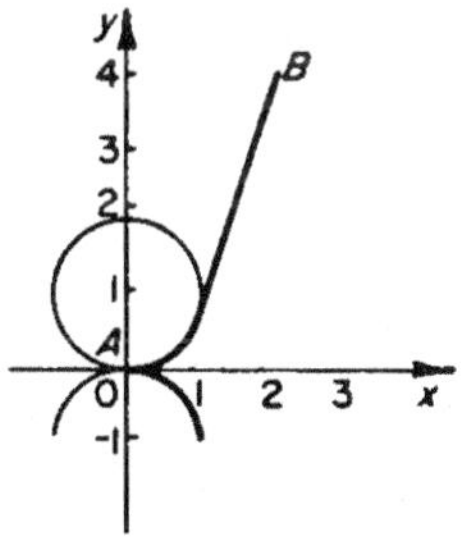

FIG. 50

distance will be achieved on a composite curve consisting of a line tangent to the upper circle and passing through the point B, and the part of the circle from the point of tangency to the point A.

Problems on the extremum of a functional dependent on several unknown functions

$$J = \int_a^b F(x; y_1, \dots, y_n; y_1', \dots, y_n')\, dx, \tag{34}$$

with a constraint of the form

$$\varphi_i(x; y_1 \dots y_n) \leqslant 0, \tag{35}$$

or even including the derivatives

$$\varphi_i(x; y_1, \dots, y_n; y_1', \dots, y_n') \leqslant 0 \tag{36}$$

may also be encountered.

Let us assume that the extremum is achieved on the curve

$$y_1 = y_1(x), \dots, y_n = y_n(x).$$

Let us fix all the variables except y_1 and let us add the variation δy to y_1. Then the increment in the functional will depend only on one variable, and therefore, as we have already proved in the beginning of the section, the extremum will be achieved on a composite curve composed of pieces of extremals of the functional (34) and pieces of the domain boundaries where the inequalities (35) and (36) become equalities:

$$\varphi_i(x; y_1, \dots, y_n) = 0. \tag{37}$$

The tangents at the junction point of the extremal and the boundary of the domain should coincide.

In the case of a functional of one unknown function, the desired function $y(x)$ is determined directly from the equation of the domain boundary

$$\varphi(x; y) = 0.$$

The equation of the domain boundary for a functional (34) of n unknown functions is only a coupling equation, and we must seek the extremum of the functional (34) in the presence of the coupling equation (37) in order to determine the nature of the portions of the desired curve which pass along the domain boundary.

32. Linear Optimum Control Problems

General methods of solving problems on the extremum of functionals in the presence of constraints were considered in the preceding section. Here, the important particular case when the functionals and the coupling equations are linear will be examined. Questions of the optimum control of various production and moving objects reduce to problems of this kind.

In the majority of cases automatic control systems are described by a system of differential equations

$$\begin{aligned} \frac{dx_1}{dt} &= f_1(t; x_1, x_2, \ldots, x_n; u_1, \ldots, u_k); \\ &\cdots\cdots\cdots\cdots \\ \frac{dx_n}{dt} &= f_n(t; x_1, x_2, \ldots, x_n; u_1, \ldots u_k), \end{aligned} \tag{38}$$

where $x_1, \ldots, x_n$ are the coordinates of the control object (phase coordinates); $u_1, \ldots, u_k$ the positions of the controlling organs.

Thus, the motion of a ship (as well as of an aircraft, rocket, etc.) is described by a system such as (38), where $x_1, \ldots, x_n$ is the position, track, velocity of the ship, and $u_1, \ldots, u_k(t)$ the position of the rudder. Henceforth, we shall designate the functions $u_i(t)$ as the controls. At first, let us limit ourselves to the case of one control $u(t)$.

As a rule, the control $u(t)$ has an upper and lower bound:

$$u_1 \leqslant u \leqslant u_2. \tag{39}$$

It is convenient to write the constraint (39) as

$$|u| \leqslant 1, \tag{40}$$

as may always be done by altering the unit of measurement and the reference origin: we take $\frac{1}{2}(u_2 - u_1)$ as the unit of measuring $u(t)$ and $u_1 + \frac{1}{2}(u_2 - u_1)$ as the zero.

In this section we shall examine linear control systems for which the equations (38) are linear, i.e., are of the form

$$\begin{aligned} \frac{dx_1}{dt} &= a_{11}x_1 + a_{12}x_2 + \cdots + a_{1n}x_n + b_1 u; \\ &\cdots\cdots\cdots\cdots \\ \frac{dx_n}{dt} &= a_{n1}x_1 + a_{n2}x_2 + \cdots + a_{nn}x_n + b_n u \end{aligned} \tag{41}$$

or

$$\frac{dx_1}{dt} = \sum_{j=1}^{n} a_{1j}x_j + b_1 u;$$
$$\cdots\cdots\cdots\cdots$$
$$\frac{dx_n}{dt} = \sum_{j=1}^{n} a_{nj}x_j + b_n u$$

(some of the b_i may be zero), and the functional whose extremum we must determine is the time for the system to reach equilibrium, i.e.,

$$J = \int_0^T dt; \qquad x_i(T) = 0, \tag{42}$$

and constraints are imposed only on the control $u(t)$.

Linear problems are often encountered in practice. Thus, automatic control systems usually maintain a given regime (or given motion) of the object by overcoming the effect of various kinds of perturbing forces. If the deviations of the coordinates of an object from their values in a given regime are taken as x, we then obtain the perturbed motion equation for which $x_i \neq 0$ at $t = 0$ and it will be the problem of the control system to assure such control effects as will return the system to the assigned regime in the briefest time, i e., $x_i(T) = 0$. Since the deviations of the system from the steady-state regime are customarily small, by expanding the functions $f_i(x_i; u_k)$ in series and discarding higher order of smallness terms, we may then write the perturbed motion equations in the form of the linear system (41), and the important problem of the most rapid recovery of the assigned regime will reduce, according to the Lagrange multiplier rule, to a problem on the minimum of the linear functional

$$\int_0^T H\,dt = \int_0^T [1 + \sum_{j=1}^{n} \lambda_1(t)(x_i' - \sum_{j=1}^{n} a_{ij}x_j - b_i u)]\,dt, \tag{43}$$

with the boundary conditions $x_i(0) = x_{i0}$; $x_i(T) = 0$ and a constraint on the absolute value (40).

Compliance with the system of Euler equations

$$\frac{\partial H}{\partial u} = 0; \qquad \frac{\partial H}{\partial x} - \frac{d}{dx}\frac{\partial H}{\partial x_i'} = 0 \quad (i = 1, 2, \ldots, n) \tag{44}$$

is the necessary condition for the extremum not to be achieved on the domain boundary.

But the first Euler equation is

$$\frac{\partial H}{\partial u} = - \sum_{i=1}^{n} \lambda_i(t)\, b_i = 0,$$

and it may only be satisfied in the special case when

$$\sum_{i=1}^{n} \lambda_i b_i = 0, \tag{45}$$

i.e., when the functions $\lambda_i(t)$ are interrelated by the linear relationship (45).

Therefore, no extremum exists except in the special (singular) case; the extremum may be achieved on the domain boundary where $|u| = 1$, i.e., either $u = +1$ or $u = -1$. Since derivatives $u'(t)$ do not enter into the intermediate function H, then, as has been shown in Chapter IV, the extremum may be achieved on the discontinuous function $u(t)$ which jumps from the value $u = +1$ to the value $u = -1$ and back (Fig. 51).

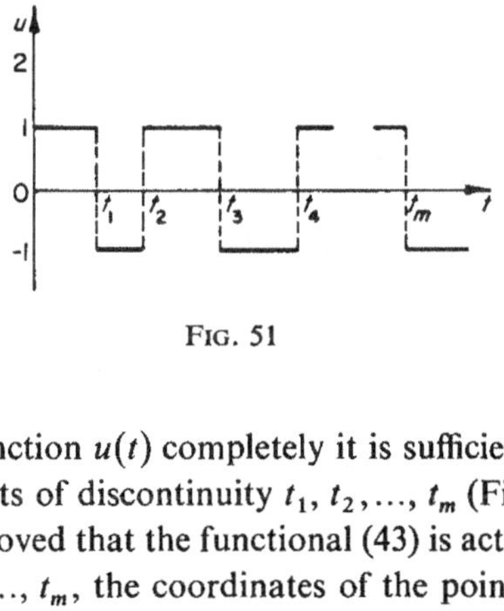

FIG. 51

To determine the function $u(t)$ completely it is sufficient now to find the abscissas of the points of discontinuity $t_1, t_2, \ldots, t_m$ (Fig. 51).

Hence, we have proved that the functional (43) is actually a function of the variables $t_1, t_2, \ldots, t_m$, the coordinates of the point of discontinuity, and the values $t_1, t_2, \ldots, t_m$ yielding the extremum of the function H may be sought by customary differential calculus methods.

The calculus of variations problem may hence be considered solved: we have reduced it to a simpler problem, in principle, to the problem of the extremum for a finite number of variables.

However, in practice it is not easy to seek the points of discontinuity by differential calculus methods, especially if it is taken into account that their number is not known.

To find them we use the following recipe: the condition $|u| = 1$ is equivalent to the condition

$$\int_0^T u^{2m}\, dt = T,$$

where $m \to \infty$.

Indeed, if $|u| > 1$, then $u^{2m} \to \infty$ as $m \to \infty$ and the integral tends to infinity; conversely, if $|u| < 1$, on at least a small section, then $u^{2m} \to 0$ and the value of the integral will be less than T.

Hence, the problem of the extremum of the functional (43) under the condition $|u| = 1$ is equivalent to the isoperimetric problem: Find the extremum of the functional (43) under the condition that the integral

$$\int_0^T u^{2m}\, dt \tag{46}$$

takes on a given value T.

The intermediate function for this isoperimetric problem is

$$H_1 = 1 + \sum_{i=1}^{n} \lambda_i \left(x_i' - \sum_{j=1}^{n} a_{ij} x_j - b_i u\right) + \lambda_0 u^{2m}, \tag{47}$$

and we obtain as the Euler equations

$$\frac{\partial H_1}{\partial u} = 0; \tag{48}$$

$$\frac{\partial H_1}{\partial x_i} - \frac{d}{dt}\frac{\partial H_1}{\partial x_i'} = 0 \tag{49}$$

the following system of equations

$$-\sum_{i=1}^{n} \lambda_i b_i + 2m\lambda_0 u^{2m-1} = 0; \tag{50}$$

$$\lambda_i' + \sum_{j=1}^{n} \lambda_j a_{ij} = 0. \tag{51}$$

It follows from (50) that

$$u = \left(\frac{1}{2m\lambda_0} \cdot \sum_{i=1}^{n} \lambda_i b_i\right)^{1/2m-1},$$

but the sign of the $(2m-1)$th root of any number A agrees with the sign of this number as $m \to \infty$, i.e., $A^{1/2m-1} = 1$ if $A > 0$ and $A^{1/2m-1} = -1$ if $A < 0$.

Symbolically this is written thus:

$$u = \operatorname{sign} A = \operatorname{sign} \sum_{i=1}^{n} \frac{\lambda_i b_i}{2m\lambda_0}, \tag{52}$$

where the symbol sign means that $u = +1$ if $\sum_{i=1}^{n} \lambda_i b_i / 2m\lambda_0 > 0$, $u = -1$ if $\sum_{i=1}^{n} \lambda_i b_i / 2m\lambda_0 < 0$ and $u = 0$ if $\sum_{i=1}^{n} \lambda_i b_i = 0$.

Krasovskii [16] and Kirillova [36] proposed and gave a foundation for the replacement of the constraint $|u| \leqslant 1$ by the constraint $\int_0^T u^{2m}\, dt \leqslant T$ and a subsequent passage to the limit.

To determine completely the control $u(t)$, it is sufficient to solve the system of linear homogeneous equations with constant coefficients (51) and to find the sign of the expression

$$\sum_{i=1}^{n} \lambda_i b_i . \tag{53}$$

Example. Let us consider a linear second order automatic regulation system whose behavior is described by the equations

$$dx_1/dt = x_2; \qquad dx_2/dt = u\,, \tag{54}$$

and let us determine the form a control $u(t)$ should have, subject to the condition $|u| \leqslant 1$ and transferring the system from the regime $x_1 = x_{10}$; $x_2 = x_{20}$ into a given regime $x_1 = 0$; $x_2 = 0$ (the origin) in the briefest time.

Let us replace $|u| \leqslant 1$ by the constraint $\int_0^T u^{2m}\, dt \leqslant T$.

Since both the functional (the time is $T = \int_0^T dt$) and the coupling equation are linear, the extremum is achieved on the domain boundary for $\int_0^T u^{2m}\, dt = T$, and we may consider our problem as isoperimetric with the intermediate function

$$H = 1 + \lambda_1(x_1' - x_2) + \lambda_2(x_2' - u) + \lambda_0 u^{2m}. \tag{55}$$

From the Euler equation follows

$$\lambda_1' = 0; \tag{56}$$

$$\lambda_2' + \lambda_1 = 0; \tag{57}$$

$$u = [(1/2m\lambda_0)\,\lambda_2]^{1/2m-1} = \operatorname{sign}\lambda_2, \tag{58}$$

i.e.,

$$\lambda_1 = \text{const}; \qquad \lambda_2 = C_1 - C_2 t; \qquad u = \operatorname{sign}(C_1 - C_2 t). \tag{59}$$

Hence, the desired function $u(t)$ may have not more than one transition from $u = +1$ to $u = -1$, and conversely. This condition will permit us to construct the desired control completely later (see Section 34).

A general theorem on the number of switchings from $u = +1$ to $u = -1$ in linear systems may also be proved.

Theorem on n Intervals

For the linear nth order system (41) for which all the roots of the characteristic equation are real, the optimum high-speed control $u(t)$ (i.e., that one transferring the system from one state $x_i = x_i(0)$, say, into another $x_i = x_i(T)$), will contain not more than $(n-1)$ switchings, i.e., not more than n intervals of constancy $u = +1$ or $u = -1$.

Proof. We have shown that the optimum control is subject to the condition

$$u = \operatorname{sign} \sum_{i=1}^{n} \frac{\lambda_i b_i}{2m\lambda_0},$$

where the λ_i are the solutions of the system of equations (51).

But if all the roots of the characteristic equation for the original system (41) are real, they are also real for the system (51); therefore, as is known from the theory of linear equations with constant coefficients, each of the functions $\lambda_i(t)$ may be represented as

$$\lambda_i = f_1(t)\, e^{k_1 t} + \cdots + f_m(t)\, e^{k_m t}, \tag{60}$$

where the k_j are all pairwise different roots of the characteristic equation of the system (51), and the f_j are either constants (if the k_j are simple roots), or polynomials of degree not higher than $(r-1)$ (if the k_j are roots of multiplicity r).

A linear combination of the functions λ_i, the sum $\sum_{i=1}^{n} \lambda_i b_i$, will also have the form (60).

For a later proof, let us use the following lemma on functions of the type (60): If the k_j are real pairwise different numbers, and the f_j are polynomials of degree $a_1; a_2; \ldots; a_m$, then a function of the type (60) may have not more than $a_1 + a_2 + \cdots + a_m + m - 1$ real roots (the proof of this lemma is given by Pontriagin *et al.* [42]).

The proof of the theorem can easily be carried through to completion by using this lemma. In fact, in our case $a_1 = r_1 - 1$; $a_2 = r_2 - 1; \ldots$; $a_m = r_m - 1$, therefore

$$\begin{aligned} a_1 + a_2 + \cdots + a_m + m - 1 &= (r_1 - 1) + (r_2 - 1) + \cdots \\ &\quad + (r_m - 1) + m - 1 \\ &= r_1 + r_2 + \cdots + r_m - 1 = n - 1, \end{aligned}$$

since $r_1 + r_2 + \cdots + r_m = n$.

A. A. Fel'dbaum first proved the theorem on n intervals. The theorem is widely utilized in computations of the optimum high-speed control for linear systems since it permits reduction of the variational problem to a problem of the extremum of a function of $n - 1$ variables.

33. The Maximum Principle

Methods of solving variational problems going back mainly to Euler and Lagrange were examined in the previous exposition. Some results of investigations of the outstanding Soviet mathematicians L. S. Pontriagin, V. G. Boltianskii, R. V. Gamkrelidze, and E. F. Mishchenko, which they obtained between 1955 and 1961, will be presented in this section. These results are elucidated briefly and without proofs. The reader desiring more detailed acquaintanceship with the investigations of L. S. Pontriagin and his colleagues may turn directly to their book "Mathematical Theory of Optimal Processes" (Fizmatgiz, 1961; Wiley (Interscience), New York, 1962).

The theory developed by L. S. Pontriagin and his associates is often called the "maximum principle." Since the "maximum principle" was the result of research on the optimum control of various automatic units, the terminology and the formulation of the problem itself are rather different from the terminology customarily utilized in the calculus of variations.

Theorems on the "maximum principle" refer to systems whose behavior may be described by the differential equations

$$\begin{aligned}\frac{dx_1}{dt} &= f_1(x_1; \dots x_n; u_1, \dots, u_k);\\ \frac{dx_n}{dt} &= f_n(x_1; \dots x_n; u_1, \dots, u_k),\end{aligned} \tag{61}$$

where the x_i are coordinates of the object, and the u_i are controls. The problem is posed: Find the control $u_j(t)$ transferring a system from the position $x_i = x_i(0)$ to the position $x_i = x_i(T)$ within the time T and yielding the minimum of the functional

$$J = \int_0^T f_0(x_i; u_j)\, dt. \tag{62}$$

We remark that, in contrast to the customary problems of the calculus of variations where all the desired functions were equivalent, the phase coordinates x_i and the controls are separated in the "maximum principle." This separation is convenient in those cases when the constraints are imposed only on the control and not on the phase coordinates; for example, if

$$|u_j| \leqslant 1 \tag{63}$$

is given.

The auxiliary variables $\psi_0; \psi_1: \dots; \psi_n$ and the intermediate function

$$H = \sum_{i=0}^{n} \psi_i f_i(x_1, \dots, x_n; u_1, \dots, u_k) \tag{64}$$

play an important part in the "maximum principle."

By using this function, the fundamental system of equations (61) and the equations required to determine the auxiliary variables $\psi_i(t)$, are written thus:

$$\frac{\partial x_i}{dt} = \frac{\partial H}{\partial \psi_i}; \tag{65}$$

$$\frac{d\psi_i}{dt} = -\frac{\partial H}{dx_i}. \tag{66}$$

In fact, since

$$\frac{\partial H}{\partial \psi_i} = f_i,$$

the equations (65) are equivalent to equations (61); at the same time, the auxiliary variables $\psi_i(t)$ may be found from (66). The fundamental necessary condition which the control $u_j(t)$ should satisfy so that it would be optimum is formulated as a theorem of the maximum: If $u_j(t)$ is an optimum control, it yields the maximum of the function H (formula (64)), i.e.,

$$H(\psi_i; f_i; u_j = u_{j\,\mathrm{opt}}) = M(\psi_i; f_i) \tag{67}$$

(M is the sign of the maximum).

Moreover, at the final instant ($t = T$) the relationships

$$\psi_0(T) \leqslant 0; \qquad M[\psi_i(T); f_i(T)] = 0 \tag{68}$$

are satisfied.

For the problem of maximum fast response, when the functional whose minimum is sought is the time

$$J = \int_0^T f_0(x_i; u_j)\, dt = \int_0^T dt, \tag{69}$$

the equation for the variable ψ_0 drops out and the function H becomes

$$H = \sum_{i=1}^{n} \psi_i f_i(x_1, \ldots, x_n; u_1, \ldots, u_k).$$

The optimum control $u_j(t)$ may actually be determined by using the theorem of the maximum. Let us note that the solution is sought here not in the class of piecewise-smooth functions, but in the more extensive class of piecewise-continuous functions.

Example 1. Let us turn to the system we examined in the previous section

$$\frac{dx_1}{dt} = x_2; \qquad \frac{dx_2}{dt} = u,$$

and let us find the control $u(t)$ assuring the fastest transfer of the system from the state $x_1 = x_{10}$; $x_2 = x_{20}$ to the state $x_1 = 0$; $x_2 = 0$ under the condition that $|u| \leqslant 1$. Let us seek the solution this time by using the "maximum principle."

In this case we have $H = \psi_1 x_2 + \psi_2 u$.

Under the condition that $|u| \leqslant 1$, the maximum of H will be achieved for $u = \operatorname{sign}\psi_2$, i.e., when the control $u(t)$ will equal $+1$ for $\psi_2 > 0$ and -1 for $\psi_2 < 0$. But we have the system of equations

$$\frac{\partial\psi_1}{dt} = -\frac{\partial H}{\partial x_1} = 0; \tag{70}$$

$$\frac{d\psi_2}{dt} = -\frac{\partial H}{\partial x_2} = -\psi_1, \tag{71}$$

for the determination of the auxiliary variables ψ_i, from which

$$\psi_1 = C_1; \qquad \psi_2 = C_2 - C_1 t; \tag{72}$$

therefore

$$u = \operatorname{sign}(C_2 - C_1 t),$$

i.e., the control does not change sign more than once.

Hence, we have obtained the same result as in the previous section, but this time by a simpler means, without passing to the limit, because of utilizing the "maximum principle."

This is the most important role of the "maximum principle." In those cases when there is no extremal, and the optimum control passes along the boundary of the admissible domain, the structure of the optimum control is successfully established at once by using the "maximum principle." It will be shown in the next section how, by knowing the structure of $u(t)$, an optimum system may be synthesized.

The "maximum principle" is particularly convenient for the investigation of systems where the desired functionals and coupling equations are linear and the constraints are imposed only on the controls.

If the functionals and the coupling equations are linear, and the roots of the characteristic equation are real, then by using the "maximum principle" the Fel'dbaum theorem on n intervals may easily be proved.

If the roots of the characteristic equation are complex, the number of intervals may be infinitely large.

Example 2. Let us consider the system

$$dx_1/dt = x_2, \qquad dx_2/dt = -x_1 + u, \tag{73}$$

and let us pose the problem of finding the control $u(t)$ assuring the most rapid transfer of the system from the position $x_1 = x_{10}$; $x_2 = x_{20}$ to the origin $x_1 = 0$; $x_2 = 0$.

The characteristic equation of the system $k^2 + 1 = 0$ has the complex roots $k = \pm i$. The function H is

$$H = \psi_1 x_2 - \psi_2 x_1 + \psi_2 u \, .$$

On the basis of the "maximum principle" the optimum control $u(t)$ is expressed by the formula $u = \text{sign}\, \psi_2$.

To determine ψ_1 and ψ_2 let us use the system of equations

$$\frac{d\psi_1}{dt} = -\frac{\partial H}{\partial x_1} = \psi_2 ; \qquad \frac{d\psi_2}{dt} = -\frac{\partial H}{\partial x_2} = -\psi_1 ,$$

from which $\psi_2 = A \sin(t - \varphi)$.

Hence, the optimum control $u(t)$ consists of the sections $u = +1$ and $u = -1$, alternating by a time $t = \pi$. These results are sufficient for the synthesis of an optimum control (see Section 34). The number of switchings from $u = +1$ to $u = -1$ may be as great as desired for large T.

We have examined examples when the extremal did not exist and the optimum control passed along the boundary of the admissible domain. If extremals exist (if a constraint is not imposed on the control), then the "maximum principle" leads to the customary Euler equations.

Example 3. Let us examine the system

$$x_1' = x_2 , \qquad x_2' = u , \tag{74}$$

and let us look for the control $u(t)$ yielding the minimum of the integral $\int_0^T u^2 \, dt$ under the boundary conditions $x_2(0) = 0$; $x_2(T) = 0$; $x_1(0) = 0$; $x_1(T) = \alpha_0$.

It is easy to see that this problem coincides with the problem, analyzed in Section 19, of seeking the optimum current diagram if we put $u = i$; $x_2 = v$; $x_1 = \alpha$.

This time let us find the solution by utilizing the "maximum principle." We have

$$H = \psi_0 u^2 + \psi_1 x_2 + \psi_2 u \, .$$

We find the maximum of H in u from the condition $\partial H / \partial u = 0$.

Since

$$\frac{\partial H}{\partial u} = 2\psi_0 u + \psi_2 ,$$

then $u = -\psi_2 / 2\psi_0$.

To determine the auxiliary variables ψ_0; ψ_1; ψ_2 we have the equations

$$\frac{d\psi_0}{dt} = -\frac{\partial H}{\partial x_0} = 0; \qquad \frac{d\psi_1}{dt} = -\frac{\partial H}{\partial x_1} = 0; \qquad \frac{d\psi_2}{\partial t} = -\frac{\partial H}{\partial x_2} = \psi_1,$$

from which follow $\psi_0 = C_0$; $\psi_1 = C_1$; $\psi_2 = C_2 + C_1 t$.

Substituting the equation for ψ_2 into the coupling equation (74), we obtain the equation

$$x_2'' = v'' = C_2,$$

for $x_2 = v$ which coincides with the Euler equation we obtained in Section 19.

The proof, in general form, that the "maximum principle" for an open domain leads to the customary Euler equations is given by Pontriagin *et al.* [42].

The manifold of problems solved in the work of Pontriagin *et al.* [42] is naturally not exhausted by the fundamental theorem on the maximum we have examined. Problems with free endpoints, optimum control with a parameter, control for constraints on the phase coordinates of the system, and controls for systems described by differential equations with retarded arguments are also examined there.

On the whole, the "maximum principle" discloses a new fruitful approach to the solution of variational problems, which differs somewhat in the method and the symbolics from the customary methods of the calculus of variations. The "maximum principle" is particularly convenient in problems where the functionals and the coupling equations are linear with respect to the desired functions. The advantages of the "maximum principle" are indisputable here. But the conventional variational methods often turn out to be more convenient for the solution of nonlinear problems in the desired functions as well as for problems where constraints are imposed on the phase coordinates of the system as well as on the control.

34. Synthesis of an Optimum Control

It has been shown in previous sections that the optimum control for systems which are linear in the control functions is piecewise-constant, and a theorem on the number of switchings has been proved. Now, let us show how the synthesis of an optimum control may be accomplished by using these data.

Let us consider a system whose behavior is described by the equations

$$dx_1/dt = x_2, \qquad dx_2/dt = u, \tag{75}$$

and let us pose the problem of finding the control assuring the most rapid drop to the origin (i.e., $x_1 = 0$; $x_2 = 0$) for each initial condition $x_1(0) = x_{10}$; $x_2 = x_{20}$. We have already analyzed this system in previous sections, and it has been found that the optimum control passes from the value $u = +1$ to $u = -1$, or conversely, and not more than one switching is necessary for any initial condition.

Let us consider the behavior of the system being studied in the phase plane, i.e., the plane where the x_1 coordinate is plotted along the horizontal, and the x_2 coordinate along the vertical. Let us investigate the behavior of the system for the control $u = +1$.

It follows from (75) that for $u = +1$

$$x_1 = \tfrac{1}{2}t^2 + C_1 t + C_2; \qquad x_2 = t + C_1, \tag{76}$$

from which

$$x_1 = \tfrac{1}{2}x_2^2 + C. \tag{77}$$

The solution (77) may also be obtained directly without integrating the system (75). It is sufficient to divide the first equation of the system (75) by the second. As a result (taking into account that $u = 1$) we have

$$dx_1/dx_2 = x_2$$

from which we again obtain (77) by integrating.

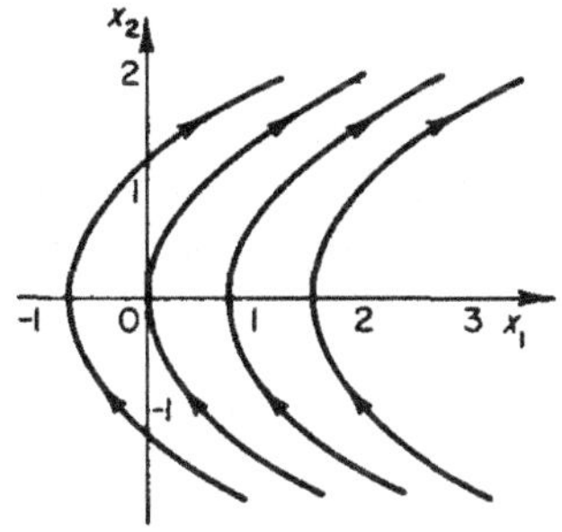

FIG. 52

The solution (77) is pictured in the phase plane as a family of parabolas (Fig. 52). The arrows on the parabolas characterize the system behavior with time. For example, let the system be in the fourth quadrant of the phase plane at the initial instant. As time passes, the x_2 coordinate will always increase, the x_1 coordinate first starts to decrease and then (after x_2 has passed through zero) also starts to increase.

Fig. 52 shows that only one parabola will pass through the origin, i.e., the origin may be achieved for a control $u = +1$ only under completely specified boundary conditions on $x_1(0)$ and $x_2(0)$.

Now, let us consider the system behavior for the control $u = -1$. Dividing the first equation of the system (75) by the second this time, we obtain

$$dx_1/dx_2 = -x_2,$$

from which

$$x_1 = -\tfrac{1}{2}x_2^{\,2} + C, \tag{78}$$

i.e., also a family of parabolas, but disposed differently in the phase plane (Fig. 53).

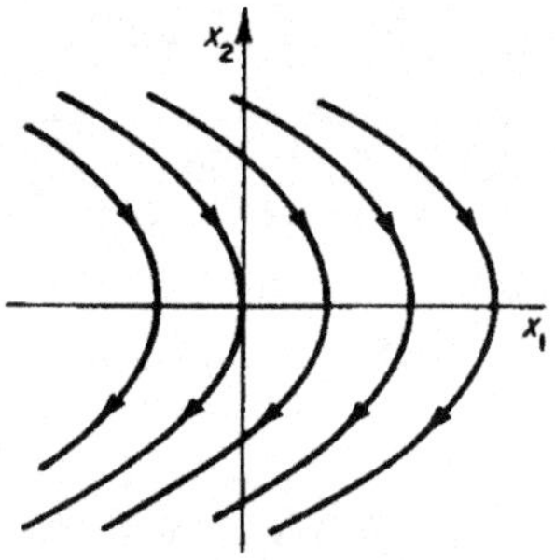

FIG. 53

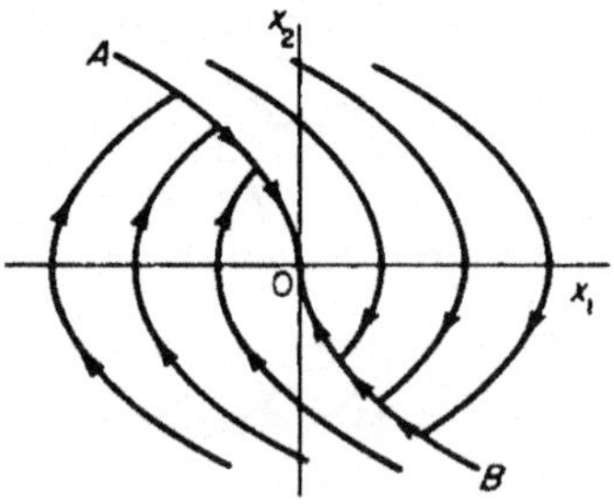

FIG. 54

If the control were piecewise-constant, i.e., would pass from the value $u = +1$ to $u = -1$, or conversely, then the system behavior in the phase plane will be as pictured in Fig. 54. The line AB is the line of switchings. Let the system be in the third quadrant of the phase plane (x_2 and x_1 negative) at the initial instant. The control $u = +1$ is applied to the system, and under its effect the system moves as is shown by the arrows in Fig. 54, until the line of switchings AB is reached. At this time, switching of the control occurs, and under the effect of the control $u = -1$ the mapping point moves along the line AB until it arrives at the origin. Fig. 54 shows that from any point of the phase plane, i.e., for any initial conditions $x_1(0)$ and $x_2(0)$, it is possible to drop into the origin by using a control $u(t)$ containing not more than one switching.

It is now easy to solve the question of synthesizing an optimum control system. The optimum system should assure a signal $u = +1$ at the output if x_1 and x_2 are such that the point mapping the system behavior is below the switching line AB in the phase plane, and the signal $u = -1$ if the mapping point is above the line AB. The system changes its x_1 and x_2 coordinates under the effect of the control signal; the point mapping the position of the system moves over the phase plane. When the point falls on the curve AB, switching of the signal from $u = +1$ to $u = -1$ or from $u = -1$ to $u = +1$ occurs at the system output.

Hence, an optimum system is a relay system switching the control signal at the output according to the following dependences: $u = +1$ for $x_1 < 0$ and $x_2 < 0$; $u = -1$ for $x_1 > 0$ and $x_2 > 0$.

If $x_1 < 0$, and $x_2 > 0$, then we have $u = +1$ for $x_1 < \frac{1}{2}x_2^2$ and $u = -1$ for $x_1 \geqslant \frac{1}{2}x_2^2$. If $x_2 < 0$, and $x_1 > 0$, we then have $u = -1$ for $x_1 > \frac{1}{2}x_2^2$ and $u = +1$ for $x_1 \leqslant \frac{1}{2}x_2^2$. Further examples of optimum control synthesis may be found in the work of Pontriagin *et al.* [42].

35. Dynamic Programming

Dynamic programming is one other method of solving optimum control problems for closed domains. Dynamic programming differs from both classical variational methods and from the "maximum principle," although it is closely related to the latter. It was developed by the American mathematician Bellman and is expounded in his book [33] which has been translated into Russian.

Underlying dynamic programming is the following "optimality principle" proposed by Bellman as a hypothesis: Optimum behavior possesses the property that no matter what the initial state and the solution (control) at the initial instant, subsequent solutions (controls) should be the optimum behavior relative to the state which has been obtained as a result of the first solution.

It should be kept in mind that the theory of dynamic programming was developed by Bellman for a broader class of processes than the processes described by systems of ordinary differential equations. Consequently, Bellman also relied on so general a principle as the "optimality principle." The optimality principle has not been proved in so general a form as that expressed above, but its validity for systems described by differential equations follows from the simple fact that each segment of an extremal is also an extremal and every portion of an optimum control is also an optimum control.

Starting from the optimality principle, Bellman derived a partial differential equation. This equation (analogous to the Euler equation) permits the determination of curves on which the extremum can be achieved.

Indeed, let us consider the control system described by Eqs. (61), and let us solve the problem of the most rapid drop of the mapping point onto the origin from the point $x_i = x_{i0}$. The time T of the passage from the point $x_i = x_{i0}$ to the origin is a function of the point, i.e., $T = T(x_{i0})$. We introduce a function of x_i with the form $\omega(x_i) = -T(x_i)$, i.e., the time of passage with the reverse sign, and we assume that the function $\omega(x_i)$ has continuous partial derivatives with respect to all the coordinates x_i. If $x_i(t)$ is an optimum trajectory, then

$$\omega[x_i(t)] = -T(x_{i0}) + t - t_0$$

and therefore $d\omega/dt = 1$, but

$$\sum_{i=1}^{n} \frac{\partial \omega}{\partial x_i} f_i(x_k; u) = \sum_{i=1}^{n} \frac{\partial \omega}{\partial x_i} \frac{dx_i}{dt};$$

hence

$$\sum_{i=1}^{n} \frac{\partial \omega}{\partial x_i} f_i(x_k; u) = 1. \tag{79}$$

Now consider the motion of a point mapping the state of a system in phase space under the effect of some control $u(t)$ which is not optimum. The system will be in the position $x_i(t)+dx_i$ after an infinitesimal time interval dt, where on the basis of (61)

$$dx_i = f_i(x_k; u)\, dt \tag{80}$$

The time of system motion between the positions $x_i = x_{i0} + dx_i$ and $x_i = x_{i0}$ cannot be less than the time of motion under an optimum control, i.e.,

$$\omega(x_i + dx_i) - \omega(x_i) \leqslant dt.$$

On the basis of (80) this inequality may be written as

$$\sum_{i=1}^{n} \frac{d\omega}{dx_i} f_i(x_k; u)\, dt \leqslant dt$$

or

$$\sum_{i=1}^{n} \frac{\partial\omega}{\partial x_i} f_i(x_k; u) \leqslant 1. \tag{81}$$

From relationships (79) and (81) results

$$\sup \sum_{i=1}^{n} \frac{\partial\omega}{\partial x_i} f_i(x_k; u) = 1, \tag{82}$$

where the sup denotes the "upper bound" of the expression after this symbol. This "upper bound" is one and in this case is achieved if the control $u(t)$ is optimal.

Equation (82) is a specific partial differential equation (the Bellman equation) from which the desired function $\omega(x)$ may be determined by integration.

Integrating a partial differential equation is a considerably more complex problem than integrating the Euler equations, which are ordinary differential equations. Hence, dynamic programming does not generally result in simplification but a significant complication of the mathematical computations, as compared with ordinary variational methods. However, in a number of cases, in compiling programs of computations to determine the function $u(t)$ on a high-speed computer, say, utilization of the dynamic programming method may turn out to be very convenient.

Let us note that the Bellman equation (82) was derived under the assumption of differentiability of the function $\omega(x)$ everywhere. Meanwhile, in many important cases $\omega(x)$ has no derivatives at individual points, at points lying on the switching line, say. Hence, Eq. (82) still does not have a sufficiently rigorous foundation.

36. Nonstandard Functionals

In preceding sections we studied the extremum of functionals having the form of a definite integral

$$J = \int_a^b F(x; y; y')\, dx,$$

or of functionals which could be reduced to this form. Such functionals may be called standard. In general, the majority of practical problems reduces successfully to standard functionals, but sometimes functionals of nonstandard form must be dealt with.

Thus, for example, it is known that the abscissa of the center of gravity of a material curve $y(x)$ passing through the points a and b will be expressed by

$$J = \frac{\int_a^b x(1 + y'^2)^{1/2}\, dx}{\int_a^b (1 + y'^2)^{1/2}\, dx}. \tag{83}$$

Hence, the problem of seeking the curve for which the center of gravity is disposed lowest as compared with all other curves passing through the same points will reduce to studying the extremum of the functional (83), the quotient of two definite integrals.

To seek the extremum of functionals having the form of certain functions of integrals, it is useful to keep in mind that the variation is subject to the same rules as is differentiation [2] i.e., if

$$J_3 = J_1/J_2 \tag{84}$$

then

$$\delta J_3 = \frac{J_2\, \delta J_1 - J_1\, \delta J_2}{{J_2}^2}. \tag{85}$$

Let $y = y_e(x)$ yield the extremum of the functional J_3. Then $\delta J_3 = 0$ and, therefore (if $J_2 \neq 0$)

$$J_2(y_e)\,\delta J_1 - J_1(y_e)\,\delta J_2 = 0\,.$$

Using the notation

$$\frac{J_1(y_e)}{J_2(y_e)} = \lambda_0\,,$$

we obtain

$$\delta J_1 - \lambda_0\,\delta J_2 = \delta(J_1 - \lambda_0 J_2)\,,$$

and we arrive at the following theorem: The function $y(x)$ yielding the extremum of the quotient of two functionals J_1 and J_2 should satisfy the Euler equation for the intermediate functional

$$H = J_1 - \lambda_0 J_2\,.$$

The constant λ_0 is determined from the condition

$$\frac{J_1(y_e)}{J_2(y_e)} = \lambda_0\,.$$

Example. Find $y(x)$ yielding the minimum of the expression

$$J_3 = \int_0^1 y'^2\,dx \Big/ \int_0^1 y^2\,dx$$

under the boundary conditions $y(0) = 0$; $y(1) = 0$.

The Euler equation for the intermediate functional

$$H = y'^2 - \lambda_0 y^2 \tag{86}$$

is the equation

$$y'' + \lambda_0 y = 0\,.$$

Its solutions which satisfy the boundary conditions are

$$y = \sin\sqrt{\lambda_0}\,x\,,$$

where $\lambda_0 = \pi^2;\ 4\pi^2;\ldots;\ n^2\pi^2$.

On the extremals

$$J_3 = \frac{\int_0^3 n^2\pi^2 \cos^2 n\pi x\,dx}{\int_0^1 \sin^2 n\pi x\,dx} = n^2\pi^2\,;$$

and the minimum is achieved for $n = 1$ when $y = \sin \pi x$.

For functionals which are the product of two integrals

$$J_3 = J_1 J_2 = \int_a^b F_1(x; y; y')\, dx \int_a^b F_2(x; y; y')\, dx\,, \tag{87}$$

we arrive, on the basis of the formula $\delta(J_1 J_2) = J_1\, \delta J_2 + J_2\, \delta J_1$, and utilization of notation that λ_0 is $J_1(y_e)/J_2(y_e)$, at the theorem: the function $y = y_e(x)$, yielding the extremum of the functional (87) should satisfy the Euler equation for the intermediate functional

$$H = J_1 + \lambda_0 J_2\,. \tag{88}$$

The general rule for calculating the extremum of functionals having the form of certain functions of definite integrals was given by Euler in 1744.

Another example of a nonstandard functional might be the functional

$$J = \varphi(y_m) \int_a^b F(x; y; y')\, dx\,, \tag{89}$$

i.e., the product of a standard integral functional by a function of y_m, the maximum ordinate of the curve $y(x)$ connecting the points A and B. The problem of determining the current diagram for which the least generator power is achieved in a motor-generator system (see Section 39), say, will lead to functionals of this kind.

The extremum of functionals of the type (89) (for definiteness, we shall henceforth speak of the minimum) is logically sought not in the general class of piecewise-smooth curves $y(x)$ connecting the points A and B but in the special class of curves with a given maximum ordinate y_m, i.e., those subject to the inequality

$$y \leqslant y_m\,, \tag{90}$$

where the equality sign is achieved in at least one point of the interval $(a; b)$. In this class the first member of the functional (89) remains constant. As has been shown in Section 31, the minimum of the second factor is achieved on a curve composed of segments of the extremals of the second member in (89) and segments of the boundary of the admissible domain, the line $y = y_m$. Values of the functional on such a curve generate a function of y_m. If this function has a minimum in y_m, then the value y_{m0} corresponding to this minimum will yield the minimum of the functional (89). An example of the solution is presented in Section 39.

The reader will meet still another example of a nonstandard functional (the magnitude of the stability domain) in Section 43.

37. Approximate Methods of Solution

Practical determination of the extremals requires solution of the Euler or Euler-Poisson equations, generally nonlinear differential equations of high order.

Solution of such equations is very difficult, hence, approximate methods have been worked out in the calculus of variations (they are called direct methods), which permit finding the extremals directly without preliminary solution of the system of Euler differential equations.

One of the most convenient methods is the Ritz method, developed in 1908. The crux of the method is that the solution of a variational problem, i.e., the problem of the extremum of a function of an infinite number of variables, reduces to the solution of a finite number of equations with a finite number of unknowns.

Let it be required to find the minimum of the functional

$$J(y) = \int_a^b F(x; y; y')\, dx. \tag{91}$$

Let us represent the desired function $y(x)$ as a series with n terms:

$$y_n(x) = \sum_{i=1}^{n} a_i \varphi_i(x), \tag{92}$$

where $\varphi_i(x)$ are certain functions of x (most often polynomials).

For such functions $y_n(x)$, the functional $J(y)$ degenerates into a function of n variables, the coefficients $a_1; a_2; \ldots; a_n$.

Now, let us seek that function among the $y_n(x)$ which will yield the minimum of the functional $J(y_n)$, where $J(y_n)$ is the result of substituting (92) into the functional (91). To seek this function it is sufficient to take the derivatives $\partial J(y_n)/\partial a_i$ and to equate them to zero. We obtain a system of n equations in n unknowns

$$\frac{\partial J(y_n)}{\partial a_i} = 0. \tag{93}$$

By solving it we find the function $y_n(x)$ which is the approximation to the desired function $y(x)$ which yields the minimum of the original functional (91). In general, the approximation will be the more exact, the greater the number of terms taken into account in the series (92). However, computational difficulties grow rapidly with the increase in the number of terms in the series. Academician Krylov [4] made important estimates of the error in the approximations.

For example, let us find the minimum of $\int_{-1}^{+1} y'^2\,dx$ under the condition that $\int_{-1}^{+1} y^2\,dx = 1$, and the boundary conditions $y(-1) = y(1) = 0$.

In this case it is easy to find the exact solution. The minimum is achieved by the function $y = \cos\frac{1}{2}\pi x$ and equals $\frac{1}{4}\pi^2 = 2.47$.

Let us solve this problem by the Ritz method.

Let us seek the extremum among polynomials of degree not higher than the third, i.e., in the class of functions of the form

$$y = a_0 + a_1 x + a_2 x^2 + a_3 x^3 \tag{94}$$

with four coefficients to be determined. Two coefficients are determined from the boundary conditions. It follows from the conditions $y(-1) = y(1) = 0$ that the polynomial (94) has the form

$$y = (1 - x^2)(a + bx).$$

Furthermore, let us evaluate

$$\int_{-1}^{+1} y^2\,dx = \int_{-1}^{+1} [(1 - x^2)(a + bx)]^2 = \frac{16}{15}a^2 + \frac{16}{105}b^2,$$

and

$$\int_{-1}^{+1} y'^2\,dx = \frac{8}{3}a^2 + \frac{8}{5}b^2.$$

It is now easy to establish by conventional methods of differential calculus that the minimum of the expression $(8/3)\,a^2 + (8/5)\,b^2$ under the condition $(16/15)\,a^2 + (16/105)\,b^2 = 1$ is achieved for $b = 0$; $a = \sqrt{15}/4$ and equals $(8/3)(15/16) = 2.5$.

The absolute error with which the minimum has been determined is 0.03, and the relative error is 1.2%. The extremal is shown by the solid line in Fig. 55, and the solution by the Ritz method:

$$y = \frac{\sqrt{15}}{4}(1 - x^2)$$

by dashes.

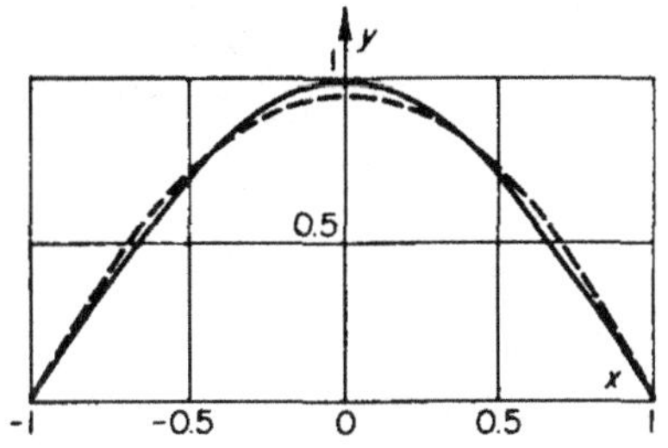

FIG. 55

Let us present still another example of the application of the Ritz method. In Sections 19 and 24 we considered the optimum control of a dc electric motor with a constant or velocity-dependent resistance moment. This problem is successfully reduced to an integrable second-order equation. However, the resistance moment on the shaft of the electric motor may depend not only on the velocity but also on its path. Traction motors of electric locomotives are an important example of such an electric motor. The resistance moment of these motors depends on what point of the path the electric locomotive is on, an ascent, a descent, a curve, i.e., is a function of the path traversed by the electric locomotive from the beginning of the run. For motors of independent excitation the equation of equilibrium of moments on the shaft may be written in this case as

$$i = \frac{d^2 s}{d\tau^2} + \mu(s) \tag{95}$$

and the optimum control problem is formulated as a problem of the minimum of the functional

$$Q = \int_0^T [s'' + \mu(s)]^2 \, d\tau \tag{96}$$

under the boundary conditions: $s = s_0$ and $s' = s_0'$ for $\tau = 0$; $s = s(T)$ and $s' = s'(T)$ for $\tau = T$.

The Euler-Poisson equation for the functional (96) will be

$$s^{\mathrm{IV}} + 2\frac{d\mu}{ds} s'' + \frac{d^2\mu}{ds^2} s'^2 + \mu\frac{d\mu}{ds} = 0. \tag{97}$$

Instead of solving the boundary value problem for the fourth order equation (97), the extremum of the functional (96) may be sought by the direct method.

Let us consider an example. Let $\mu = 1 + \sin 2\pi s$, and let $s = 0$ and $s' = 1$ for $\tau = 0$ and $s = 1$ and $s' = 1$ for $\tau = 1$. This example corresponds to the motion of an electric locomotive on a run with a varying profile, where there are both ascents and descents.

Let us seek the function $s(\tau)$, yielding the extremum of the integral (96) in the class of polynomials not higher than the seventh (i.e., having eight coefficients to be determined). Four coefficients are determined from the boundary conditions. A seventh power polynomial of the form

$$s = \tau + \tau^2 (1 - \tau)^2 (a_0 + a_1\tau + a_2\tau^2 + a_3\tau^3) \tag{98}$$

satisfies the assigned boundary conditions.

We determine the coefficients a_i from the system of equations

$$\partial Q / \partial a_1 = 0.$$

Results of a computation are given in Fig. 56. The velocity of the motion (s') and the armature current ($i = s' + \mu$) are shown. The armature losses are $Q = 1.295$. If the motion were to occur at constant velocity,

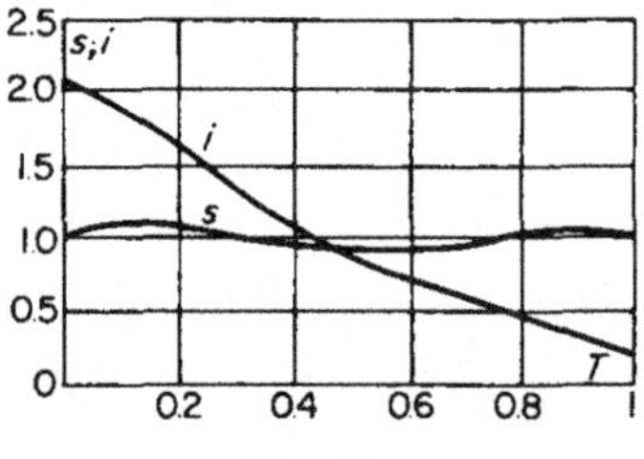

FIG. 56

then $i = 1 + \sin 2\pi\tau$ in this case and the armature losses would be $Q = 1.5$, i.e., would have grown 15.8% in comparison with the motion according to an optimum law.

In addition to the Ritz method, other direct methods of solving variational problems exist, for example, the Galerkin method, the Chebyshev method, etc. [2].

VI Examples of the Application of Variational Methods

38. Optimum Control of DC Electric Motors with Velocity and Armature Current Constraints

Examples are presented in this chapter of the application of variational methods to solve the most widespread class of technical problems, i.e., when the desired functions must be sought in a closed domain and various constraints must be imposed on the desired functions, and the independent variables must be taken into account.

Both the classical variational methods and the "maximum principle" are used in the solution, depending on which method is more convenient for the specific problem.

Let us return to the problem we have already considered in Section 19 of Chapter III, the problem of seeking the best current and velocity diagrams which will assure the highest efficiency and fast response of dc electric motors. This time, however, let us take account of an additional constraint on the rotational velocity and armature current (in addition to the constraint on heating taken into account in Chapter III).

As a rule, the constraint on the velocity is connected with the mechanical integrity of the motor armature and is written in the form of the inequality

$$v \leqslant v_0 . \tag{1}$$

For a parabolic velocity diagram the maximum velocity $v_m = \frac{3}{2}\alpha/T$ is $1\frac{1}{2}$ times greater than the mean velocity $v_{\text{mean}} = \alpha/T$.

If it turns out that $v_0 < v_m$, then the optimum velocity diagram consists of pieces of the extremal (parabola) and the domain boundary $v = v_0$.

Since $H_{v'v'} \neq 0$, the tangents to the extremal and the domain boundary coincide at the junction point, i.e., at the junction points $v' = 0$ and $i = \mu_0$. Hence, the optimum current and velocity diagrams take the form shown in Fig. 57. The abscissas of the transition points from the extremal to the boundary and conversely are to be determined in these diagrams, i.e., the values T_1 and T_2.

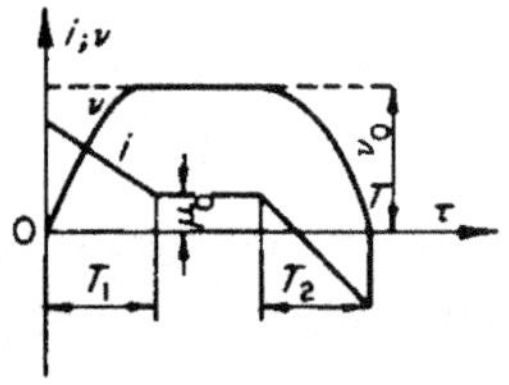

FIG. 57

Integrating the rotational velocity and the square of the armature current separately on the sections where $v(\tau)$ is an extremal, and on the sections where $v(\tau)$ goes along the domain boundary, we obtain

$$Q = \frac{8}{3} v_0^2 \left(\frac{1}{T_1} + \frac{1}{T_2} \right) + \mu_0^2 T; \qquad (2)$$

$$\alpha = v_0 T - \tfrac{1}{3} v_0 (T_1 + T_2).$$

These equations permit expressing T_1 and T_2 either in terms of α and v_0 (if the magnitude of the displacement is given and the heat loss is minimized), or in terms of Q and v_0 (if the heating is given and it is necessary to assure the greatest possible displacement of the load):

$$T_1 = T_2 = \frac{3}{2} \left(T - \frac{\alpha}{v_0} \right);$$

$$T_1 = T_2 = \frac{8}{3} \left(\frac{v_0^2}{Q - \mu_0^2 T} \right).$$

Hence, we see that the theorem on continuity of the tangent at the junction points of the extremal and the boundary (see Section 31) permits formation of the equations needed for the complete solution of a problem with constraints, i.e., to find the points of transition from extremal to boundary, or conversely.

Let us determine the optimum current and velocity diagrams in the presence of constraints on the armature current. The magnitude of the current is constrained primarily by the commutation conditions on the collector. Assuming that the commutation conditions are independent of the rotational velocity, we obtain that the armature current is bounded in absolute value:

$$|i| \leqslant i_m. \tag{3}$$

Since the desired function is $v(\tau)$, the inequality (3) imposes a constraint on its derivative:

$$|v' + \mu_0| \leqslant i_m.$$

If the armature current of the linear current diagram found in Section 19 violates the constraint (3), the optimum current diagram assumes the form shown in Fig. 58, or for large values of μ_0, that shown in Fig. 59.

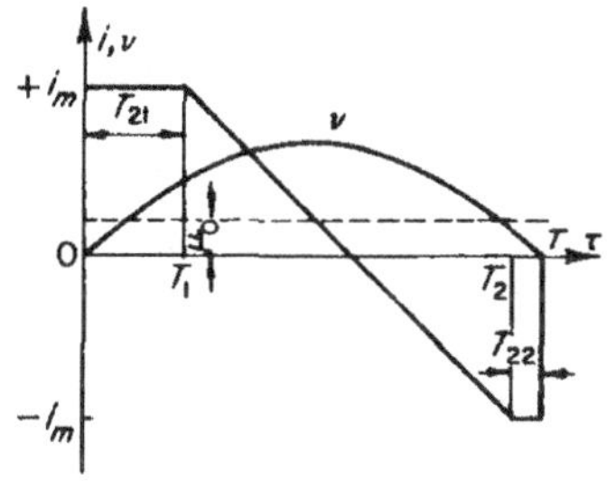

FIG. 58

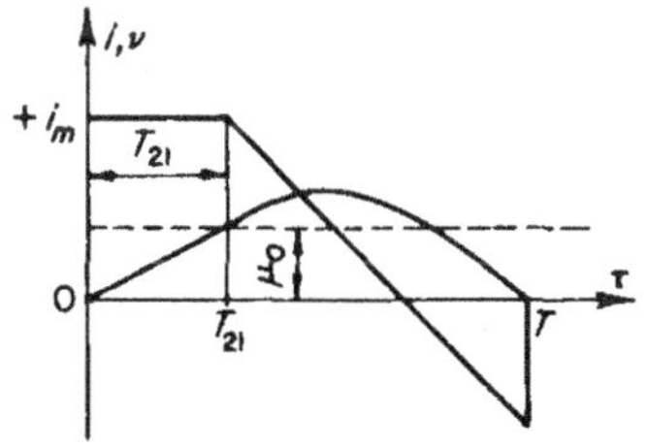

FIG. 59

The condition of continuity of the tangents to the velocity diagram at the junction points of the extremal and the domain boundary is satisfied automatically for the current diagrams pictured in Figs. 58 and 59.

Let us determine the abscissas of the transition points from the extremal to the boundary by starting with the case when there are two points (Fig. 58).

It follows from the condition $v(0) = v(T)$ that

$$\int_0^T (i - \mu)\, d\tau = 0.$$

But on the other hand

$$\int_0^T (i - \mu)\, d\tau = \int_0^{T_1} i_m\, d\tau + \int_{T_1}^{T_2} i\, d\tau - \int_{T_2}^{T} i_m\, d\tau - \int_0^T \mu_0\, d\tau,$$

and since

$$\int_{T_1}^{T_2} i\, d\tau = 0,$$

then

$$i_m(T_{21} - T_{22}) = \mu_0 T. \qquad (4)$$

Now integrating the square of the armature current over the sections from 0 to T_1, from T_1 to T_2, and from T_2 to T, we obtain

$$Q = \tfrac{1}{3} i_m^2 T + \tfrac{2}{3} i_m^2 (T_{21} + T_{22}) \qquad (5)$$

Utilizing formulas (4) and (5), we finally determine T_{21} and T_{22}:

$$T_{21} = \frac{3Q_0}{4i_m^2} - \frac{T}{4} + \frac{\mu_0 T}{2i_m};$$

$$T_{22} = \frac{3Q_0}{4i_m^2} - \frac{T}{4} - \frac{\mu_0 T}{2i_m}; \qquad (6)$$

$$T_{21} + T_{22} = \tfrac{1}{2}\left(\frac{3Q_0}{i_m^2} - T\right).$$

If it turns out in (6) that $T_{21} + T_{22} > 0$ but $T_{22} < 0$, it means that there is just one point of transition from the boundary to the extremal (Fig. 59). In this case (6) may not be utilized to evaluate T_{21}; an individual investigation is necessary.

On the first section of the current diagram (Fig. 59) $i = i_m$; $v = (i_m - \mu_0)\tau$, on the second section $i = i_m - a\tau$;

$$v = (i_m - \mu_0)\, T_{21} + (i_m - \mu_0)\, \tau - \tfrac{1}{2} a\tau^2.$$

The coefficient a is determined from the condition $v(T) = 0$. Since the armature losses on the first section equal $i_m^2 T_{21}$, and the integral

$$\int_{T_{21}}^{T} (i_m - a\tau)^2 \, d\tau,$$

on the second section, then by substituting the value of the coefficient a we will have the possibility of expressing T_{21} in terms of the given quantities Q, i_m, T, μ_0:

$$T_{21} = T\left(1 - \frac{4}{3}\frac{i_m^2 T - 2i_m\mu_0 T + \mu_0^2 T}{i_m^2 T - 2i_m\mu_0 T + Q}\right). \tag{7}$$

Formulas (6) and (7) show that the form of the optimum current diagram depends essentially on the relationship between the armature current permitted by the commutation conditions i_m, and the armature current permitted by the heating $i = Q/T$.

If

$$i_m \geqslant (3Q/T)^{1/2},$$

then the length of the sections of the optimum diagram passing along the domain boundary vanishes; the maximum productivity is achieved on the extremal.

If

$$(Q/T)^{1/2} < i_m < (3Q/T)^{1/2},$$

then the extremum is achieved on a composite curve composed of pieces of the extremal and pieces of the domain boundary, and finally, if

$$i_m \leqslant (Q/T)^{1/2},$$

then the lengths of the extremal sections vanish, the armature current jumps from the value $i = i_m$ to $i = -i_m$ (Fig. 60) at $\tau = T_{21}$. The values of

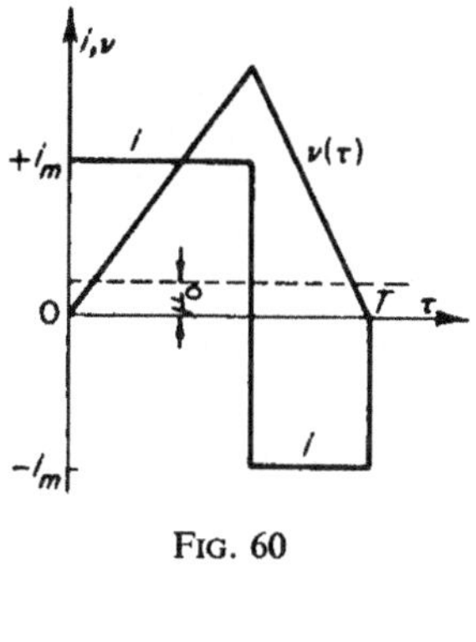

FIG. 60

T_{21} and T_{22} may be determined by means of (6) taking into account that $T_{21} + T_{22} = T$ in this case. We thus obtain

$$T_{21} = \frac{T}{2} + \frac{\mu_0 T}{2i_m}; \qquad T_{22} = \frac{T}{2} - \frac{\mu_0 T}{2i_m}. \tag{8}$$

Let us consider in more detail the question of current and velocity diagrams for motors in a brief repeated start-stop operating regime. The mean-square current of such motors under optimum control is

$$i_{\text{mean quad.}} = \left(\frac{Q}{T + kt_{\text{pause}}}\right)^{1/2} = \left(\frac{T}{T + kt_{\text{pause}}} \cdot \frac{Q}{T}\right)^{1/2}$$
$$= \left(\left\{\frac{T}{T + kt_{\text{pause}}}\right\}\left\{\mu_0^2 + \frac{12\alpha^2}{T^4}\right\}\right)^{1/2},$$

where t_{pause} is the length of the pause between operating cycles of the motor; k is a coefficient taking account of degradation of the motor cooling conditions during idle time. For motors cooled by a separate fan $k = 1$; for motors cooled by vanes on a shaft $k = 0.25 - 1$.

Let us consider the case $\mu_0 = 0$. Here

$$i_{\text{mean quad.}} = \left(\frac{12\alpha^2}{T^4} \cdot \frac{T}{T + kt_{\text{pause}}}\right)^{1/2} = 3.46 \frac{\alpha}{T^2}\left(\frac{T}{T + kt_{\text{pause}}}\right)^{1/2},$$

while the maximum current of the optimum diagram is

$$i_m = \frac{6\alpha}{T^2}.$$

Taking into account that the maximum admissible current for normal dc motors is usually thrice the mean-square current (i.e., for a brief time the armature current may exceed threefold the admissible current according to the heating conditions), we arrive at the conclusion that the optimum control diagram will not include sections going along the domain boundary if the length of the pause does not exceed twice the length of the operating cycles of the motor, i.e., if

$$\frac{T}{T + kt_{\text{pause}}} \leqslant \frac{1}{3}.$$

For longer pauses it is necessary to revert to a diagram composed of pieces of the extremal and pieces of the domain boundary, and finally, for pauses more than eightfold greater than the duration of motor operation the optimum control goes entirely along the domain boundary.

39. Control Assuring Minimum Rated Generator Power (Example with a Nonstandard Functional)

For a machine chosen according to its heat capacity, the rated generator power in a motor-generator system is the product of the nominal voltage by the nominal current, i.e., by $(Q/T)^{1/2}$. The voltage, in turn, is proportional to the maximum ordinate of the velocity diagram (if the small voltage drop in the generator and motor armatures is neglected). Therefore, to assure minimum rated generator power it is necessary to find the velocity diagram $v(\tau)$, yielding the minimum of the functional

$$N = v_m (Q/T)^{1/2}$$

or, equivalently, of the functional

$$N^2 = \frac{v_m^{\,2}}{T} \int_0^T (v' + \mu_0)^2 \, d\tau . \tag{9}$$

The functional (9) resembles the nonstandard functionals analyzed in section 36. As was mentioned there, the extremum of the functional (9) must be sought in the class of curves with given maximum ordinate and with fixed endpoints, i.e., those satisfying the conditions:

$$v \leqslant v_0 ; \tag{10}$$

$$v(0) = 0; \qquad v(T) = 0. \tag{11}$$

The first factor of the functional (9) is fixed in this class of curves; it is necessary to seek the curve minimizing the second member taking the constraint (10) into account. We have already solved this problem in the preceding section, and we obtained that the relationships (2), which may be written as

$$Q = \frac{16}{9} \frac{v_0^{\,3}}{(v_0 T - \alpha)} + \mu_0^{\,2} T$$

should be satisfied on the optimum curve.

Therefore, on the optimum curve the functional (9) takes the value

$$N^2 = \frac{{v_0}^2 Q}{T} = \frac{16}{9} \frac{{v_0}^5}{T(v_0 T - \alpha)} + {\mu_0}^2 {v_0}^2 . \tag{12}$$

The value of the ordinate v_0 in (12) may be arbitrary, i.e., selection of the class of curves with ordinate subject to the condition (10) as comparison curves does not restrict the generality of the solution. Now, differentiating (12) with respect to v_0 and equating the derivative to zero, we find the value of the v_0 ordinate yielding the minimum of the functional (9). Since we obtain $v_0 = \frac{5}{4}\alpha/T$ for $\mu_0 = 0$ it hence follows that $T_1 = T_2 = 0.3T$, i.e., minimum power yields a velocity diagram containing the section $v = v_0 = \frac{5}{4}\alpha/T$, consuming 0.4 of the total time in the complete displacement cycle (Fig. 61). Analogous solutions may also be obtained for $\mu_0 \neq 0$.

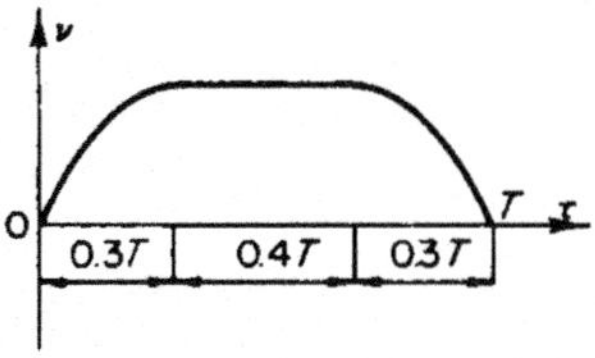

FIG. 61

Let us compare the rated generator power needed to perform the given program of load mechanism displacement for optimum and nonoptimum velocity diagrams. It is easy to verify that for $\mu_0 = 0$

$$N = v_0 \left(\frac{Q}{T}\right)^{1/2} = B \frac{\alpha^2}{T^3},$$

where B is a number dependent only on the shape of the velocity diagram and characterizing the efficiency of this diagram from the viewpoint of the magnitude of the rated power.

For an optimum diagram $B = 4.66$. For a "triangular" velocity diagram (to which a "rectangular" current diagram with a unit filling factor corresponds) $B = 9$, i.e., is 71% greater than with optimum control.

It should be noted that the rated power in the electric drive motor in the motor-generator system also diminishes simultaneously with the diminution in the rated generator power decrease, but this plays a minor part.

If the generator cost is determined by its power, then the cost of the motor is determined primarily by the moment rather than the power. Hence, it is expedient to insert a section $v = v_0$ in the velocity diagram from the viewpoint of decreasing the size and cost of the generator.

40. Control of a Compound Motor with Independent Excitation in the Armature and Excitation Loops

There are two parameters in a motor with independent excitation, which can be controlled independently of each other. These are the armature current and the magnetic flux. Hence, seeking a pair of functions $i(\tau)$ and $\Phi(\tau)$, assuring, as a set, the best operating results of an electric drive (minimum loss for given efficiency, maximum efficiency for given loss level, highest speed response, etc.) enters into the problem of optimum control of a motor with independent excitation.

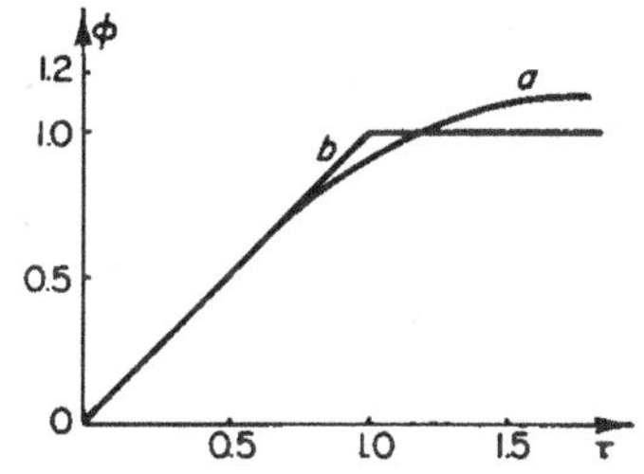

FIG. 62

When controlling the magnetic flux, saturation of the magnetic loop of the motor should certainly be taken into account. It is hence logical to replace the actual magnetic characteristic of the motor (Fig. 62, curve *a*) by an idealized, piecewise-linear characteristic (curve *b*), i.e., to assume that for $\Phi_{\text{motor}} \leqslant \Phi_m$ or (if the magnetic flux is expressed in fractions of Φ_m) for $\Phi \leqslant 1$ saturation does not affect the motor operation, and the value $\Phi = 1$ is the maximum value of the magnetic flux, i.e., the constraint

$$\Phi \leqslant 1 \tag{13}$$

is satisfied.

Under such an assumption, the hysteresis losses and the losses in the excitation windings of the motor turn out to be proportional to the square of the magnetic flux. As is known, the losses in the armature windings are proportional to the square of the armature current.

Utilization of the motor is customarily constrained by the hot-spot temperature. In motors of the short repeated start-stop operating mode, the hot-spot is, as a rule, in the armature windings. Hence, the hysteresis losses and the losses in the excitation windings affect the armature heating to some degree; hence, the hot-spot temperature is determined by the magnitude of the integral

$$Q = \int_0^T (i^2 + k_{\text{losses}} \Phi^2)\, d\tau, \tag{14}$$

where k_{losses} is a coefficient taking account of the influence of the losses proportional to the magnetic flux squared, on the heating of the armature winding.

Usually k_{losses} is a very small number, and it is normally assumed to be zero.

Now, a mathematical formulation of the problem of optimum control of a compound motor with independent excitation can be given: Find the functions $i(\tau)$ and $\Phi(\tau)$ yielding the maximum of the integral

$$\alpha = \int_0^T \nu\, d\tau \tag{15}$$

for a given value of the integral (14), the coupling equation

$$i\Phi = \nu' + \mu_0 \tag{16}$$

and the constraint (13).

In the first stage of the solution, we shall not take account of the constraint (13) and we shall seek the functions $i(\tau)$ and $\Phi(\tau)$ in an open domain. Expressing $i(\tau)$ in terms of $\Phi(\tau)$ on the basis of the coupling equation, we obtain the isoperimetric problem: Find the functions $\nu(\tau)$ and $\Phi(\tau)$ yielding the maximum of the integral (15) for a given value of the integral

$$Q = \int_0^T \left[\frac{(\nu' + \mu_0)^2}{\Phi^2} + k_{\text{losses}} \Phi^2 \right] d\tau . \tag{17}$$

Let us form the intermediate function

$$H = \lambda_0 \left[\frac{(\nu' + \mu_0)^2}{\Phi^2} + k_{\text{losses}} \Phi^2 \right] + \nu . \tag{18}$$

Let us note that the function H is degenerate relative to $\Phi(\tau)$, therefore, the extremal of $\Phi(\tau)$ may have discontinuities and jumps (see Section 29). At the same time

$$H_{v'v'} = 2\lambda_0/\Phi^2,$$

i.e., the functional is not degenerate relative to $v(\tau)$, the extremals (if they exist) are smooth curves and the maximum of load displacement is reached on them (for $\lambda_0 < 0$).

The desired functions should satisfy two Euler equations for the intermediate function H. These equations are

$$\frac{2(v' + \mu_0)^2}{\Phi^3} = 2k_{\text{losses}}\Phi; \tag{19}$$

$$\frac{d}{d\tau}\frac{2\lambda_0(v' + \mu_0)}{\Phi^2} = 1. \tag{20}$$

As is easily verified by substitution, (19) and (20) are contradictory; extremals do not exist.

To illustrate the physical meaning of the result which has been obtained, let us examine the particular case $\mu_0 = 0$; $v(0) = 0$; $v(T) = 0$, and let us investigate the behavior of the motor for v and Φ satisfying just the first Euler equation (19) when

$$i = \frac{v' + \mu_0}{\Phi^2} = \pm\sqrt{k_{\text{losses}}}\,\Phi,$$

i.e., $i = +\sqrt{k_{\text{losses}}}\,\Phi$ on the motor acceleration section with $v' \geqslant 0$, and $i = -\sqrt{k_{\text{losses}}}\,\Phi$ on the deceleration portion with $v' \leqslant 0$.

We obtain $Q = 2\sqrt{k_{\text{losses}}}\,\Delta v$ on the acceleration section, and again $Q = 2\sqrt{k_{\text{losses}}}\,\Delta v$ on the deceleration section.

Therefore, the magnitude of the integral (14) depends only on the maximum ordinate of the velocity diagram $v(\tau)$. But among all the curves with given maximum ordinate and boundary conditions $v(0) = v(T) = 0$, the greatest value of the integral (15) is achieved on a discontinuous function (recalling the outline of a rectangle, Fig. 63) by a jump from the value $v = 0$ at $\tau = 0$ and $\tau = T$ to the value $v = v_m$ for $0 < \tau < T$. For such

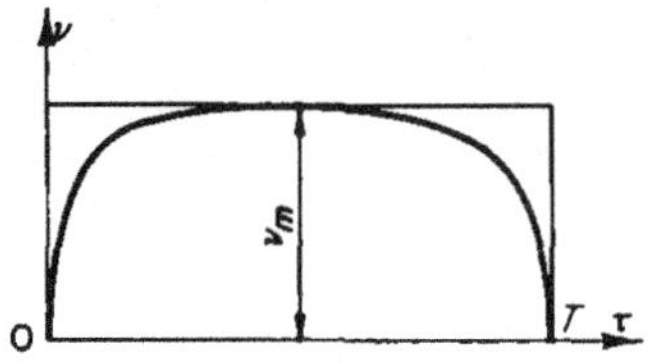

FIG. 63

a function $v' \to \infty$ at $\tau = 0$, and therefore, $i \to \infty$, $\Phi \to \infty$, and $v' \to -\infty$ for $\tau = T$, i.e., $i \to -\infty$, $\Phi \to \infty$.

Hence, the reason for the absence of extremals is that the extremum is achieved outside the limits of the class of piecewise-smooth functions. No matter what smooth curve $v(\tau)$, connecting the points $(0; 0)$ and $(T; 0)$ we take, another smooth curve with the same maximum ordinate may be found but which will approximate the outline of the rectangle more closely. The value of the integral (15) will be greater for this curve than for the original curve.

Thus, we arrive at the following deduction: The higher the value of the magnetic flux at the beginning and ending of the displacement cycle, the higher the efficiency and fast-response of the electric motor. However, raising the magnetic flux is constrained by (30), and the extremum is achieved on the domain boundary. To attain the highest efficiency the magnetic flux of the motor should be kept constant and equal to the maximum value; as regards the armature current, the optimum current diagram under the condition of constant magnetic flux has already been found in Chapter III, it is the linear diagram.

41. Control with a Voltage Constraint

The input voltage to the motor $u(\tau)$ consists of two components: the counter-emf of the armature which equals the product of the magnetic flux and the rotational velocity, and the voltage drop in the armature winding:

$$u = \Phi v + mi,$$

where m is a constant coefficient.

The magnitude of the voltage at the motor terminals is constrained, firstly, by the insulation, and secondly, by the maximum voltage of the supplying generator. Hence, the voltage constraint

$$u \leqslant u_m \tag{21}$$

must be considered.

Let us analyze an accelerating motor and let us find the control, which for given armature loss

$$Q = \int_0^T i^2 \, d\tau \,, \tag{22}$$

will assure the greatest change in rotational velocity

$$\Delta v = \int_0^T v' \, d\tau \tag{23}$$

in a given time T, taking account of the constraints (13) and (21).

First, let us consider the control in an open domain. Expressing $i(\tau)$ in terms of Φ and v on the basis of the coupling equation (16), we reduce the problem under consideration to an isoperimetric problem with the intermediate function

$$H = \left[\frac{(v' + \mu_0)^2}{\Phi^2}\right] \lambda_0 + v' .$$

The extremals of $v(\tau)$ and $\Phi(\tau)$ (if they exist) should satisfy the Euler equations

$$\frac{\partial H}{\partial \Phi} = 0; \qquad \frac{\partial H}{\partial v} - \frac{d}{d\tau}\frac{\partial H}{\partial v'} = 0 .$$

However, no function of $\Phi(\tau)$ (if the trivial case of $v' + \mu_0 = 0$ is excluded, which corresponds to the regime $i\Phi = 0$, i.e., absence of a rotational moment at the shaft) can satisfy the first Euler equation

$$\frac{\partial H}{\partial \Phi} = -\frac{2(v' + \mu_0)}{\Phi^3} = 0 .$$

Therefore, no extremals exist. In this case the extremum is achieved on the domain boundary, i.e., at $\Phi = 1$. We find the optimum armature current from the second Euler equation, which becomes for $\Phi = 1$

$$2\lambda_0 v'' = 0 ,$$

from which $v = C_1 + C_2 \tau$ and, therefore, $i = \text{const}$.

Hence, the optimum control of an accelerating motor in the absence of any voltage constraint will be to maintain constant magnetic flux and armature current. The rotational velocity and voltage at the motor terminals will hence grow according to a linear law.

When it turns out that the constraint (21) is violated with such a control, this means that the optimum control should include a section of the domain boundary, i.e., $u = u_m$.

Let us now find the laws for the change of $i(\tau)$ and $\Phi(\tau)$ on the domain boundary where the constraint (21) goes over into the additional coupling equation

$$u_m = \Phi v + mi. \tag{24}$$

The two coupling equations (24) and (16) may be combined into one by eliminating the variable $\Phi(\tau)$. We obtain an equation connecting i and v:

$$vv' + \mu_0 v = u_m i - mi^2. \tag{25}$$

The problem has now been reduced to seeking the functions $i(\tau)$ and $v(\tau)$ yielding a maximum of the integral (23) for given values of the integral (22) and the coupling equation (25). This is a Lagrange problem. The desired functions should satisfy the Euler equation for the intermediate function

$$H = \lambda_0 i^2 + v' + \lambda_1 (vv' + \mu_0 v - u_m i + mi^2),$$

where λ_1 is a function of τ.

Integration is completed easily for the particular case of $\mu_0 = 0$. The Euler equations become

$$\lambda_1{}' v = 0; \qquad 2\lambda_0 i - \lambda_1 (u_m - 2mi) = 0,$$

from which follows

$$i = i_2 = \text{const}; \qquad v = \left(v(0) + 2(u_m i_2 - mi_2{}^2)\,\tau\right)^{1/2}, \tag{26}$$

and substituting (26) into the coupling equation (16), we obtain

$$\Phi = \frac{u_m - mi_2}{v}. \tag{27}$$

Hence, the optimum acceleration of a motor with independent excitation will consist of two stages. In the first the magnetic flux is kept a maximum, and the armature current constant. The rotational velocity and the voltage at the motor terminals increase linearly. When the voltage has reached the limit, the magnetic flux should be attenuated according to (27), while maintaining the armature current constant (Fig. 64). It follows from the condition of continuity of the tangent to the curve $v(\tau)$ that

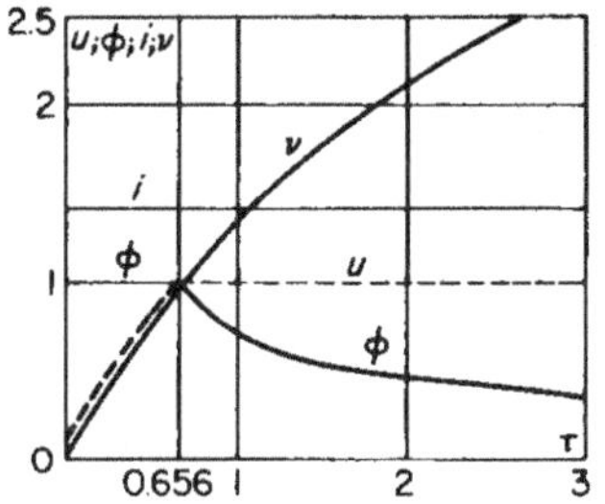

FIG. 64

the armature current in the first stage of the acceleration equals the current in the second stage. This permits finding all the optimum control parameters rather simply.

Example. Given $Q = 6$ and $T = 3$, the maximum voltage $u_m = 1$ and $m = 0.05$, find the optimum regime of motor acceleration and the velocity at $\tau = T$ if $v = 0$ at $\tau = 0$.

According to the given Q and T we find the armature current

$$i_1 = i_2 = (Q/T)^{1/2} = 1.41 .$$

In the first stage of the acceleration, the velocity grows according to the equation $v = i_1 \tau$. The time T_1 during which the voltage on the motor terminals reaches the limit is found from the equation

$$1 = mi_1 + i_1 T_1 ,$$

from which $T_1 = 0.656$ and $v(T_1) = 0.93$.

In the second stage, the velocity grows more slowly

$$v = (0.93^2 + 2(1.41 - 0.05 \cdot 1.41^2)(\tau - 0.656))^{1/2} ,$$

and we have $v = 2.66$ and $\Phi = 0.35$ for $\tau = T$.

The change in armature current, rotational velocity, magnetic flux and voltage as a function of the time in an optimum acceleration regime is shown in Fig. 64.

Let us note that while the tangent to the function $v(\tau)$ changes continuously during passage from the region where $\Phi = 1$ to the domain where $u = u_m$, the derivative of the function $\Phi(\tau)$ undergoes a discontinuity. But this is associated with the fact that the functional under consideration is degenerate relative to $\Phi(\tau)$, i.e., is independent of $\Phi'(\tau)$.

42. Determination of the Maximum Allowable Dynamic Effect

Many components and structures operate under variable loading conditions, whose law of variation we do not know in advance. In this case the problem of estimating the greatest possible stresses and strains in the structure's elements is of great interest. To do this it is necessary to determine which effect is most dangerous to the structure, after which it is sufficient to calculate the stress and strain originating from this effect.

Let us consider the simplest element of a structure (a mass on an elastic beam), whose behavior may be described by the equation

$$mx'' + nx' + kx = f(t), \tag{28}$$

where m is the mass of the element; x the beam displacement, n the friction coefficient characterizing the vibration damping; k a proportionality (or spring) coefficient between the force and the displacement; and f the effective force.

With respect to the force $f(t)$ it is known only that it is bounded in absolute value

$$|f| \leqslant f_m. \tag{29}$$

We are required to find the maximum allowable effect $f(t)$ subject to the constraint (29), for which the strain at some time $t = T$ will reach the greatest value as compared with any other effects $f(t)$ subject to the same constraint.

The constraint (29) may be considered as the limit of

$$\int_0^T (f/f_m)^{2p}\, dt \leqslant T \tag{30}$$

as $p \to \infty$, and the demand for the maximum displacement x at the time $t = T$ may be treated as the demand to reach the maximum of the integral

$$x(T) = \int_0^T x' \, dt \,. \tag{31}$$

It is easy to see that the extremum will not be achieved within the admissible domain; the extremum will be reached on the boundary where the inequality (30) transforms into the equality

$$\int_0^T (f/f_m)^{2p} \, dt = T \,. \tag{32}$$

Consequently, we arrive at the general Lagrange problem: Find the functions $f(t)$ and $x(t)$ which will yield the maximum of the integral (31) in the presence of the coupling equation (28) and a given value of the integral (32). The desired functions should satisfy the Euler-Poisson equations for the intermediate function

$$H = x' + \lambda_0 (f/f_m)^{2p} + \lambda(mx'' + nx' + kx - f) \,. \tag{33}$$

It follows from the equation

$$\partial H / \partial f = 0$$

for the function f that

$$\frac{f}{f_m} = \frac{1}{2p\lambda_0} \lambda^{1/2p-1} \,,$$

from which we obtain $f = f_m \operatorname{sign} \lambda$ by passing to the limit.

From the equation for x

$$\frac{\partial H}{\partial x} - \frac{d}{dt}\frac{\partial H}{\partial x'} + \frac{d^2}{dt^2}\frac{\partial H}{\partial x''} = m\lambda'' - n\lambda' + k\lambda = 0 \,,$$

we have

$$\lambda = A e^{\frac{n}{2m}t} \sin\left(\frac{(4km - n^2)^{1/2}}{2m} t + \varphi\right),$$

therefore

$$f(t) = f_m \operatorname{sign} \sin\left(\frac{(4km - n^2)^{1/2}}{2m} t + \varphi\right), \tag{34}$$

i.e., the maximum allowable dynamic effect is piecewise-constant, and changes sign in the time

$$t = \frac{2m}{(4km - n^2)^{1/2}} \pi,$$

which is equal to half the period of the free vibrations of the element under consideration.

The maximum allowable effect is a static loading effect, and the greatest displacement is

$$x_{CT} = f_m/k$$

for high damping when $n^2 > 4km$ and the element characteristic is aperiodic in nature.

If the element characteristic is oscillatory in nature, the greatest displacement may exceed many times the motion due to the static loading.

The maximum displacement is achieved when the force defined by (34) acts a long time. To determine the maximum displacement it is sufficient to find the periodic solution of Eq. (28) for a function $f(t)$ changing in conformity with (34).

The greatest displacement will equal

$$x_{\max} = x_{CT} \frac{1 + z}{1 - z}$$

where

$$z = \exp\left[- \frac{n}{(4km - n^2)^{1/2}} \pi \right].$$

For small n (i.e., for slight damping)

$$x_{\max} \to \frac{4}{\pi} \frac{(km)^{1/2}}{n} x_{CT}. \tag{35}$$

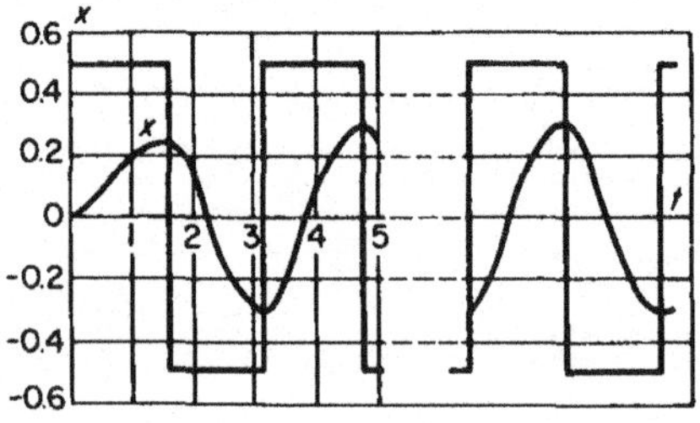

FIG. 65

Hence, for a piecewise-constant effect (Fig. 65) in resonance with the natural vibrations of the structure, the greatest displacement (for small n) will exceed the static $(4/\pi)(\{km\}^{1/2}/n)$-fold. Let us note that for a sinusoidal external effect with amplitude f_m which is in resonance with the natural vibrations, we will have (for small n)

$$x_{\max} = \frac{(km)^{1/2}}{n} x_{CT}.$$

Hence, contrary to widely held opinion, a sinusoidal external effect in resonance with the natural vibrations is not the maximum allowable. The maximum allowable (for a given maximum amplitude) is a piecewise-constant external effect.

Formula (35) may be utilized to select the strength factor for elements of a structure if only an estimate of their absolute value is known for the external forces.

Let us note that by using (34), the inverse problem may also be solved of destruction of a structure, i.e., of imparting displacements up to the yield point. If the stress resultants at our disposal are bounded in absolute value, the best results will be afforded by the application of a piecewise-constant stress resultant (formula (34)).

If the energy of the effect is bounded, i.e.,

$$\int_0^T f^2(t)\, dt \leqslant A, \tag{36}$$

then a piecewise-constant effect will not be the maximum allowable. In this case the desired function $f(t)$ should yield the maximum of the integral (31) for a given value of the integral (36) and the coupling equation (28). Forming the intermediate function according to the customary rules

$$H = x' + \lambda_0 f^2(t) + \lambda(mx'' + nx' + kx - f),$$

we obtain the Euler equations

$$\frac{\partial H}{\partial f} = 2\lambda_0 f - \lambda = 0;$$

$$\frac{\partial H}{\partial x} - \frac{d}{dt}\frac{\partial H}{\partial x'} + \frac{d^2}{dt^2}\frac{\partial H}{\partial x''} = m\lambda'' - n\lambda' + k\lambda = 0,$$

from which it follows that

$$f(t) = \frac{1}{2\lambda_0} \exp\left[\frac{n}{2m} t\right] \sin\left(\frac{(4km - n^2)^{1/2}}{2m} t + \varphi\right),$$

i.e., an effect varying according to a sine law whose amplitude increases exponentially will result in the greatest strain for a given energy.

Shown in Fig. 65 is an example of the growth of displacement in an element of a structure described by (28) for $m = 1$ kg; $n = 2$ kg/sec; $k = 5$ kg/sec^2 and $|f| \leqslant 1$ kg·m/sec^2 (i.e., the force is bounded in absolute value), and with the application of the most dangerous stress $f(t)$ equal to $f_m = 1$ kg·m/sec^2 in absolute value and changing in sign every half-period $\pi/2$ sec of the free vibrations of the element. The displacements in the steady-state regime under prolonged application of the maximum allowable loading are shown in the right side of Fig. 65.

The figure shows that the displacements are close to the limit even at the third change in sign, and exceed the static strain 1.52-fold.

Chebotarev, Bulgakov, and Kuzovkov analyzed problems on the maximum allowable law of loading and stress-resultant variation by a considerably more complicated means, without applying the calculus of variations. Variational methods permit a more simple solution of these problems, not only for the simplest element described by (28), but also for more complicated structures.

The problem of the greatest possible deviation in automatic control systems subject to perturbations constrained in absolute value or in energy is also solved by these methods.

43. Control of the Excitation of a Synchronous Machine Assuring the Highest Degree of Stability

Stable parallel operation of a synchronous machine from a power grid is characterized by constant, steady-state values of the angle of displacement θ between the rotor axis and the stator field, and constant values of the rotor and stator interlinkages.

The behavior of a synchronous machine, operating in parallel with a grid, is described by the Park-Gorev equations:

$$\frac{d\psi_d}{dt} = e \sin\theta + \psi_q(1 + s) + r(A_d\psi_d + A_f\psi_f + A_{ed}\psi_{ed});$$

$$\frac{d\psi_q}{dt} = e \cos \theta - \psi_d(1 + s) + r(D_q\psi_q + D_{eq}\psi_{eq});$$

$$\frac{d\psi_f}{dt} = e_f - r_f(B_f\psi_f + B_{ed}\psi_{ed} + B_d\psi_d);$$

$$\frac{d\psi_{ed}}{dt} = - r_{ed}(C_d\psi_d + C_f\psi_f); \tag{37}$$

$$\frac{d\psi_{eq}}{dt} = - r_{eq}(F_q\psi_q - F_{eq}\psi_{eq});$$

$$\frac{ds}{dt} = \frac{1}{H_j}[M_T - \psi_q(A_d\psi_d - A_f\psi_f + A_{ed}\psi_{ed}) + \psi_d(D_q\psi_q + D_{eq}\psi_{eq})];$$

$$\frac{d\theta}{dt} = s,$$

where ψ_d and ψ_q are the interlinkages of the stator windings and ψ_{ed} and ψ_{eq} the interlinkages of the damper windings along the longitudinal axis d and the transverse axis q; ψ_f is the interlinkage of the excitation winding; s the slip of the rotor relative to the stator field; θ the angle between the rotor and the stator; M_T the moment applied to the rotor; e the grid voltage; e_f the voltage on the excitation winding; r and r_f the stator winding and excitation winding resistances; $A_d, A_f, \ldots, D_{eq}$ and H_j constant coefficients.

In the steady-state regime the derivatives of all the variables are zero. Sudden violations of the steady-state regime (short circuits in the grid, circuit breaker action, switching in or taking off loads) cause deviations of the variables in (37) from their steady-state values. Depending on the magnitude of these deviations, the machine may either return to the steady-state (generally different from the initial state) or may go out of synchronization, which is characterized in particular by an unlimited growth of the angle θ with passing time. Going out of synchronization is a serious emergency, it is hence very important to expand the possibility of stable machine operation so that even strong perturbing effects on the machine and system would not result in its going out of synchronization.

An effective means of raising the stability is regulation of the voltage e_f

at the terminals of the excitation winding. The quantity e_f is bounded in an absolute value

$$-e_{f\,\max} \leqslant e_f \leqslant e_{f\,\max},$$

or, taking the voltage $e_{f\,\max}$ as unity, we obtain

$$|e_f| \leqslant 1. \tag{38}$$

We neglect constraints on the rate of increase of the exciter voltage.

Let us consider the variables $\psi_d, \psi_q, \ldots, s$ and θ in (37) as coordinates of a seven-dimensional phase space. By an appropriate selection of the measuring unit, it is possible to establish that the stable synchronized regime resulting after cancellation of the consequences of an accident would correspond to the origin ($\psi_d = \psi_q = \cdots = s = \theta = 0$).

As a result of an external effect (a short circuit, say), let a state occur which is characterized by the initial conditions $\psi_d(0); \psi_q(0); \cdots; s(0); \theta(0)$. Depending on the force of the effect (in particular, on the duration of the short circuit) the machine will either return to the stable, synchronized regime, the origin, after its deviation, or it will not. Evidently a domain (we call it the stability domain) may be separated out of the seven-dimensional phase space, within which all points (initial conditions) are found from which the machine will return to the origin, and outside this domain are points from which return to the origin is impossible.

The magnitude of the stability domain depends on the law controlling the voltage on the excitation winding. It is of interest to find the optimum control law, i.e., that function e_f subject to the constraint (38) which would assure the maximum stability domain as compared with all other functions subject to the same constraint.

We encounter here a rather extraordinary problem of the calculus of variations, since in this case the functional is the magnitude of the stability domain, which does not reduce to the "standard" form of the integral $\int_a^b F(x; y; y')\, dx$.

The method of the "maximum principle" (see Section 33) permits determination of the optimum fast response control e_f. Let us prove that the optimum fast-response control simultaneously assures also the greatest magnitude of the stability domain. For the proof, let us assume that in the phase space a domain has been constructed within which are included points from which the origin is attainable with an optimum fast-response control within the finite time T ($T \to \infty$ may correspond to the boundary of the domain). Let us now assume that at least one point lies outside this domain from which the origin is attainable within a finite time T_1 with a control belonging to the class of admissible controls, but which is not an optimum fast-response. But then the origin will also be attainable from this point within a finite time T_2 with an optimum control, where $T_2 \leqslant T_1$. This contradicts the assumption made above that the considered point lies outside the limits of the stability domain.

This proof may be extended to any system described by an nth order differential equation, and we arrive at the following general conclusion: An optimum fast-response control simultaneously assures the greatest stability domain also; if the stable regime is not attainable with an optimum fast-response control for some initial conditions, then it is even more not attainable with any control different from the optimum control.

As applied to a synchronized machine, it is rational to seek the optimum fast-response control by using the "maximum principle." The optimum function e_f should yield the maximum of the expression

$$\begin{aligned} H = {} & p_1 [(e \sin\theta + \psi_q(1 + s) + r(A_d\psi_d + A_f\psi_f + A_{ed}\psi_{ed})] \\ & + p_2 [e \cos\theta - \psi_d(1 + s) + r(D_q\psi_q + D_{eq}\psi_{eq})] \\ & + p_3 [e_f - r_f(B_f\psi_f + B_{ed}\psi_{ed} + B_d\psi_d)] - \\ & - p_4 r_{ed}(C_d\psi_d + C_f\psi_f) - p_5 r_{eq}(F_q\psi_q - F_{eq}\psi_{eq}) \\ & + p_6(1/H_j)[M_T - \psi_q(A_d\psi_d - A_f\psi_f) + A_{ed}\psi_{ed} \\ & + \psi_d(D_q\psi_q + D_{eq}\psi_{eq})] + p_7 s, \end{aligned}$$

where the functions $p_1, p_2, \ldots, p_7$ satisfy the system of differential equations:

$$\begin{gathered} \frac{dp_1}{dt} = -\frac{\partial H}{\partial \psi_d}; \quad \frac{dp_2}{dt} = -\frac{\partial H}{\partial \psi_q}; \quad \frac{dp_3}{dt} = -\frac{\partial H}{\partial \psi_f}; \\ \frac{dp_4}{dt} = -\frac{\partial H}{\partial \psi_{ed}}; \quad \frac{dp_5}{dt} = -\frac{\partial H}{\partial \psi_{eq}}; \quad \frac{dp_6}{dt} = -\frac{dH}{\partial s}; \\ \frac{dp_7}{dt} = -\frac{\partial H}{\partial \theta}. \end{gathered} \tag{39}$$

In the presence of the constraint (38), the maximum of H will be achieved for

$$e_f = \operatorname{sign} p_3. \tag{40}$$

Hence, a relay control will be optimum, the alternate maximum forcing of the voltage ($e_f = 1$) and the maximum forcing of the opposite sign ($e_f = -1$). To seek the transition points from forcing to unforcing and back, it is necessary to determine the sign of the function p_3. As a whole, Eqs. (37) and (39), in combination with (40) form a system of 15 equations which are adequate to determine 15 unknowns: the 7 variables $\psi_d, \psi_q, \ldots, s$ and θ in (37), the 7 functions $p_1, \ldots, p_7$ and the function e_f. This system may be solved by numerical methods.

However, even without having solved the equations, an investigation permits the important deduction that the optimum control system for excitation of a synchronous machine is a system which supplies the maximum voltage of alternating polarity to the excitation winding. This deduction has a high degree of generality and is valid for all synchronous machines, both generators and motors, for any law of variation of the moment on the shaft M_T.

In the simplest cases, alternation of the switching is sufficiently evident. Let us consider the most frequent accident to a synchronous generator, a short circuit in the grid and its disconnection. During the short circuit, the generator does not deliver active power to the grid, and all the energy supplied to its shaft by the turbine goes into increasing its rotational velocity, the angle θ increases. After the short circuit has been disconnected by the relay, coupling between the generator and grid is restored, gradual deceleration of the rotor starts, but at the initial instant the angle θ continues to grow and may reach the critical value which will result in the generator going out of synchronization before the rotor is braked. To prevent this, it is attempted to increase the decelerating effect of the grid prior to the maximum by forcing the excitation. However, this means a new danger: under powerful and prolonged forcing, the decelerating

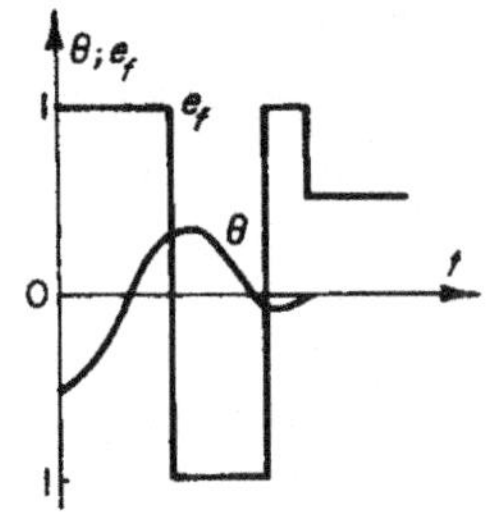

FIG. 66

effect of the grid may turn out to be so abrupt that the angle θ will start to reverse and the generator may go out of synchronization at negative angles. To prevent this danger, the polarity of the excitation voltage should be switched at a specific instant (Fig. 66). The greatest possible degree of stability of a synchronous machine is achieved with such regulation.

44. Optimum Control of Locomotive Motion

Let us consider the problem of optimum control of a diesel engine and the regime of motion of a locomotive with electrical transmission. It is here necessary to achieve complex optimization by connecting the optimum regime of the diesel with the optimum graph of the motion of the train during the run. The problem is also of interest in that it leads to a degenerate functional.

The equation of motion of the train may be written as

$$\frac{d}{dt}\left(\frac{m}{2}v^2\right) + \omega v = \eta p, \tag{41}$$

where m is the mass of the train, v its velocity, ω is the drag, η the efficiency of the transmission from the diesel to the driving axes, and p is the power of the diesel.

It may be assumed with adequate accuracy that the efficiency of the transmission is independent of the power and is a constant. The drag of the train depends, on the one hand, on the roadway (ascents, descents, curves), and on the other hand, it depends quadratically on the velocity of the motion, i.e.,

$$\omega = \omega(s) + kv + k_1 v^2,$$

where k and k_1 are constant coefficients, s is the moving value of the roadway traversed by the locomotive from the beginning of the run, where

$$ds/dt = v,$$

$\omega(s)$ is the drag component independent of the velocity, but is a function of s depending completely on the distribution of ascents, descents and curves on the roadway.

By making use of a logical selection of the units of measurement for the roadway, the power and time, the equation of train motion (41) may be written in the nondimensional form

$$s''s' + \omega(s)\, s' + ks'^2 + k_1 s'^3 = \eta p, \tag{42}$$

where s and p are nondimensional variables.

Since we are interested in the qualitative solution of the problem, let us not dwell on the selection of the units of measurement, but let us henceforth consider the equation of train motion to be given in the form (42).

Consider now on which of the variables the fuel consumption of the diesel locomotive depends. In the general case the fuel consumption depends on the power developed by the diesel and on its angular velocity. When there is an electrical transmission the velocity of train motion is not connected strictly to the number of rpm of the diesel, hence, an optimum number of rpm corresponding to the minimum fuel consumption may be established for each value of the diesel power. With such regulation, the fuel consumption is a function only of the diesel power. The nature of such a function for the TE-3 locomotive is shown in Fig. 67.

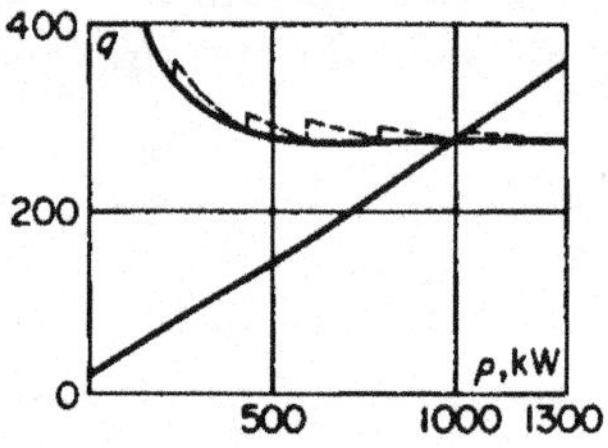

FIG. 67

The lower curve yields the total fuel consumption by the diesel in kilograms per hour, and the upper curve is the specific consumption in grams per hour per kilowatt of power of the traction generator. The dashed broken line corresponds to the specific fuel consumption under regulation using an eight-position controller, the solid line is the specific consumption with a positionless regulation system. The total fuel consumption curve may be replaced by a straight line with sufficient accuracy, i.e., it may be assumed that the fuel consumption q is a linear function of the power, i.e., in relative units

$$q = p + a \tag{43}$$

where a is a constant.

The fundamental requirement imposed on the control of the locomotive is completion of the motion schedule. If we have $s = 0$ and $v = 0$ at $t = 0$, then we should have $v = 0$ and $s = s_0$ at $t = T$, where T is the prescribed time schedule of the motion, and s_0 is the length of the run. The motion regime during the run is arbitrary to a considerable extent.

Out of all the functions $s(t)$ satisfying the boundary conditions (i.e., out of all the regimes of motion satisfying the schedule), a function $s(t)$ should be chosen which would result in least fuel consumption, i.e., would yield the minimum of the integral

$$J = \int_0^T q\,dt = \frac{1}{\eta}\int_0^T (s''s' + \omega s' + ks'^2 + k_1 s'^3)\,dt + \int_0^T a\,dt. \tag{44}$$

The desired function $s(t)$ should satisfy the following constraints:

(1) $s'' \leqslant s''_{\max}$, the constraint on maximum acceleration due to commutation and interlinkage conditions;

(2) $s' \leqslant s'_{\max}$, the constraint on the maximum velocity dependent mainly on the state of the rails on the roadbed;

(3) $p \leqslant p_{\max}$, the constraint on the diesel;

(4) $p \geqslant 0$, the constraint specifically for a locomotive which reflects the impossibility of "fuel recuperation" by the diesel during downhill motion.

Let us solve the problem by the customary variational methods, i.e., let us first seek the extremal for an open domain, and then let us find the junction points of the extremal and the boundary curves.

We find the equations of the extremal from the Euler-Poisson equation for the functional (44), which is

$$s''(2k + 6k_1 s') = 0, \tag{45}$$

i.e., which decomposes into two equations:

$$s'' = 0,$$

whose solution will be a constant velocity curve

$$v = \text{const} \tag{46}$$

and the equation

$$2k + 2k_1 s' = 0,$$

whose solution is also $v = \text{const}$.

Therefore, the least fuel consumption is achieved when the locomotive moves at constant speed, where this deduction remains valid for any function $\omega(s)$, i.e. for any roadbed profile (terms containing the function $\omega(s)$ in the Euler-Poisson equation cancel each other).*

On investigating the Legendre condition we see that the second partial derivative of the integrand of the functional (44) with respect to the highest derivative of the desired function vanishes:

$$\partial^2 q / \partial s''^2 = 0.$$

The functional (44) is a degenerate functional. This results in non-compliance with the condition of continuity of the tangents on the $s' = v(t)$ graph at the transition points from the extremal to the boundary curves, and the optimum graph of the motion has the form shown in Fig. 68. At the time the locomotive starts, the constraints on commutation

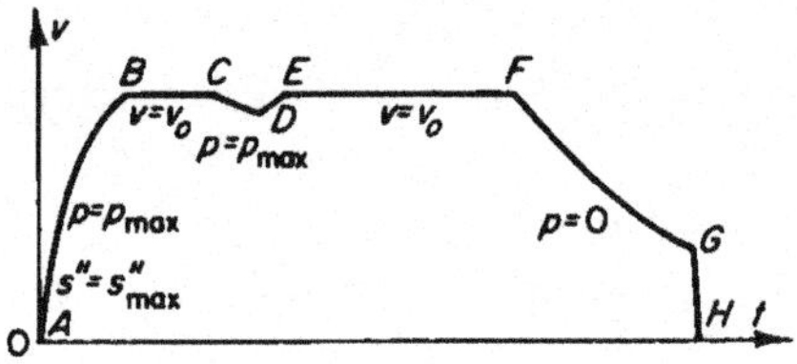

FIG. 68

of the traction engines or the interlinkage play a governing part (depending on which of these two constraints turns out to be stricter in each specific case). The motion regime with constant, maximal possible acceleration $s'' = s''_{\max}$ (the section OA) is optimum. As the train velocity increases on the section OA the power required from the diesel also increases. When this power reaches the limiting power, it is necessary to transfer to the boundary curve $p = p_{\max}$, i.e., to motion with maximum diesel power (the section AB).

* An experimental verification conducted on locomotives of the Oktiabr'sk Railroad confirmed this.

Later, the transition to the regime of motion on the extremal, $v = \text{const}$ (the section BC) occurs. The diesel power is variable on the extremal portion and depends on the declination of the roadbed. If the train encounters so steep an ascent on the roadway that the diesel power exceeds the limit during motion on the extremal, then a transition from the extremal to the boundary curve $p = p_{\max}$ occurs, the velocity of the motion is reduced (section CD). When the steep ascent has been terminated, the velocity of the train starts to grow (section DE) in the $p = p_{\max}$ regime until there is a return to the motion along the extremal (section EF). Before the end of the run a free coasting of the rolling stock occurs ($p = 0$ regime, section FG), and finally, braking by a mechanical brake (section GH) before stopping.

The magnitude of the velocity on the $v = \text{const}$ portion of the extremal is selected in such a manner that the motion schedule is executed taking account of the portions of the motion along the domain boundary, i.e., the mean velocity of the motion on the run $v_{\text{mean}} = s_0/T$ would equal that given by the schedule. The magnitude of this velocity is established from a traction computation.

It must be noted that from the solution of the variational problem there follows only that the velocities should be equal on the portions of the extremal $v = \text{const}$, but it does not follow that those on different segments of the extremal separated by the section $p = p_{\max}$, say, should.

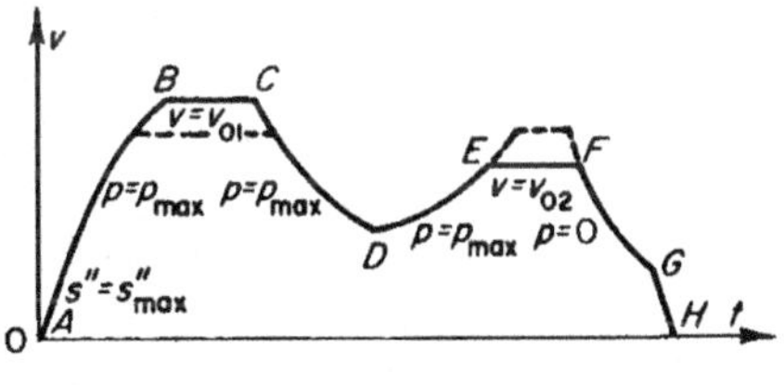

FIG. 69

The plot in Fig. 69 (solid line) may turn out to be optimum together with the graph of the motion shown in Fig. 68.

If there are long steep declines on the run, and the motion velocity on the $p = p_{\max}$ portions is successfully reduced considerably, then the fuel consumption diminishes as the velocity increases before the steep decline, i.e., upon the transition from the graph of the motion shown by the dashes in Fig. 69 to the graph shown by the solid line (the kinetic energy of the moving mass of the train is used here).

The optimum magnitude of the rise in velocity before an ascent is established after several approximate traction computations with the fuel consumption in each compared. Hence, in this case, because of the large number of constraints on the regime of train motion, the solution of the variational problem does not eliminate solution of a number of approximate computations and selecting the best out of all possible combinations.

But preliminary knowledge of the solution of the Euler-Poisson equation drastically cuts down the number of versions to be compared.

Instead of having to make a selection from among an innumerable variety of possible graphs of the motion, it is sufficient to make a selection from a number of graphs of the form pictured in Fig. 69, where only the values of the velocity on the extremal portions turn out to be unknown.

Synthesis of Control System Realizing the Optimum Regime of Motion

The motorman's throttle is the master control in existing locomotive control systems. By rotating the handle of the throttle, the motorman prescribes the supply of fuel to the diesel and its angular velocity. By constantly following the profile of the roadway, the motorman changes the throttle handle from position to position to keep watch that too great a fluctuation in the velocity of the train motion should not occur. Experienced motormen even use the inertia of the train. However, the motion regime turns out to be far from the optimum, while the control system demands constant attention of the motorman.

Existing automatic control technique permits the creation of a sufficiently simple control system which would automatically assure the optimum regime of locomotive motion.

The block diagram of an optimum control system is pictured in Fig. 70. In this diagram the parameter prescribing the regime of the diesel and the electrical transmission is calculated in advance, and the velocity of the motion on the $v = v_0$ portion of the extremal is transmitted to the motorman before dispatching the train.

In the comparison check, this velocity is compared with the true ve-

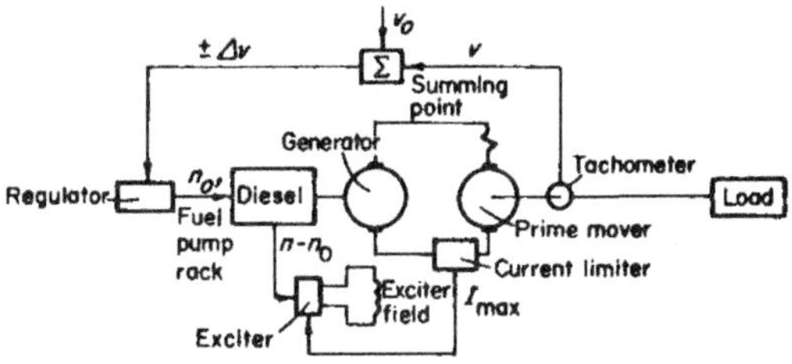

FIG. 70

locity of the train motion at the summing point $\sum$, and their difference Δv is the input of the throttle (Regulator). This unit controls the position of the rack on the fuel pump, and simultaneously establishes the optimum rotational velocity of the diesel n_0 for a given power setting for each position of the fuel pump rack.

For example, if the true velocity of train motion is less than the given velocity v_0, then in conformity with the incoming mismatch signal $\Delta v = v_0 - v$, the regulator unit increases the delivery of fuel to the diesel by operating on the rack of the fuel pump, and simultaneously adjusts the diesel to a number of revolutions n_0 which is optimum for the given fuel delivery. If the true number of revolutions of the diesel n turns out to be less than the setting n_0 of the regulator, then this means that the generator requires too much power from the diesel. The mismatch signal $n - n_0$ at the input of the generator exciter diminishes the excitation current of the generator and equalizes the power balance.

Hence, the diesel always operates in the optimum regime.

If the locomotive approaches a steep grade, where its velocity will diminish, then the throttle (Regulator) will increase the fuel supply until the rack of the fuel pump reaches the detent. Then the control system automatically goes over into the $p = p_{max}$ regime, and will remain there until the ascent has been overcome, after which it returns automatically to the regime of motion along the extremal $v = v_0$. The current limiter in the armature circuit of the generator reduces excitation of the generator when the armature current reaches the maximum admissible value I_{max}, and therefore, the locomotive automatically goes over into the regime $s'' = s''_{max}$ at low velocities. A conventional field-attenuation system (not shown in Fig. 70) regulates the magnetic flux of the traction engines (prime mover).

The control system pictured in Fig. 70 is semi-automatic. It assumes the participation of the motorman, but his role is reduced to adjusting the value of the velocity v_0 and to selecting the time to disconnect the diesel before stopping the locomotive so as to assure the train's being just at the designated location when the durations of the coasting and deceleration portions are taken into account. Moreover, the motorman may disconnect the automatic system and go over to manual control in emergency situations (appearance of strange objects on the roadway, appearance of a signal requiring a reduction in velocity, etc.). The amount of work for the motorman is reduced substantially with such a control system, which permits the motorman to turn all his attention to assuring the safety and economy of the motion.

Hence, the optimum motion regime may be realized by a simpler control system than the existing system, and may, at the same time, lighten the motorman's workload considerably.

Let us note that this control system may also realize the regime of the greatest capability of the locomotive when the fuel consumption is not restricted but it is necessary to complete the run in the shortest time (or to haul the greatest possible weight within a given time). The regime of greatest capability consists entirely of motion along the domain boundaries, i.e., either $s'' = s''_{max}$ or $p = p_{max}$ or $v = v_{max}$. This regime will be realized by the control system shown in Fig. 70 if the limiting admissible velocity v_{max} is inserted instead of the velocity v_0 of motion along the extremal.

45. Amplitude and Frequency Control of Asynchronous Electric Motors

Asynchronous squirrel-cage motors may be controlled by changing either the amplitude of the voltage applied to the motor terminals, or the frequency. Correspondingly, we shall differentiate amplitude control, when the delivered voltage changes only in amplitude at a constant frequency, and frequency control, when the amplitude and frequency change simultaneously.

Let us consider amplitude control for such an asynchronous motor. Let us make the following assumptions, which are customary in the theory of asynchronous machines.

(1) We replace the actual by an idealized magnetization curve (Fig. 62, curve *b*), i.e., we assume no saturation for $\Phi < 1$. Hence, the magnetic flux

of the motor will be sinusoidal. Henceforth, when speaking of the magnitude of the magnetic flux and the voltage we shall mean their effective values.

(2) We neglect the free components in the stator and rotor currents, i.e., we do not take account of electromagnetic transients which occur immediately after energizing the motor into the grid.

Taking these assumptions into account, the torque of a squirrel-cage motor may be expressed by the following formula

$$M = \Phi^2 \frac{\psi(s)}{s}, \tag{47}$$

where s is the slip.

The equation of equilibrium of the moments at the shaft becomes

$$\Phi^2 \frac{\psi(s)}{s} = -\frac{ds}{dt} + M_{\text{resist.}}, \tag{48}$$

and the rotor losses are expressed by the integral

$$Q = \int_0^T \Phi^2 \psi(s)\, dt \tag{49}$$

(we shall not consider the selection of the measurement units assuring absence of dimensional coefficients in (47)–(49)).

In these formulas $\psi(s)$ is some function of the slip s dependent on the dimensions and shape of the rotor cage. As we shall see below, the specific form of this function is not essential, hence, the deductions obtained later will be equally valid for motors with a squirrel cage of circular rods as well as for deep groove and two-cage motors.

Let us consider the starting process of an asynchronous motor. As is known, a considerable quantity of heat is evolved in the rotor during start-up and this may lead to overheating of the rotor with frequent starts.

Let us pose the problem: Find the control law for the voltage on the motor terminals which would assure minimum losses in the rotor during acceleration of the motor from the initial slip $s = 1$ to the final slip s_{final} (it is customary to take $s_{\text{final}} = 0$), taking account of the constraint $\Phi \leqslant 1$ and the constraints of the voltage drop in the grid when starting the motor.

It is difficult to seek the optimum voltage control law directly. It is much more convenient to find the law of magnetic-flux change first.

Replacing the variable t in the integral (49) by the variable s on the basis of the coupling equation (48), we arrive at the following problem of the calculus of variations: Find the function $\Phi^2(s)$ yielding the minimum of the integral

$$Q = \int_{s_{\text{final}}}^{1} \Phi^2\psi(s)\, ds \bigg/ \left(\frac{\Phi^2\psi(s)}{s} - M_{\text{resist.}} \right). \tag{50}$$

Since the integrand is independent of the derivative of the desired function, the functional (50) is degenerate.

Taking the derivative, we see that

$$\frac{\partial}{\partial \Phi^2}\left[\Phi^2\psi(s) \bigg/ \left(\frac{\Phi^2\psi(s)}{s} - M_{\text{resist.}} \right)\right] = -\frac{M_{\text{resist.}}\psi(s)}{(M - M_{\text{resist.}})^2}, \tag{51}$$

and the derivative does not vanish for any $\Phi^2(s)$ for $M_{\text{resist.}} > 0$; it remains negative and tends to zero as $\Phi^2(s) \to \infty$. This indicates that the armature losses diminish monotonely for $M_{\text{resist.}} > 0$ as the magnetic flux increases and tend to a limit as $\Phi \to \infty$ equal to

$$Q_{\min} = \int_{s_{\text{final}}}^{1} s\, ds. \tag{52}$$

For $M_{\text{resist.}} = 0$ the rotor losses are independent of Φ^2 and equal

$$Q_{\text{x.x}} = \int_{s_{\text{final}}}^{1} s\, ds. \tag{53}$$

It is proved in the theory of asynchronous motors that the integral (53) is numerically equal to the kinetic energy of the mass of the rotor and the load set into motion. This is the minimal possible value of the losses in the rotor of an asynchronous motor. For $M_{\text{resist.}} > 0$ the losses in the rotor increase. The role of the magnetic-flux regulation is constrained so as to minimize the increase in rotor losses caused by the presence of a resistance moment.

No extremals exist for the functional (50). The extremum is achieved on the domain boundary, at $\Phi = 1$. Hence, the optimum regulation of the voltage on the motor terminals should maintain its magnetic flux constant and equal to the maximal possible value according to saturation conditions. Knowing the active and inductive resistances of the stator and rotor, the voltage regulation law may be found as a function of the slip $u(s)$, which would assure constant magnetic flux in the motor.

Results of a computation for a motor with the following specifications are given in Fig. 71.

Power	155 kW
Synchronized rotational velocity	1500 rpm
Nominal voltage	220 V
Stator resistance: active	0.0102 ohm
inductive	0.06 ohm
Rotor resistance: active	0.0127 ohm
inductive	0.0552 ohm

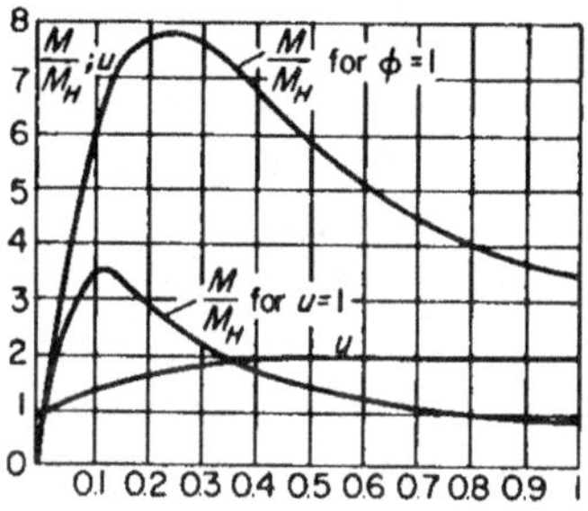

FIG. 71

The voltage $u(s)$ (in portions of the nominal voltage), assuring constant magnetic flux, and the moments of the motor (in portions of the nominal moment) for constant voltage on the motor terminals and constant magnetic flux are shown in Fig. 71. The motor torque for the control law $\Phi = 1$ increases substantially as compared with the $u = 1$ regime. The high-speed of the driver increases, but the rotor losses are lowered. However, it should be taken into account that significant current surges, several times greater than the nominal current, occur in starting up an asynchronous motor. These current surges may cause undesirable voltage fluctuations in the power net.

The magnitude of the starting current in the $\Phi = 1$ regime increases as compared with the $u = 1$ regime. Hence, in those cases when the motor is fed from an insufficient power net, the voltage at the motor terminals is not increased at start-up, but conversely, is decreased although this also leads to a stretching out of the start-up time and an increase in rotor losses.

We have examined squirrel-cage motors whose resistance depends on the slip, but is independent of the current.

Motors with a heavy ferromagnetic rotor whose parameters are functions of both the slip and the rotor current are also of interest. Among this type of motor are intrinsically asynchronous motors with a heavy smooth steel rotor and synchronous motors with heavy poles.

As a rule synchronous motors are started up in the asynchronous regime, and it is particularly important to seek the optimum voltage regulation law for them at the start, since an asynchronous start-up often results in an undesirable temperature rise in the rotor body (particularly for high-power motors).

In the case of a heavy rotor the rotating magnetic field of the stator induces a current in the surface layer which creates a torque during interaction with the stator field. The depth of penetration of these currents depends on the frequency in the rotor, i.e., on the slip of the motor. The depth of penetration is small at the initial instant of start-up, and this results in a high current density and saturation of the steel. Hence, the currents in the rotor, and therefore, the torque of the motor depend on both the slip and on the rotor current, i.e., $M = M(I; s)$. The equation of equilibrium of moments at the shaft becomes

$$M(I; s) = -\frac{ds}{dt} + M_{\text{resist.}} \tag{54}$$

and the rotor losses are expressed by the integral

$$Q = \int_0^T Ms\, dt. \tag{55}$$

Replacing the variable t in (55) by the variable s on the basis of the coupling equation, we obtain the following problem of the calculus of variations: Find the function $I(s)$ yielding the minimum of the degenerate functional

$$Q = \int_{s_{\text{final}}}^{1} \frac{Ms}{M - M_{\text{resist.}}}\, ds = \int_{s_{\text{final}}}^{1} F(I; s)\, ds. \tag{56}$$

Evaluating the derivative

$$\frac{\partial F}{\partial I}=\frac{\dfrac{\partial M}{\partial I}\,s(M-M_{\text{resist.}})-\dfrac{\partial M}{\partial I}\,Ms}{(M-M_{\text{resist.}})^2}=-\frac{\partial M}{\partial I}\cdot\frac{M_{\text{resist.}}s}{(M-M_{\text{resist.}})^2}, \tag{57}$$

we see that we will have $\partial F/\partial I<0$ for $M_{\text{resist.}}>0$ in the case of compliance with the inequality

$$\partial M/\partial I>0. \tag{58}$$

Therefore, when the condition (58) is satisfied the rotor losses will diminish monotonely as the rotor current increases (i.e., as the voltage on the motor terminals increases). Taking account of the constraint $\Phi\leqslant 1$ we establish that $\Phi=1$ is the optimum voltage regulation law for all motors satisfying the condition (58).

Condition (58) is sufficiently general and practically all synchronous and asynchronous motors satisfy it. Thus, for the Shenfer motor

$$M=I^{1.5}s^{-0.5} \tag{59}$$

and

$$\frac{\partial M}{\partial I}=1.5I^{0.5}s^{-0.5}>0.$$

The constraint on the admissible voltage fluctuations in the power net should understandably be taken into account also in the practical realization of voltage regulation during start-up of large synchronous motors. Hence, it is often attempted to diminish, rather than increase, the starting current in the interests of the net, although this results in a rise in rotor heat losses, as has been proved above.

Let us turn to an investigation of the optimum frequency control of an asynchronous motor. Realization of frequency control is more complicated than realization of amplitude control. To regulate the amplitude it is sufficient to use a saturation choke, regulating transformer or autotransformer while to accomplish frequency control it is necessary to have a separate variable frequency supply source. Furthermore the efficiency of frequency control is much higher than of amplitude control.

In considering frequency control, let us introduce a new assumption which we did not use in the analysis of the amplitude control, namely; let us assume that the rotor parameters are independent of the frequency. Consequently, we see that this assumption is valid and applicable since the motor operates all the time at such small slips, under optimum frequency control, that displacement of the current in the rotor rods can be completely neglected.

We have two independent parameters in frequency control, which can be utilized for the control: these are the supply voltage u and its frequency f. However, it is difficult to seek the law of variation of these parameters directly (a complicated equation relating the voltage and the moment must be considered, and as complicated a constraint is imposed by the saturation conditions of the magnetic circuit on the limiting supply voltage at the variable frequency). Hence, instead of a direct determination of u and f, let us seek optimum control laws for the magnetic flux Φ of the motor and the frequency ω in the rotor. Knowing these quantities, we may find the supply voltage and its frequency.

Let us derive the equation relating the motor torque and the magnetic flux and frequency in the rotor. The torque is directly proportional to the rotor losses and inversely proportional to the current frequency; therefore,

$$M_{\text{motor}} = \frac{I^2 r}{\omega_P}, \tag{60}$$

where I is the rotor current; r its active resistance; ω_P the frequency in the rotor.

Since

$$I^2 = E^2/Z^2, \tag{61}$$

where E is the rotor emf proportional to the product of the magnetic flux of the motor Φ by the rotor frequency ω, and Z is the total impedance of the rotor equal to $Z = (r^2 + L^2\omega^2)^{1/2}$, where L is the rotor inductance then

$$M_{\text{motor}} \equiv \frac{\Phi^2 \omega_P}{r^2 + L^2 \omega_P{}^2}. \tag{62}$$

Now, if the frequency in the rotor is expressed in fractions of the critical frequency at which the active resistance of the rotor equals its inductive impedance (i.e., $r = L\omega_{\text{crit.}}$), and the torque is expressed in fractions of the maximum moment (i.e., the moment at $\Phi = 1$ and $\omega_P = \omega_{\text{crit.}}$), then it is possible to go from proportionality to equality in (62) and to write

$$M = \frac{2\Phi^2\omega}{1+\omega^2}. \tag{63}$$

Expressing the rotational velocity of the motor in fractions of the synchronous velocity at the greatest possible supply frequency f_m and the time in fractions of the mechanical time constant

$$T_{\text{mech.}} = GD^2 n_C / 375 M_{\text{crit.}}$$

where GD^2 is the flywheel moment of the motor and the load ($\text{kg}\cdot\text{m}^2$) referred to the motor shaft; n_C is the synchronous number of revolutions per minute; and $M_{\text{crit.}}$ is the maximum torque of the motor ($\text{kg}\cdot\text{m}$) (for $\Phi = 1$ and $\omega = \omega_{\text{crit.}}$) we obtain the following equilibrium equation for the moments at the motor shaft:

$$M = \frac{dv}{d\tau} + \mu, \tag{64}$$

where

$$v = \frac{n_{\text{motor}}}{n_C}; \qquad \mu = \frac{M_{\text{resist.}}}{M_{\text{crit.}}}; \qquad \tau = \frac{t}{T_{\text{mech.}}}.$$

The rotor losses in the motor will equal the integral

$$Q = \int_0^T \frac{2\Phi^2\omega^2}{1+\omega^2}\, d\tau, \tag{65}$$

where the rotor losses for $M = M_{\text{crit.}}$ at the time $t = T_{\text{mech.}}$ are taken as the unit.

Now, a mathematical formulation of the optimum control problem may be given. Let us start with accelerating motors for which to find the optimum control law; this means to find that pair of functions $\Phi(\tau)$ and $\omega(\tau)$, connected by the coupling equation (64), which, by assuring a given level of motor acceleration in a given time (i.e., for a given value of the integral $\Delta v = \int_0^T v'\, d\tau$), would yield minimum losses in the rotor, i.e., would yield the minimum of the integral (65) taking account of the constraint $\Phi \leqslant 1$.

This is the general Lagrange problem of the calculus of variations with the intermediate function

$$H = \frac{2\Phi^2\omega^2}{1+\omega^2} + \lambda_0 v' + \lambda\left(\frac{dv}{d\tau} + \mu_0 - \frac{2\Phi^2\omega}{1+\omega^2}\right), \tag{66}$$

where λ_0 is a constant, and λ a function of τ.

The desired functions ω, v, Φ^2 should satisfy three Euler equations for H.

The first Euler equation (for the function ω) is

$$\frac{2\omega}{1-\omega^2} = \lambda. \tag{67}$$

The second equation (for the function v) is

$$d\lambda/d\tau = 0, \tag{68}$$

and, finally, the third Euler equation requires that the derivative $\partial H/\partial\Phi^2$ should vanish. But

$$\frac{\partial H}{\partial \Phi^2} = \frac{2\omega^2}{1+\omega^2} - \lambda\frac{2\omega}{1+\omega^2}. \tag{69}$$

Substituting λ from (67) in this expression, we obtain

$$\frac{\partial H}{\partial \Phi^2} = -\frac{2\omega^2}{1-\omega^2},$$

i.e., the derivative does not vanish anywhere (since $\omega \leqslant 1$). The extremum is achieved on the domain boundary where $\Phi = 1$.

It follows from (67) and (68) that $\omega = \text{const}$, meaning that $M = \text{const}$, for optimum control.

To verify the Legendre condition it is convenient to reduce the Lagrange problem to an isoperimetric problem. To do this, let us replace the variable ω in the integral (65) by the variable v on the basis of the coupling equation (64), and taking account of $\Phi = 1$, we obtain an isoperimetric problem with the intermediate function

$$H_1 = 1 - (1 - (v' + \mu_0)^2)^{1/2} + \lambda_0 v', \tag{70}$$

for which

$$\frac{\partial^2 H_1}{\partial v^2} = \frac{1}{(1-M^3)^{3/2}}, \tag{71}$$

where $M = \nu' + \mu_0$. Since $|M| \leqslant 1$, then $\partial^2 H_1/\partial \nu'^2 > 0$ and the minimum loss in the armature is achieved on the extremals $\omega = \text{const}$.

For $\omega = \text{const}$ and $M = \text{const}$ the rotational velocity of the rotor will increase linearly, and therefore, the frequency of the supply source should also change linearly.

The final result may now be formulated: In optimum frequency control of an accelerating asynchronous motor the supply frequency varies linearly, the motor torque remains constant, and the voltage changes in such a way that the magnetic flux of the motor remains constant and equal to the maximal possible value according to saturation conditions.

Frequency control is effective also for motors used to displace a load as well as for accelerating motors. The optimum control law will however be altogether different than for accelerating motors.

In this case the optimum control problem is formulated as a problem for the functions $\Phi^2(\tau)$, $\omega(\tau)$, $\nu(\tau)$, to yield the maximum of the integral

$$\alpha = \int_0^T \nu \, d\tau$$

(the displacement angle of the load) for a given value of the integral (65) (the rotor losses) and the coupling equation (64). This is the general Lagrange problem with the intermediate function

$$H = \nu + \lambda_0 \frac{2\Phi^2\omega^2}{1+\omega^2} + \lambda\left(\nu' + \mu_0 - \frac{2\Phi^2\omega}{1+\omega^2}\right). \tag{72}$$

Exactly as for the intermediate function (66), we see that the derivative $\partial H/\partial \Phi^2$ does not vanish and the extremum is achieved on the domain boundary for $\Phi = 1$. Therefore, the optimum voltage regulation law reduces to the simple condition $\Phi = 1$ even in this case, i.e., to maintain the magnetic flux of the motor constant.

For $\Phi = 1$ the Euler equations for the intermediate function (72) are

$$\frac{2\omega}{1+\omega^2} = \frac{\lambda}{\lambda_0}; \qquad \lambda' - 1 = 0, \tag{73}$$

from which we obtain by eliminating λ,

$$\frac{2\omega}{1-\omega^2} = C + \frac{\tau}{\lambda_0}. \tag{74}$$

To verify the Legendre condition, it is convenient to eliminate λ in advance by expressing ω in terms of v on the basis of the coupling equation, and to reduce the Lagrange problem to an isoperimetric problem with the intermediate function

$$H_1 = v + \lambda_0(1 - (1 - (v' + \mu_0)^2)^{1/2}),$$

for which

$$\frac{\partial^2 H_1}{\partial v'^2} = \lambda_0 \frac{1}{(1 - M^2)^{3/2}}. \tag{75}$$

Therefore, the sign of $\partial^2 H_1/\partial v'^2$ agrees with the sign of λ_0 and the maximum displacement will be achieved for $\lambda_0 < 0$, i.e., when the frequency in the rotor and the torque will decrease with time.

Since the sign of $\partial^2 H_1/\partial v'^2$ is independent of v and τ, the Weierstrass condition is then satisfied and a strong (local) maximum is reached on the extremals.

Examples of optimum frequency control are given in Figs. 72 and 73. The law of torque variation as a function of the time is almost linear for small control effects, when the motor torque is small.

A control (the acceleration section of a drive) taking account of the constraint on the maximal possible supply frequency is shown in Fig. 74. The tangent to the extremal $v(\tau)$ at the point conjugating the extremal and the boundary curve is continuous.

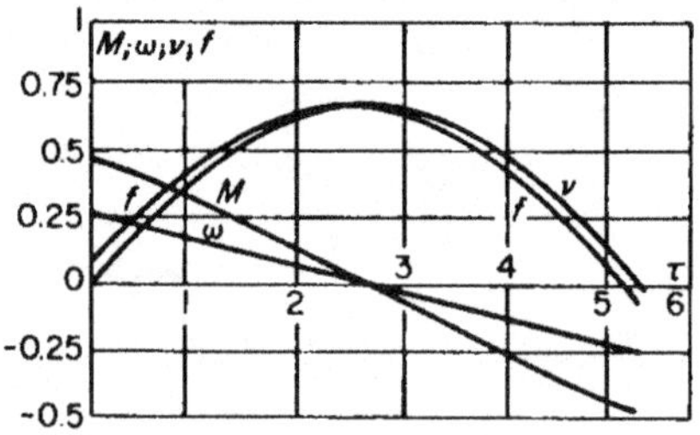

FIG. 72

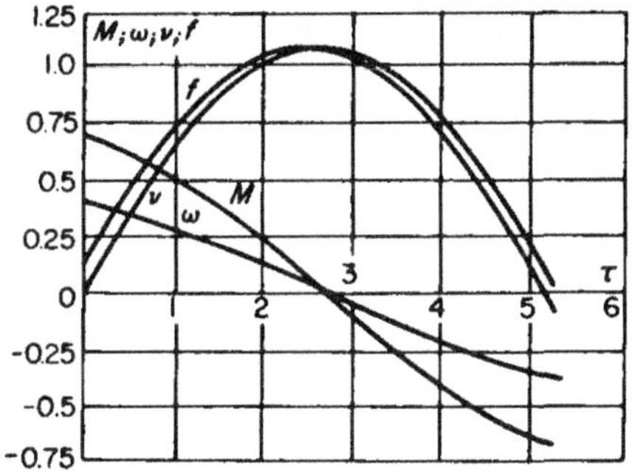

FIG. 73

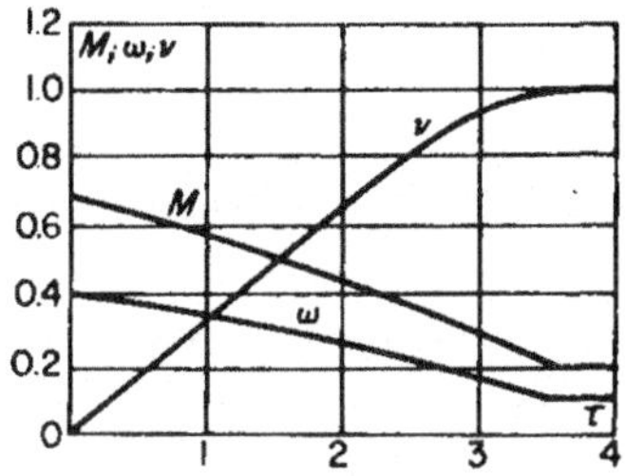

FIG. 74

More detailed results on the method of determining the coefficients in the extremal equations, on reduction of rotor losses with an optimum control as compared with other possible control laws, as well as on the control of a motor with a phase rotor may be found in the work of Petrov [111].

Appendix I: Historical Survey

The calculus of variations was born at the very end of the seventeenth century. This was the time of explosive and rapid development of mathematical methods, the time of the very great upheaval in mathematics about which Engels wrote in "Dialectics of Nature": "The turning point in mathematics was the Cartesian *variable.* Because of it, *motion* and *dialectics* entered mathematics, and consequently, differential and integral calculus rapidly became necessary, immediately originated, and was generally and wholly perfected, and not invented by Newton and Leibniz."*

The newly discovered methods of differential calculus were used at once to solve many important practical maximum and minimum problems. Problems where the maximum and minimum depended not on the selection of some value of the independent variable but on the selection of the function as a whole occupied a special niche. An example of such a problem, first considered by Newton in 1687, was the choice of the shape of a ship's hull to assure minimum drag of the water. This is a typical variational problem.

However, the Swiss mathematician J. Bernoulli (1667–1748) was the first to observe the specifics of a new kind of extremum problem. In June 1696 Bernoulli posed the brachistochrone problem to mathematicians. The problem was formulated thus: Among all lines connecting two given points, to find that curve traversed in the shortest time by a material body under the effect of gravity.

Leibniz solved this, by his own definition, "beautiful but as yet unheard of problem," and asked Bernoulli to give mathematicians a year to cope

* F. Engels, "Dialectics of Nature," p. 206. Gospolitizdat, 1952.

with its solution. Bernoulli agreed and again published his problem in January 1697, accompanying it with the following appeal: "I, Jean Bernoulli, greet the cleverest mathematicians in the world! Nothing is more attractive to highly intelligent people than a difficult, and moreover, honorable problem whose solution is possible and will endow fame and remain an eternal memorial. I hope to earn the gratitude of the whole scientific community if, by the example of Pascal, Fermat, etc., I set a problem before the best mathematicians of our time, which would afford them the opportunity of testing whether those methods they possess are good, and how great is the strength of their intellect. If someone finds the solution of the proposed problem and communicates it to me, I shall then publicly declare him to be worthy of praise."

Three solutions were given before the time had elapsed: one was due to Jacob Bernoulli, another to L'Hopital, and the third was published without the author's signature. Jean Bernoulli recognized the author "by his lion's claws," as he expressed it. The solution was Newton's.

In subsequent years, Jean Bernoulli, his older brother Jacob, Leibniz and others solved separate variational problems. However, the honor of creating a single method of solving variational problems belongs exclusively and indubitably to Leonhard Euler (1707–1783).

In 1732, when Euler was only 25 years old, he brought forth the work "General Solution of the Isoperimetric Problem Taken in Its Most General Sense." Euler did not consider separate particular problems therein, but generally, "problems where curves are sought which possess the maximum or minimum property." In subsequent years, Euler returned over and over again to variational problems, and finally, surveyed his research in 1744 [1].

In contrast to his predecessors, Euler considers concrete variational problems as a particular case of the general problem: Find the curve $y(x)$ yielding the extremum of some "integral expression" of the form

$$W = \int_{x_0}^{x_1} Z(x; y; y'; y'', \dots, y^{(n)})\, dx. \tag{1}$$

Euler found that the desired curve should satisfy the differential equation

$$Z_y - \frac{d}{dx} Z_{y'} + \frac{d^2}{dx^2} Z_{y''} - \cdots = 0. \tag{2}$$

Later, Euler used (2) directly in solving specific examples, thereby reducing the variational problem to the problem of integrating differential equations. Hence, Euler created the algorithm for solving variational problems.

Besides standard functionals of the type (1), Euler also investigated functionals which are a product, quotient, or generally, an arbitrary function of definite integrals. Euler also derived formulas (85) and (88) of Section 36.

In addition to the simplest problems, Euler also considered the conditional extremum and proved the mnemonic rule, which permits reduction of the isoperimetric to the simplest problem.

The content of the Euler treatise is generally astounding in its bounty, although the rigor of the exposition is certainly far from modern requirements. In deriving (2) Euler replaces the desired function $y(x)$ by a broken line with a large number of links, whereupon the variational problem reduces to the usual determination of the extremum of a function of a large number of variables, and he then passes to the limit without troubling to find a basis for the validity of the passage to the limit.

The disadvantages of the Euler method, awkward even for functionals dependent on one variable, are perceived particularly acutely in investigations of problems on the extremum of multiple integrals.

The creation of a specific method for the investigation of variational problems, the method of variations, is associated with the name of Lagrange (J. L. Lagrange, 1736–1813). Lagrange first expounded his method in a letter of 12 August 1755 to Euler. Euler was then already a universally known scientist, while Lagrange was 19 years old and had not yet published any scientific work. Euler rapidly responded to the Lagrange letter, warmly endorsed the new method, and a correspondence lasting many years was established between them. On Euler's recommendation, Lagrange was elected a foreign member of the Berlin Academy in 1756. Euler found what he had long sought, a simple and convenient analytical method of investigation, in the letters of the young Lagrange.

In later years, Euler worked intensively on perfecting and developing the Lagrange method. However, Euler did not publish his results, awaiting the publication of the Lagrange work. On 2 October 1759, Euler wrote to Lagrange, "Your analytical solution of the isoperimetric problem contains, insofar as I can see, all that may be desired in this area, and I am extremely happy that this theory, which I hardly touched upon after my first attempts, has been brought to such very great perfection by you.

"The importance of the question stimulated me to the extent that I, by using your illumination, derived a very analytical solution; however, I resolved to hide it until you had published your results, since I do not in any way wish to deprive you of any part of the honor due you."

Lagrange's works were published in 1760–1761. A solution of the variational problems with moving ends is given there; the transversality conditions are derived. Lagrange also investigated the problem of the extremum of multiple integrals, although M. V. Ostrogradskii gave the complete solution only in 1834. Equation (2) was derived in a modern manner in the Lagrange works, in terms of variations, although the very name "calculus of variations" appeared somewhat later in the work of Euler, continuing and expanding the Lagrange work [10].

The Lagrange-Euler methods reduce to a study of the first variation of the functional. Nothing was said about sufficient conditions. Euler clearly recognized that a maximum or minimum may be reached on the extremals, but neither a maximum nor a minimum may be generally achieved. However, Euler did not give a method to distinguish between maximums and minimums, but recommended making a judgment each time directly from the physical sense of the formulated problem.

The French mathematician A. M. Legendre (1752–1833) gave the criterion for differentiating between the maximum and minimum in 1786.

Investigating the second variation of the functional

$$J = \int_a^b F(x; y; y')\, dx,$$

Legendre reduced it to the form

$$\delta^2 J = \frac{1}{2} \int_a^b F_{y'y'} \left(\delta y' + \frac{F_{yy'} + v}{F_{y'y'}} \delta y \right)^2 dx, \tag{3}$$

where v satisfies the differential equation

$$F_{y'y'} \left(F_{yy} + \frac{dv}{dx} \right) = (F_{yy'} + v)^2, \tag{4}$$

from which the deduction is made that a minimum of the functional is reached for $F_{y'y'} > 0$ and a maximum for $F_{y'y'} < 0$. Legendre also made analogous studies of functionals dependent on higher order derivatives. Legendre soon recognized that his investigations could not possibly be considered rigorous because it was still necessary to prove the existence of the solution of (4). Lagrange raised a decisive objection against the Legendre theory in 1797. He showed that the Legendre criterion permits differentiation between the maximum and minimum if they exist and are reached on the extremals, but does not yield sufficient conditions for the existence of the extremum.

The sufficient conditions for the (weak) extremum were found by the German mathematician Jacobi (1804–1851), a professor at Koenigsberg University, and he published them in 1837. Jacobi first went from the investigation of individual curves to the investigation of the field of extremals, and thereby found his criterion which he formulated as the absence of any intersection of two infinitely close extremals.

The complete proof of the Jacobi criterion was given by Hesse (1811–1874) in 1857.

However, exactly as Lagrange, Euler, and others, Jacobi did not distinguish between the concept of a strong and a weak extremum. In utilizing the variations it was tacitly assumed that both δy, as well as $\delta y'$ are small. This led to many difficulties and paradoxes.

Weierstrass (1815–1897) gave a rigorous theory for the weak and strong extremums.

Weierstrass showed the inadequacy of the intuitive conceptions on the absolute existence of extremals for a bounded functional. He presented the example of the functional

$$\int_{-1}^{+1} x^2 y'^2 \, dx,$$

whose minimum, zero, is achieved outside the limits of the class of piecewise-smooth functions.

Besides the smooth extremals, extremals having a break point or discontinuity have been studied since the second half of the nineteenth century. In 1865 Weierstrass and Erdmann in 1875 established conditions which an extremal should satisfy at a break point.

The theory of discontinuous extremals has been worked out by the Soviet mathematician A. M. Razmadze (1890–1929), and more recently by Krotov [5, 6].

Direct methods of solving variational problems were proposed by Ritz (1878–1909) and B. A. Galerkin (1871–1915) in 1915.

Variational problems taking into account the constraints imposed on the desired functions or their derivatives (i.e., problems of finding the extremum in a closed domain) have been considered off-and-on by mathematicians even in the nineteenth century. Apparently the first such problem was solved by Goldschmidt in 1831. Later, Airy solved problems with constraints in 1861, Todhunter in 1871, and others [11]. In 1889, Markov [16] examined a problem where the constraints were imposed not only on the desired function but also on its derivative.

In 1913, Garnett [11] gave a general formulation of the fundamental theorem of the calculus of variations for a closed domain: in the general case, the curve on which the extremum is achieved is a composite curve consisting of integral curves of the solution of the Euler equations and segments of the domain boundary.

Conditions permitting the finding of transition points from the extremals to the domain boundary and back are also presented in the Garnett work [11].

Variational methods did not receive widespread acceptance in the engineering practice of the late nineteenth and early twentieth centuries. A sudden transition set in with the development of aviation, especially rocketry. Numerous problems on the best control of aircraft, rockets, artificial earth satellites revived interest in variational methods. If variational methods had been applied earlier, primarily to problems where the extremals could be sought in an open domain of variation of the variables, now variational methods were applied to the determination of optimum control laws, first for aircraft and rockets, and then for other engineering objects such as electric motors, heat-treatment furnaces, etc.

Numerous works on this topic appeared both here and abroad [76–122].

A new branch of automatic regulation, optimum control theory, was created. In optimum control theory it is necessary to deal with numerous problems of the control of systems in whose equations the desired functions enter linearly. For such cases the length of portions of the extremal usually vanishes, and it is necessary to find the point of transition from one constraint to another. Classical variational methods are inconvenient for such problems (an additional passage to the limit is required). The demand arose for new mathematical methods. A number of works devoted to the "maximum principle" appeared. This principle was first proposed by Boltianskii *et al.* as a hypothesis in 1956 [15].

This principle was proved soon after; first in 1957 for linear systems [18], and then in 1958 for the general case of optimality of fast response [20, 21]. Finally, a summary of the researches of Pontriagin *et al.* was presented in 1961 [42]. The set of works of L. S. Pontriagin and his colleagues was awarded the Lenin Prize in 1962.

Appendix II: Glossary

Functional A variable quantity dependent on a function (or several functions). Examples of functionals: (1) the quantity of heat being liberated in an armature winding during the time T; the function on which the functional depends is the armature current (a function of the time); (2) fuel consumption by a locomotive traversing a given portion of a run; the function on which the functional depends is the velocity of locomotive motion (a function of time).

Continuous Functions Functions without discontinuities and jumps; an infinitesimal increment in the function corresponds to infinitesimal increments in the independent variable.

Smooth Functions Functions with a continuous first derivative are understood to be smooth functions in this book. Such functions may not have breakpoints.

Piecewise-Smooth Functions Functions which are smooth everywhere except at individual isolated points.

Class of Functions A set of functions united by a common property. These properties may be of generally theoretical nature (as for example, it is possible to speak of the class of continuous functions, the class of piecewise-smooth functions), or may consist of compliance with some inequality, $y \leqslant y_m$, say, or an equation, whereupon we speak of the class of functions with given maximum ordinate, or the class of functions satisfying a given equation, etc. Extremums of functionals are always sought among functions of a definite class.

Zero-Order Distance between the Functions $y(x)$ and $y_1(x)$ The maximum of the absolute value of the distance between $y(x)$ and $y_1(x)$.

First-Order Distance between the Functions $y(x)$ and $y_1(x)$ The maximum of the absolute value of the distance between either the functions themselves, or between their derivatives $y'(x)$ and $y_1'(x)$, depending on which of the maximums is greater.

Extremum Extreme value of the variable; its maximum or minimum.

Absolute Extremum of a Functional The extremum as compared with all other functions (curves) of the given class.

Relative Extremum of a Functional Extremum as compared with nearby functions, i.e., those to which the distance does not exceed some given number ε prescribed in advance. A relative extremum may be either strong or weak.

Weak Relative Extremum An extremum as compared with functions to which the first-order distance is small.

Strong Relative Extremum An extremum as compared with functions to which the zero order distance is small but the first-order distance may be arbitrary.

Variation of a Function The difference between two functions, customarily the difference between the desired function $y(x)$, on which the extremum of the functional is achieved, and a nearby function $y_1(x)$. The variation is denoted by the letter δ, i.e.,

$$\delta y = y(x) - y_1(x).$$

Variating of the Function $y(x)$ A change in the function, the addition of an arbitrary variation δy to the function $y(x)$.

Varied Function Function to which a variation has been appended.

Increment of a Functional The difference in values of the functional for a function $y(x)$ and for another function $y + \delta y$. The increment of a functional ΔJ may be expanded in a series of variations:

$$\Delta J = \delta J + \delta^2 J + \cdots,$$

where δJ, $\delta^2 J$, etc., are respectively, the first, second, etc., variations of the functional.

First Variation of a Functional The smooth, linear portion of the increment of a functional. It depends linearly on the variation of the desired function and may be written thus

$$\delta J = \int_a^b \left[F_y - \frac{d}{dx} F_{y'} \right] \delta y \, dx,$$

i.e., equal to the integral of the product of the variation of the desired function δy by the expression in the square brackets, called the functional derivative.

Extremal Integral curve of the Euler equation.

Broken-Line Extremal A curve composed of different integral curves of the solutions of the Euler equation, where the Weierstrass-Erdmann conditions are satisfied at the juncture points.

Simplest Problem of the Calculus of Variations Finding the function (curve) yielding an extremum of the functional, which depends on one unknown function and its first derivative, under the condition that the ends of the desired function are given.

Problem with Moving Endpoints Determination of the extremum of a functional when the endpoints of the desired function are not given in advance but are determined on the basis of the transversality condition.

Conditional Extremum Problem Seeking the function yielding the extremum of the functional and simultaneously satisfying some additional conditions (the coupling equations).

General Lagrange Problem A conditional extremum problem when some of the coupling equations are differential equations. This is the most general of all the problems of calculus of variations. The rest of the problems are particular cases or its equivalent.

Single-Sided Extremum Problem A problem to seek the function yielding the extremum of the functional and simultaneously satisfying some inequality (or system of inequalities). Such problems are still called extremum problems in a closed domain.

Closed Domain A bounded domain of variation of the variables, including the boundary itself. Thus, all values of $y(x)$ satisfying the inequality $y \leqslant y_m$ (i.e., all $y < y_m$ and $y = y_m$) form a closed domain.

Field A family of curves disposed in the domain D in such a way that one and only one curve of the family passes through each point.

Local Extremum If the Euler, Lagrange, and Weierstrass conditions are satisfied, then a local extremum is achieved, i.e., the extremum is reached at infinitesimal portions of the extremal, but to verify that the extremum is maintained even at large sections of the extremal it is still necessary to check the Jacobi condition.

REFERENCES

A. On Calculus of Variations

1. L. Euler, "Metod Nakhozhdeniia Krivykh Linii, Obladiaiushchikh Svoistvami Maksimuma Libo Minimuma, Ili Reshenie Izoperimetricheskoi Zadachi, Vziatoi v Samom Shirokom Smysle" ("Method of Finding Curves Possessing Maximum or Minimum Properties, or The Solution of the Isoperimetric Problem Taken in Its Broadest Sense") (translated from the 1744 ed.). GITTL, 1934.
2. M. A. Lavrent'ev and L. A. Liusternik, "Kurs Variatsionnogo Ischisleniia ("Calculus of Variations"). Gostekhizdat, 1950.
3. N. M. Giunter, "Kurs Variatsionnogo Ischisleniia" ("Calculus of Variations"). Gostekhizdat, 1941.
4. M. A. Lavrent'ev and L. A. Liusternik, "Osnovy Variatsionnogo Ischisleniia" ("Principles of the Calculus of Variations"). ONTI, 1935.
5. V. F. Krotov, Razryvnye resheniia variatsionnykh zadach (Discontinuous solutions of variational problems). *Izv. Vysshikh Uchebn. Zavedenii Mat.* No. 5 (1960); No. 2 (1961).
6. V. F. Krotov, Osnovnaia zadacha variatsionnogo ischisleniia na sovokupnosti razryvnykh funktsii (Fundamental calculus of variations problem in the set of discontinuous functions). *Dokl. Akad. Nauk.* **137,** No. 1 (1961).
7. G. A. Bliss, Lectures on Calculus of Variations, 1911.
8. L. E. Elsgol'ts, "Variatsionnoe Ischislenie" ("Calculus of Variations"). Gostekhizdat, 1958.
9. I. M. Gel'fand and S. V. Fomin, "Variatsionnoe Ischislenie" ("Calculus of Variations"). Fizmatgiz, 1961.
10. L. Euler, "Integral'noe Ischislenie", t. 3 ("Integral Calculus," vol. 3) (translated from the 1770 ed.). Fizmatgiz, 1958.
11. N. Garnett, "Ob Osnovnoi Prosteishei Zadache Variatsionnogo Ischisleniia" ("On the Fundamental Simplest Problem of Calculus of Variations"). SPB, 1913.

11a. F. Engels, "Dialectics of Nature," p. 206. Gospolitizdat, 1952.

B. On Theoretical Optimum Control Principles

12. A. A. Fel'dbaum, Optimal'nye protsessy v sistemakh avtomaticheskogo regulirovaniia (Optimum processes in automatic regulation systems). *Avtomat. i Telemeh.* **14,** No. 6 (1953).
13. A. Ia. Lerner, O predel'nom bystrodeistvii sistem avtomaticheskogo upravleniia (On the limiting fast response of automatic control systems). *Avtomat. i Telemeh.* **15,** No. 6 (1954).
14. A. A. Fel'dbaum, O sinteze optimal'nykh sistem s pomoshch'iu favozogo prostranstva (On synthesis of optimum systems using phase space). *Avtomat. i Telemeh.* **16,** No. 2 (1955).

15. V. G. Boltianskii, R. V. Gamkrelidze and L. S. Pontriagin, K teorii optimal'nykh protsessov (On the theory of optimum processes). *Dokl. Akad. Nauk SSSR*, **115**, No. 1 (1956).
16. N. N. Krasovskii, K teorii optimal'nogo regulirovaniia (On optimum regulation theory). *Avtomat. i. Telemeh.* **18**, No. 11 (1957).
17. N. N. Krasovskii, Ob odnoi zadache optimal'nogo regulirovaniia (On an optimum regulation problem). *Prikl. Mat. Meh.* **21**, No. 5 (1957).
18. R. V. Gamkrelidze, K teorii optimal'nykh protsessov v lineinykh sistemakh (On the theory of optimum processes in linear systems). *Dokl. Akad, Nauk SSSR* **116**, No. 1 (1957).
19. R. V. Gamkrelidze, Teoriia optimal'nykh po bystrodeistviiu protsessov v lineinykh (Optimum fast-response process theory in linear systems). *Izv. Akad. Nauk SSSR Ser. Mat.* **22**, No. 4 (1958).
20. R. V. Gamkrelidze, K obshchei teorii optimal'nykh protsessov (On the general theory of optimum processes). *Dokl. Akad. Nauk SSSR* **123**, No. 2 (1958).
21. V. G. Boltianskii, Printsip maksimuma v teorii optimal'nykh protsessov (Maximum principle in the theory of optimum processes). *Dokl. Akad. Nauk SSSR* **119**, No. 6 (1958).
22. F. M. Kirillova, O korrektnosti postanovki odnoi zadachi optimal'nogo upravleniia (On the correctness of the formulation of an optimum control problem). *Izv. Vysshikh Uchebn. Zavedenii Mat.* No. 4 (1958).
23. R. V. Gamkrelidze, Optimal'nye po bystrodeistviiu protsessy pri ogranichennykh fazovykh koordinatakh (Optimum fast-response processes with bounded phase coordinates). *Dokl. Akad. Nauk SSSR* **125**, No. 3 (1959).
24. L. S. Pontriagin, Optimal'nye protsessy regulirovaniia (Optimum regulation processes). *Usp. Mat. Nauk* **14**, No. 1 (1959).
25. N. N. Krasovskii, Ob odnoi zadache optimal'nogo regulirovaniia nelineinykh sistem (On an optimum regulation problem for nonlinear systems). *Prikl. Mat. Meh.* **23**, No. 2 (1959).
26. N. N. Krasovskii, K dostatochnykh usloviam optimal'nosti (On sufficient conditions for optimality). *Prikl. Mat. Meh.* **23**, No. 3 (1959).
27. N. N. Krasovskii, K. teorii optimal'nogo regulirovaniia (On optimum regulation theory). *Prikl. Mat. Meh.* **23**, No. 4 (1959).
28. V. G. Boltianskii, Optimal'nye protsessy s parametrami (Optimum processes with parameters). *Dokl. Akad. Nauk Uz. SSR* No. 10 (1959).
29. L. I. Rozonoer, O dostatochnykh usloviiakh optimal'nosti (On sufficient conditions for optimality). *Dokl. Akad. Nauk SSSR* **127**, No. 3 (1959).
30. L. I. Rozonoer, Printsip maximuma L. S. Pontriagina v teorii optimal'nykh sistem (L. S. Pontriagin maximum principle in the theory of optimum systems). *Avtomat. i Telemeh.* **20**, No. 10, 11, 12 (1959).
31. A. A. Fel'dbaum, "Vychislitel'nye Ustroistva v Avtomaticheskikh Sistemakh" ("Computer Units in Automatic Systems"). Fizmatgiz, 1959.
32. A. F. Filippov, O nekotorykh voprosakh teorii optimal'nogo regulirovaniia (On some questions of optimum regulation theory). *Vestn. Moscow Univ.* No. 2 (1959).

33. R. Bellman, "Dynamic Programming." IL, 1960.
34. V. G. Boltianskii, R. V. Gamkrelidze, and L. S. Pontriagin, Teoriia optimal'nykh protsessov (Theory of optimum processes). *Izv. Akad. Nauk SSSR Ser. Mat.* **24,** No. 1 (1960).
35. A. G. Butkovskii and A. Ia. Lerner, Ob optimal'nom upravlenii sistemami s raspredelennymi parametrami (On optimum control of systems with distributed parameters). *Avtomat. i Telemeh.* **21,** No. 6 (1960).
36. F. M. Kirillova, O predel'nom perekhode v reshenii odnoi zadachi optimal'nogo regulirovaniia (On the passage to the limit in the solution of one optimum regulation problem). *Prikl. Mat. Meh.* **24,** No. 2 (1960).
37. N. N. Krasovskii, Ob optimal'nom regulirovanii pri sluchainykh vozmushcheniiakh (On optimum regulation with random disturbances). *Prikl. Mat. Meh.* **24,** No. 1 (1960).
38. N. N. Krasovskii, O priblizhennom vychislenii optimal'nogo upravleniia priamym metodom (On the approximate calculation of an optimum control by a direct method). *Prikl. Mat. Meh.* **24,** No. 2 (1960).
39. A. M. Letov, Analiticheskoe konstruirovanie reguliatorov (Analytic construction of regulators). *Avtomat. i Telemeh.* **21,** No. 4, 5, 6 (1960).
40. Sun Tsian, Sintez optimal'noi sistemy upravleniia na osnovanii polia izokhron (Synthesis of an optimum control system on the basis of an isochrone field). *Izv. Akad. Nauk SSSR, Otd. Tekhn. Nauk Energ. i Avtomat.* No. 5 (1960).
41. Ia. Z. Tsypkin, Optimal'nye protsessy v impul'snykh avtomaticheskikh sistemakh (Optimum processes in pulsed automatic systems). *Izv. Akad. Nauk SSSR, Otd. Tekhn. Nauk Energ. i Avtomat.* No. 4 (1960).
42. L. S. Pontriagin, V. G. Boltianskii, R. V. Gamkrelidze, and E. F. Mishchenko, "Matematicheskaia Teoriia Optimal'nykh Protsessov" ("Mathematical Theory of Optimum Processes"). Fizmatgiz, 1961; Wiley (Interscience), New York, 1962.
43. V. G. Boltianskii, Dostatochnye usloviia optimal'nosti (Sufficient conditions for optimality). *Dokl. Akad. Nauk* SSSR **140,** No. 5 (1961).
44. A. G. Butkovskii, Printsip maksimuma dlia optimal'nykh sistem s raspredelennymi parametrami (Maximum principle for optimum systems with distributed parameters). *Avtomat. i Telemeh.* **22,** No. 10 (1961).
45. A. G. Butkovskii, Nekotorye priblizhennye metody resheniia zadach s raspredelennymi parametrami (Some approximate methods of solving problems with distributed parameters). *Avtomat. i Telemeh.* **22,** No. 12 (1961).
46. F. M. Kirillova, K probleme sushchestvovaniia optimal'nykh traektorii nelineinykh sistem (On the problem of the existence of optimum trajectories of nonlinear systems). *Izv. Vysshikh Uchebn. Zavedenii Mat.* No. 2 (1961).
47. N. N. Krasovskii, Ob odnom metode postroeniia optimal'nykh traektorii (On a method of constructing optimum trajectories). *Mat. Sb.* **43,** No. 2 (1961).
48. N. N. Krasovskii and E. A. Lidskii, Analiticheskoe konstruirovanie reguliatorov v sisteme so sluchainymi svoistvami (Analytic construction of regulators in a system with random properties). *Avtomat. i Telemeh.* **22,** No. 9, 10, 11 (1961).
49. E. F. Mishchenko and L. S. Pontriagin, Ob odnoi statisticheskoi zadache op-

timal'nogo upravleniia (On a statistical optimum control problem). *Izv. Akad. Nauk SSSR Ser. Mat.* **24**, No. 4 (1960).

50. V. A. Troitskii, Zadacha Maiera-Bol'tsa variatsionnogo ischisleniia i teoriia optimal'nykh sistem (Mayer-Bolza problem of the calculus of variations and the theory of optimum systems). *Prikl. Mat. Meh.* **25**, No. 4 (1961).
51. V. A. Troitskii, Zadacha Lagranzha variatsionnogo ischisleniia i teoriia optimal'nykh sistem (Lagrange problem of the calculus of variations and the theory of optimum systems). *Nauchn.-Tekhn. Inform. Byul.* (*Leningr. Politekhni. Inst.*) No. 7 (1961).
52. G. L. Kharatashvili, Printsip maksimuma v teorii optimal'nykh protsessov s zapazdyvaniem (Maximum principle in the theory of optimum processes with lag). *Dokl. Akad. Nauk SSSR* **131**, No. 1 (1961).
53. V. S. Balakirev, Printsip maksimuma v teorii optimal'nykh sistem vtorogo poriadka (Maximum principle in the theory of second order optimum systems). *Avtomat. i Telemeh.* **23**, No. 8 (1962).
54. G. Gabasov, K voprosu ob edinstvennosti optimal'nogo upravleniia v diskretnoi sisteme (On the question of the uniqueness of an optimum control in a discrete system). *Izv. Akad. Nauk SSSR Otd. Tekhn Nauk Energ. i Avtomat.* No. 5 (1962).
55. L. S. Gnoenskii, Ob odnoi zadache optimal'nogo regulirovaniia (On an optimum regulation problem). *Prikl. Mat. Meh.* **26**, No. 1 (1962).
56. L. S. Gnoenskii, K optimizatsii slediashchikh sistem (On the optimization of following systems). *Prikl. Mat. Meh.* **26**, No. 4 (1962).
57. L. S. Gnoenskii, K zadache presledovaniia (On the pursuit problem). *Prikl. Mat. Meh.* **26**, No. 5 (1962).
58. V. N. Zhigulev, Sintez optimal'nykh sistem odnogo klassa (Synthesis of one class of optimum systems). *Avtomat. i Telemeh.* **23**, No. 7 (1962).
59. D. L. Kelendzheridze, Ob odnoi zadache optimal'nogo presledovaniia (On an optimum pursuit problem). *Avtomat. i Telemeh.* **23**, No. 8 (1962).
60. N. N. Krasovskii and A. M. Letov, K teorii analiticheskogo konstruirovaniia reguliatorov (On the theory of the analytic construction of regulators). *Avtomat. i Telemeh.* **23**, No. 6 (1962).
61. N. N. Krasovskii, Ob analiticheskom konstruirovanii optimal'nogo reguliatora v sisteme s zapazdyvaniiami vremeni (On analytic construction of an optimum regulator in a system with time lags). *Prikl. Mat. Meh.* **26**, No. 1 (1962).
62. N. N. Krasovskii, Ob odnoi zadache presledovaniia (On a pursuit problem). *Prikl. Mat. Meh.* **26**, No. 2 (1962).
63. I. A. Krylov and F. L. Chernous'ko, O metode posledovatel'nykh priblizhenii dlia resheniia zadach optimal'nogo upravleniia (On a successive approximations method to solve optimum control problems). *Zh. Vychisl. Mat. i Mat. Fiz.* **2**, No. 2 (1962).
64. E. A. Lidskii, Ob analiticheskov konstruirovanii reguliatorov v sisteme so sluchainymi svoistvami (On the analytic construction of regulators in a system with stochastic properties). *Prikl. Mat. Meh.* **26**, No. 2 (1962).

65. V. S. Kisliakov, Sintez optimal'nykh sistem s posledeistviem (Synthesis of optimum systems with after-effect). *Izv. Akad. Nauk Otd. Tekhn. Nauk SSSR Energ. i Avtomat.* No. 3 (1962).
66. V. N. Novosel'tsev, Optimal'nye po bystrodeistviiu sistemy pri nalichii sluchainykh pomekh (Optimum fast-response systems in the presence of random interference). *Avtomat. i Telemeh.* **23,** No. 12 (1962).
67. M. E. Salukvadze, Ob analiticheskom konstruirovanii optimal'nykh reguliatorov pri postoianno deistvyiushchkikh vozmushcheniiakh (On the analytic construction of optimum regulators with constantly acting disturbances). *Avtomat. i Telemeh.* **23,** No. 6 (1962).
68. A. B. Savvin, Fazovye traektorii sistem, optimal'nykh po bystrodeistviiu, otnositel'no zadannoi oblast fazovoi ploskosti (Phase trajectories of optimum fast-response systems relative to a given phase-plane domain). *Izv. Akad. Nauk SSSR Otd. Tekhn. Nauk Energ. i Avtomat.* No. 1 (1962).
69. Ia. N. Roitenberg, Nekotorye zadachi dinamicheskogo programmirovaniia dlia nelineinykh impul'snykh sistem (Some dynamic programming problems for nonlinear pulse systems). *Prikl. Mat. Meh.* **26,** No. 5 (1962).
70. Ia. N. Roitenberg, O privedenii k transtsendentnym uravneniiam nekotorykh zadach dinamicheskogo programmirovaniia dlia nelineinykh sistem (On the reduction of some dynamic programming problems for nonlinear systems to transcendental equations). *Prikl. Mat. Meh.* **26,** No. 4 (1962).
71. V. A. Troitskii, O variatsionnykh zadachakh optimizatsii protsessov upravleniia (On variational problems of control process optimization). *Prikl. Mat. Meh.* **26,** No. 2 (1962).
72. V. A. Troitskii, Variatsionnye zadachi optimizatsii protsessov upravleniia dlia uravnenii s razryvnymi pravymi chastiami (Variational problems of optimizing control processes for equations with discontinuous right sides). *Prikl. Mat. Meh.* **26,** No. 1 (1962).
73. V. A. Troitskii, Variatsionnye zadachi optimizatsii protsessov upravleniia v sistemakh s ogranichennymi koordinatami (Variational problems of optimizing control processes with constrained coordinates). *Prikl. Mat. Meh.* **26,** No. 3 (1962).
74. V. A. Troitskii, Variatsionnye zadachi optimizatsii protsessov upravleniia s funktsionalami, zavisiashchimi ot promezhutochnykh znachenii koordinat (Variational problems of optimizing control processes with functionals dependent on intermediate values of the coordinates). *Prikl. Mat. Meh.* **26,** No. 6 (1962).
75. A. A. Fel'dbaum, Ob optimal'nom upravlenii markovskimi protsessami (On the optimum control of Markov processes). *Avtomat. i Telemeh.* **23,** No. 8 (1962).

C. On the Application of Variational Methods to the Solution of Engineering Problems

76. D. E. Okhotsimskii, K teorii dvizheniia raket (On the theory of rocket motion). *Prikl. Mat. Meh.* **10,** No. 2 (1946).

77. B. L. Davydov, Perspektivy i zadachi teorii rudnichnogo pod'ema (Prospects and problems of mine-hoist theory). *Ugol'* **25**, No. 11 (1950).
78. B. L. Davydov, Variatsionnye metody teorii rudnichnogo pod'ema (Variational methods of mine-hoist theory). *Sb. "Rudnichnyi pod'em" (Mine Hoists) Metallurgizdat* 1953.
79. B. Ia. Levin and S. B. Brailovskii, K voprosu o naivygodneishem dinamicheskom rezhime rudnichnogo pod'ema (On the question of the most advantageous dynamic regime of a mine hoist). *Sb. "Rudnichnyi pod'em" Metallurgizdat* 1953.
80. K. I. Kozhevnikov, Diagramma toka dvigatelei vspomogatel'nykh mekhanizmov prokatnykh stanov (Current diagram of motors of auxiliary mechanisms of rolling mills). *Elektrichestvo* No. 6 (1956).
81. K. I. Kozhevnikov, Vybor peredatochnogo chisla reduktora privodov vspomogatel'nykh mekhanizmov prokatnykh stanov (Gear ratio selection for drives of auxiliary rolling-mill mechanisms). *Elektrichestvo* No. 7 (1957).
82. D. E. Okhotsimskii and T. M. Eneev, Nekotorye variatsionnye zadachi, sviazannye s zapuskom iskusstvennogo sputnika Zemli (Some variational problems associated with the launching of an artificial earth satellite). *Usp. Fiz. Nauk* **63**, No. 1 (1957).
83. E. A. Rozenman, Ob optimal'nykh perekhodnykh protsessakh v sistemakh s ogranichennoi moshchnost'iu (On optimum transients in power-limited systems). *Avtomat. i Telemeh.* **18**, No. 6 (1957).
84. E. K. Krug and O. M. Minina, Ob optimal'nykh perekhodnykh protsessakh v sisteme avtomaticheskogo regulirovaniia s ogranicheniem polozheniia reguliruiushchego organa (On optimum transients in an automatic regulation system with a constraint on the position of the regulating organ). *Avtomat. i Telemeh.* **19**, No. 1 (1958).
85. E. A. Rozenman, O predel'nom bystrodeistvii slediashchikh sistem s ogranicheniem po moshchnosti, skorosti i momentu ispolnitel'nogo mekhanizma (On the limiting fast-response of following systems with a constraint on the power, velocity and moment of the performance mechanism). *Avtomat. i Telemeh.* **19**, No. 7 (1958).
86. Sh. Sh. Khamitov, Issledovanie dvigatelia postoiannogo toka kak ob'ekta optimal'noi sistemy regulirovaniia (Investigation of a DC motor as the object of an optimum regulation system). *Elektrichestvo* No. 5 (1958).
87. Iu. P. Petrov, Optimal'nye zakony upravleniia elektroprivodom (Optimum control laws of an electric drive). *Avtomat. i Telemeh.* **20**, No. 7 (1959).
88. Iu. P. Petrov, Razgon i tormozhenie tiagovykh elektrodvigatelei po optimal'mym zakonam (Acceleration and deceleration of electric traction motors according to optimum laws). *Izv. Vysshikh Uchebn. Zavedenii Elektromekh.* **2**, No. 5 (1959).
89. E. A. Rozenman, Optimal'noe upravlenie ob'ektom s dvumia upravliaiushchimi vozdeistviiami (Optimum control of an object with two controlling effects). *Avtomat. i Telemeh.* **20**, No. 10 (1959).
90. Sbornik perevodov (Collection of translations) "Issledovanie optimal'nykh rezhimov dvizheniia raket" ("Investigation of optimum rocket-motion regimes"). Oborongiz, 1959.

91. O. V. Slezhanovskii, Optimal'noe izmenenie osnovnykh parametrov i ratsional'naia struktura sistem upravleniia elektroprivodami (Optimum change in fundamental parameters and logical structure of control systems for an electric drive). *Elektrichestvo* No. 4 (1959).
92. Sh. Sh. Khamitov, K voprosu opredeleniia optimal'nykh diagramm toka dvigatelia postoiannogo toka (On the question of determining optimum current diagrams of a dc motor). *Dokl. Akad. Nauk SSSR* **124,** No. 2 (1959).
93. Iu. A. Gorelov, O dvukh klassakh ploskikh ekstremal'nykh dvizhenii rakety v pustote (On two classes of plane extremal rocket motions in vacuo). *Prikl. Mat. Meh.* **24,** No. 2 (1960).
94. S. V. Emel'ianov and A. I. Fedorova, Postroenie optimal'noi sistemy avtomaticheskogo regulirovaniia vtorogo poriadka s ispol'zovaniem predel'nykh znachenii koeffitsientov usileniia elementov kontur (Construction of an optimum second-order automatic regulation system utilizing limiting values of the gain coefficients of the circuit elements). *Avtomat. i Telemeh.* **21,** No. 1 (1960).
95. Lan Shi-Tsiun', Novyi metod uskoreniia perekhodnykh protsessov v sisteme avtomatizirovannogo elektroprivoda (New method of accelerating the transients in an automated electric drive system). *Rep. 1st IFAC Congr. 1960.*
96. I. A. Litovchenko, Ob odnoi zadache optimal'nogo upravleniia (On an optimum control problem). *Avtomat. i Telemeh.* **21,** No. 8 (1960).
97. G. A. Nadzhafova, Predel'nye dinamicheskie kharakteristiki silovykh ispolnitel'nykh ustroistv slediashchikh sistem (Limiting dynamic characteristics of power performing units of following systems). *Avtomat. i Telemeh.* **21,** No. 7 (1960).
98. Iu. P. Petrov, Upravlenie elektrodvigateliami postoiannogo toka izmeneniem magnitnogo potoka i napriazheniia (Control of d. electric motors by a change in magnetic flux and voltage). *Izv. Akad. Nauk SSSR Otd. Tekhn. Nauk Energ. i Avtomat,* No. 1 (1960).
99. Iu. P. Petrov, Optimal'noe chastotnoe upravlenie asinkhronnymi elektrodvigateliami (Optimum frequency control of asynchronous electric motors.) *Avtomat. i Telemeh.* **21,** No. 3 (1960).
100. Iu. P. Petrov, Optimal'noe upravlenie elektroprivodom pri momenta soprotivleniia, zavisiashchem ot puti peremeshchenii (Optimum control of an electric drive with resistance moment dependent on the stroke). *Izv. Akad. Nauk SSSR Otd. Tekhn. Nauk Energ. i Avtomat.* No. 2 (1960).
101. L. P. Smol'nikov, K voprosu ob optimal'nykh rezhimakh skorosti dlia avtomatizirovannogo reversivnogo stana goriachei prokatki (On the question of optimum velocity regimes for an automated reversing hot rolling mill). *Izv. Vysshikh Uchebn. Zavedenii Energ.* **2,** No. 8 (1960).
102. Sun Tsian', Optimal'noe upravlenie v odnoi nelineinoi sisteme (Optimum control in a nonlinear system). *Avtomat. i Telemeh.* **21,** No. 1 (1960).
103. A. E. Bor-Ramenskii and Sun Tsian', Optimal'nyi slediashchii privod s dvumia parametrami upravleniia (Optimum servodrive with two control parameters). *Avtomat. i Telemeh.* **22,** No. 2 (1961).

104. J. Breakwell, Trajectory optimization (translation). *Vopr. Raketnoi Tekhn.* No. 1 (1961).

105. V. K. Isaev, Printsip maksimuma L. S. Pontriagina i optimal'noe programmirovanie tiagi raket (L. S. Pontriagin maximum principle and optimum programming of rocket thrust). *Avtomat. i Telemeh.* **22**, No. 8 (1961).

106. V. F. Krotov, Ob optimal'nom rezhime gorizontal'nogo poleta samoleta (On the optimum horizontal flight regime of an aircraft). *Sb. statei MVTU* (Collection of papers of Moscow Higher Technical Institute) No. 104 (1961).

107. G. Leitmann, Ob optimal'nykh traektoriiakh rakety (On optimum rocket trajectories). *Prikl. Mat. Meh.* **25**, No. 6 (1961).

108. A. Ia. Lerner, "Printsipy Postroeniia Bystrodeistvuiushchikh Slediashchikh Sistem i Reguliatorov" ("Principles of Constructing Fast-Response Servo-Systems and Regulators"). Gosenergoizdat, 1961.

109. D. F. Lawden, Necessary conditions for analysis of optimum rocket trajectories (translation). *Mekhanika* No. 3 (1961).

110. V. D. Matytsyn, Opredelenie zakona upravleniia samoletom dlia polucheniia optimal'noi traektorii pri polete v usloviiakh peremennogo vetra (Determination of the control law of an aircraft to obtain an optimum fight trajectory under variable wind conditions). *Avtomat. i Telemeh.* **22**, No. 1 (1961).

111. Iu. P. Petrov, "Optimal'noe Upravlenie Elektroprivodom" ("Optimum Control of an Electric Drive"). Gosenergoizdat, 1961.

112. E. V. Tarasov, Optimal'noe programmirovanie tiagi silovoi ustanovki (Optimum programming of the thrust of a power plant). *Izv. Vysshikh Uchebn. Zavedenii Aviats. Tekhn.* **5**, No. 1 (1961).

113. G. D. Shirankov, K voprosu razrabotki bystrodeistvuiushchikh avtomaticheskikh reguliatorov dlia promyshlennykh ob'ektov (On the question of developing fast-response automatic regulators for industrial objects). *Avtomat. i Telemeh.* **22**, No. 12 (1961).

114. Iu. G. Antomonov, "Avtomaticheskoe Upravlenie s Primeneniem Vychislitel'nykh Mashin (Sintez Sistem, Optimal'nykh Po Bystrodeistviiu)" ["Automatic Control Utilizing Computers (Synthesis of Optimum Fast-Response Systems")]. Sudpromgiz, 1962.

115. G. I. Kostychev and V. I. Polkovnikov, Nekotorye variatsionnye zadachi gazodinamiki dlia dvizhenii, otlichnykh ot ustanovivshikhsia (Some variational problems of gasdynamics for motions different from the steady). *Izv. Vysshikh Uchebn. Zavedenii Aviats. Tekhn.* **5**, No. 2 (1962).

116. G. I. Kostychev, Ob optimal'nom programmirovanii v sluchae razlichnykh uslovii realizatsii protsessa (On optimum programming in the case of various conditions of process realization). *Izv. Vysshikh Uchebn. Zavedenii Aviats. Tekhn.* **5**, No. 2 (1962).

117. V. F. Krotov and M. Ia. Brovman, Ekstremal'nye protsessy plasticheskogo deformirovaniia metallov (Extremal processes of plastic deformation of metals). *Izv. Akad. Nauk SSSR Otd. Tekhn. Nauk Mekhan i Mashinostr.* No. 3 (1962).

118. Iu. N. Ivanov, Optimal'noe izmenenie moshchnosti pri dvizhenii tela peremennoi

massy v gravitatsionnom pole (Optimum power change for motion of a variable-mass body in a gravitational field). *Prikl. Mat. Meh.* **26,** No. 4 (1962).

119. A. A. Pavlov, O povyshenii bystrodeistviia nekotorykh releinykh sistem tret'ego poriadka (On raising the fast-response of some third-order relay systems). *Izv. Akad. Nauk SSSR Otd. Tekhn. Nauk Energ. i Avtomat.* No. 2 (1962).
120. Iu. P. Petrov, O dvukh tipakh zadach optimal'nogo upravleniia (On two types of optimum control problems). *Sb. Rabot po Voprosam Elektromekhaniki* No. 7, 1962.
121. Iu. D. Shmyglevskii, Variatsionnye zadachi dlia sverkhzvukovykh tel vrashcheniia i sopel (Variational problems for supersonic bodies of revolution and nozzles). *Prikl. Mat. Meh.* **26,** No. 1 (1962).
122. Sh. Sh. Khamitov, Sintez optimal'nogo upravleniia dlia ob'ekta vtorogo poriadka pri nalichii integral'nogo ogranicheniia (Synthesis of the optimum control for a second-order object in the presence of an integral constraint). *Izv. Akad. Nauk SSSR Ser Tekhn. Nauk* No. 3 (1962).

D. On the History of the Calculus of Variations

123. K. A. Rybnikov, "Pervye etapy razvitiia variatsionnogo ischisleniia" ("First steps in the development of calculus of variations"). *Istor. Mat. Issled.* No. 2 (1949).
124. A. V. Dorofeeva, "Razvitie variatsionnogo ischisleniia kak ischisleniia variatsii" ("Development of variational calculus as calculus of variations"). *Istor.-Mat. Issled.* No. 14 (1961). Fizmatgiz.
125. F. Klein, "Lectures on the Development of Mathematics in the Nineteenth Century." Onti, 1937.
126. Sbornik "Variatsionnye Printsipy Mekhaniki" (Collection entitled "Variational Principles of Mechanics"). Fizmatgiz, 1961.

Author Index

Numbers in parentheses are reference numbers. Numbers in italics show the page on which the complete reference is listed.

Subject Index

Mathematics in Science and Engineering

A Series of Monographs and Textbooks

Edited by RICHARD BELLMAN, *University of Southern California*

1. TRACY Y. THOMAS. Concepts from Tensor Analysis and Differential Geometry. Second Edition. 1965
2. TRACY Y. THOMAS. Plastic Flow and Fracture in Solids. 1961
3. RUTHERFORD ARIS. The Optimal Design of Chemical Reactors: A Study in Dynamic Programming. 1961
4. JOSEPH LASALLE and SOLOMON LEFSCHETZ. Stability by Liapunov's Direct Method with Applications. 1961
5. GEORGE LEITMANN (ed.). Optimization Techniques: With Applications to Aerospace Systems. 1962
6. RICHARD BELLMAN and KENNETH L. COOKE. Differential-Difference Equations. 1963
7. FRANK A. HAIGHT. Mathematical Theories of Traffic Flow. 1963
8. F. V. ATKINSON. Discrete and Continuous Boundary Problems. 1964
9. A. JEFFREY and T. TANIUTI. Non-Linear Wave Propagation: With Applications to Physics and Magnetohydrodynamics. 1964
10. JULIUS T. TOU. Optimum Design of Digital Control Systems. 1963
11. HARLEY FLANDERS. Differential Forms: With Applications to the Physical Sciences. 1963
12. SANFORD M. ROBERTS. Dynamic Programming in Chemical Engineering and Process Control. 1964
13. SOLOMON LEFSCHETZ. Stability of Nonlinear Control Systems. 1965
14. DIMITRIS N. CHORAFAS. Systems and Simulation. 1965
15. A. A. PERVOZVANSKII. Random Processes in Nonlinear Control Systems. 1965
16. MARSHALL C. PEASE, III. Methods of Matrix Algebra. 1965
17. V. E. BENES. Mathematical Theory of Connecting Networks and Telephone Traffic. 1965
18. WILLIAM F. AMES. Nonlinear Partial Differential Equations in Engineering. 1965
19. J. ACZEL. Lectures on Functional Equations and Their Applications. 1966
20. R. E. MURPHY. Adaptive Processes in Economic Systems. 1965
21. S. E. DREYFUS. Dynamic Programming and the Calculus of Variations. 1965
22. A. A. FEL'DBAUM. Optimal Control Systems. 1965
23. A. HALANAY. Differential Equations: Stability, Oscillations, Time Lags. 1966
24. M. NAMIK OGUZTORELI. Time-Lag Control Systems. 1966
25. DAVID SWORDER. Optimal Adaptive Control Systems. 1966
26. MILTON ASH. Optimal Shutdown Control of Nuclear Reactors. 1966
27. DIMITRIS N. CHORAFAS. Control System Functions and Programming Approaches (In Two Volumes). 1966
28. N. P. ERUGIN. Linear Systems of Ordinary Differential Equations. 1966
29. SOLOMON MARCUS. Algebraic Linguistics; Analytical Models. 1967
30. A. M. LIAPUNOV. Stability of Motion. 1966

31. George Leitmann (ed.). Topics in Optimization. 1967
32. Masanao Aoki. Optimization of Stochastic Systems. 1967
33. Harold J. Kushner. Stochastic Stability and Control. 1967
34. Minoru Urabe. Nonlinear Autonomous Oscillations. 1967
35. F. Calogero. Variable Phase Approach to Potential Scattering. 1967
36. A. Kaufmann. Graphs, Dynamic Programming, and Finite Games. 1967
37. A. Kaufmann and R. Cruon. Dynamic Programming: Sequential Scientific Management. 1967
38. J. H. Ahlberg, E. N. Nilson, and J. L. Walsh. The Theory of Splines and Their Applications. 1967
39. Y. Sawaragi, Y. Sunahara, and T. Nakamizo. Statistical Decision Theory in Adaptive Control Systems. 1967
40. Richard Bellman. Introduction to the Mathematical Theory of Control Processes Volume I. 1967 (Volumes II and III in preparation)
41. E. Stanley Lee. Quasilinearization and Invariant Imbedding. 1968
42. William Ames. Nonlinear Ordinary Differential Equations in Transport Processes. 1968
43. Willard Miller, Jr. Lie Theory and Special Functions. 1968
44. Paul B. Bailey, Lawrence F. Shampine, and Paul E. Waltman. Nonlinear Two Point Boundary Value Problems. 1968
45. Iu. P. Petrov. Variational Methods in Optimum Control Theory. 1968
46. O. A. Ladyzhenskaya and N. N. Ural'tseva. Linear and Quasilinear Elliptic Equations. 1968
47. A. Kaufmann and R. Faure. Introduction to Operations Research. 1968
48. C. A. Swanson. Comparison and Oscillation Theory of Differential Equations. 1968

In preparation

N. K. Jaiswal. Priority Queues

Robert Hermann. Differential Geometry and the Calculus of Variations

Robert P. Gilbert. Function Theoretic Methods in the Theory of Partial Differential Equations

Yudell Luke. The Special Functions and Their Approximations (In Two Volumes)

Hukukane Nikaido. Convex Structures and Economic Theory

V. Lakshmikantham and S. Leela. Differential and Integral Inequalities

King-sun Fu. Sequential Methods in Pattern Recognition and Machine Learning

Printed in Dunstable, United Kingdom

91898138R00131